Tribals and Community Forest Management

Tribals and Community Forest Management

Madhusudan Bandi

Rawat Publications
Jaipur • New Delhi • Bangalore • Hyderabad • Guwahati

ISBN 978-81-316-0577-6

Published by
Prem Rawat for **Rawat Publications**
Satyam Apts, Sector 3, Jawahar Nagar, Jaipur 302 004 (India)
Phone: 0141 265 1748 / 7006 Fax: 0141 265 1748
E-mail: info@rawatbooks.com
Website: www.rawatbooks.com

New Delhi Office
4858/24, Ansari Road, Daryaganj, New Delhi 110 002
Phone: 011 2326 3290

Also at *Bangalore, Hyderabad* and *Guwahati*

Typeset by Rawat Computers, Jaipur
Printed at Chaman Enterprises, New Delhi

To my parents
Devika Bandi and Sathyanarayan Bandi

Contents

Acknowledgements

I would like to place on record my profound thanks to all those who have contributed to the successful completion of this book.

I owe a deep debt of gratitude to Dr M. Gopinath Reddy, Professor, Centre for Economic and Social Studies (CESS), Hyderabad, who has been a guiding force all through this research effort. Thanks are due to Dr V. Ratna Reddy, Director, Livelihoods and Natural Resources Management Institute, Hyderabad and Dr Amita Shah, Professor and Director, Gujarat Institute of Development Research (GIDR), Ahmedabad for their constant support while writing this book.

I am grateful to Dr V.N. Reddy, retired Professor, Indian Institute of Management, Kolkata for sparing his invaluable time in helping me design the methodology for this research study. I am obliged to Dr John Cameron, Associate Professor, School of Development Studies, University of East Anglia (UEA), Norwich (UK), and Dr Oliver Springate-Baginski, Lecturer, School of International Development, UEA, Norwich for highly valuable interactions and discussions which have helped improve the overall structure of the book.

I gratefully acknowledge the support extended by Dr B. Prabhakar, Divisional Forest Officer, Adilabad during my fieldwork there. He was always ready to help me access the relevant information whenever needed from his office. I am deeply touched by his down-to-earth attitude.

I also take this opportunity to specially thank Ms Raqia Begum, Cartographer, CESS, for helping me prepare maps for this study. My sincere thanks are also due to the library staff of CESS and UEA for their cooperation in gathering secondary information for the study. I would like to sincerely acknowledge my friend Barry Ferguson's generous gesture in allowing me to freely access his personal collection of books, which made my job not only easier in terms of identifying and selecting relevant literature, but also saving my invaluable time.

It is my pleasant duty to record my indebtedness to all the respondents, especially tribals, who may have expected my investigation to act as a conduit to make their voice heard across the outer world and help them improve their living conditions. I cannot dare claim how far my research work would contribute towards fulfilling their expectations, however, I must admit that the invaluable sessions they spent with me have benefited me not only academically but also prompted me to look at the philosophy of life altogether from a new perspective. In the same breath, I wish to oblige the services of two students of anthropology, Manohar Kandregula and Murali Ponnada, for helping me not only in the field but also eliciting opinions in local dialects from the respondents.

I am grateful to the expert contributions rendered by Dr Kameswara Rao, Professor, Department of Environmental Sciences, Andhra University, Visakhapatnam, Dr Redappa Reddy, Professor, Sri Krishna Devaraya Univeristy, Anantapur and Dr Satyanarayana Sangita, Professor, Institute for Economic and Social Change, Bangalore. They read earlier draft of this manuscript and provided valuable comments that helped me in improving upon the quality of this study. My friend and colleague, Dr Sudeep Basu, Assistant Professor, GIDR read through the draft of the manuscript in the pre-editing phase and also made useful suggestions. I thank him whole-heartedly for his help. The exercise of giving final shape to the book coincided with my joining GIDR. I am indebted to the institute for all the necessary support.

The contribution of all my friends in terms of standing by me at every stage of my life has been just incredible. Here, I wish to single out Aitharaju Prasanna Kumar, Biplab Dhak, Clement Inkhamba, Floraine Clement, Pagadala Pavan Kumar and Sanjit Kumar Rout for being closely associated with me during this research.

My sister Maniesha, brother-in-law Dinesh and their little daughters Dhriti and Briti, brother Srinivas and sister-in-law Shradha, my nieces Aditi and Shreya, my mother Devika and father Sathyanarayan may not have directly contributed towards this book, but they have remained all along my core strength. Their mere presence served as the single greatest motivating factor. 'Thanks' would be too little a word to acknowledge their love and compassion.

Madhusudan Bandi

List of Tables and Figures

Tables

Figure

Figures

List of Boxes

Abbreviations

ANM	:	Auxiliary Nurse and Midwife
AOFFPS	:	Area Oriented Fuelwood and Fodder Projects Scheme
AP	:	Andhra Pradesh
APCFM	:	Andhra Pradesh Community Forest Management
APFD	:	Andhra Pradesh Forest Department
APFDC	:	Andhra Pradesh Forest Department Corporation
APRPRP	:	Andhra Pradesh Rural Poverty Reduction Programme (*Velugu*)
ASTRP	:	Association of Scheduled Tribes and Rural Poor
BC	:	Backward Caste/Class
CBF	:	Central Board of Forestry
CEW	:	Community Extension Worker
CFM	:	Community Forest Management
CWS	:	Centre for World Solidarity
DFC	:	District Forestry Committee

DFO	:	Divisional Forest Officer
DPAP	:	Drought Prone Areas Programme
DPIP	:	District Poverty Initiatives Project
DRDA	:	District Rural Development Agency
DRDO	:	Defence Research and Development Organisation
EAS	:	Employment Assurance Scheme
EDC	:	Eco-Development Committee
EFS&T	:	Energy Forests Environment Science and Technology
FAO	:	Food and Agriculture Organisation of the United Nations
FBO	:	Forest Beat Officer
FCA	:	Forest Conservation Act
FD	:	Forest Department
FDA	:	Forest Development Agency
FGD	:	Focus Group Discussion
FIR	:	First Information Report
FPC	:	Forest Protection Committee
FPP	:	Forest People's Programme
FRO	:	Forest Range Officer
FSO	:	Forest Section Officer
GB	:	General Body
GCC	:	Girijan Cooperative Corporation
GO	:	Government Order
GoAP	:	Government of Andhra Pradesh
GoI	:	Government of India
GT	:	Grand Total
ha	:	Hectare
HH	:	Household

IAEPS	:	Integrated Afforestation and Eco-Development Projects
IFS	:	Indian Forest Service
ITC	:	Indian Tobacco Company
ITDA	:	Integrated Tribal Development Authority
J/CFM	:	Joint/Community Forest Management
JFM	:	Joint Forest Management
Km	:	Kilometres
MC	:	Managing Committee
MCV	:	Mixed Caste VSS
MFP	:	Minor Forest Produce
MLA	:	Member of Legislative Assembly
mm	:	Millimetre
MoEF	:	Ministry of Environment and Forests
MoU	:	Memorandum of Understanding
MRO	:	Mandal Revenue Officer
NABARD	:	National Bank for Agriculture and Rural Development
NCA	:	National Commission on Agriculture
NEDCAP	:	Non-conventional Energy Development Corporation of Andhra Pradesh
NGO	:	Non-Government Organisation
MGNREGS	:	Mahatma Gandhi National Rural Employment Guarantee Scheme
NRM	:	Natural Resources Management
NTFP	:	Non-Timber Forest Produce
OBC	:	Other Backward Classes
OC	:	Other Castes
OTV	:	Only Tribal VSS
PDS	:	Public Distribution System

PESA	:	Panchayat Extension to Scheduled Areas
PFM	:	Participatory Forest Management
PRA	:	Participatory Rural Appraisal
PTG	:	Primitive Tribal Group
RF	:	Reserved Forests
RIDF	:	Rural Infrastructure Development Fund
₹	:	Rupees (Indian Currency)
SC	:	Scheduled Caste
SHG	:	Self-Help Group
SKREDSS	:	Sri Sai Krishna Rural Education and Development Seva Samithi (NGO)
SMC	:	Soil and Moisture Conservation
Sq.	:	Square
ST	:	Scheduled Tribe
TWD	:	Tribal Welfare Department
UNFAO	:	United Nations Food and Agriculture Organisation
USA	:	United States of America
VSS	:	*Vana Samrakshana Samithi*
WL	:	Wildlife
ZPTC	:	Zilla Parishad Territorial Constituency

Glossary

Local and Telugu Terms

Adda Aakulu	:	Climber leaves (used for preparing leaf plates)/ *Bauhinia Vahali*
Aranyas	:	Forests
Ashwagandha	:	Winter Cherry/Indian Ginseng/*Withania Somnifera*
Bajra	:	Millet
Biduru/Viduru	:	Bamboo
Cheepiri Pullalu	:	Broomsticks
Chenega	:	Bengal Gram
Chikudukai	:	Kidney Bean/*Dolichos*
Chinta Pandu	:	Tamarind/*Tamarindus Indica*
Chipko Andolan	:	Tree-hugging movement started in Uttaranchal to save trees
Crore	:	10 million (100 crores = 1 billion)
Devasthanam	:	Temple

Fasli	:	*Fasli* is a calendar followed by the Nizams of Hyderabad. This calendar is 590 years behind the English calendar.
Faujdar	:	Forest Section Officer (FSO)
Ghat	:	Valley
Girijan	:	Hill dwellers
Gram Sabha	:	Lowest unit of Panchayat
Irsali	:	Urdu word meaning 'reserved'
Jafra	:	Annota – dye yielding plant/*Bixa Orelina*
Jama	:	Guava
Jeedi Pappu	:	Cashew-nut
Jowar	:	Milo/*Sorghum Bicolour*
Kalabandha	:	Aloe/Aloe Vera/*Barbados Aloe*
Kalyugam	:	The last of the four yugas or eons of time before *pralaya* or deluge
Kanuga	:	Pongamia Ghaira/*Dersis Indica*
Karaka Kaya	:	Black Myrobalan/*Chebula Myrobalanus*
Katla Pamu	:	Common Indian Krait (snake)
Kuccha	:	Loose or Temporary
Lakh	:	Million (10 lakhs = 1 million)
Lakka	:	Gum
Lok Sabha	:	Lower House of Indian Parliament
Mahabharatha	:	Hindu Mythological Epic
Makhbara	:	Muslim Tombstone
Mamidi	:	Mango/*Mangifera Indica*
Mandal	:	Administrative Block
Marri Pandu	:	Banyan/*Ficus Bengahalensis*
Naga Pamu	:	Cobra (snake)
Naxalism/Naxalites	:	Extremist and outlawed outfit in Andhra Pradesh

Neredu Pandu	:	Blackberry
Panchayati Raj	:	Decentralised governance at village level
Pattas	:	Landholding document
Penjeri	:	Russel's Viper (snake)
Phanasa Pandu	:	Jackfruit/*Aetocarpus Heterophyllus*
Podu	:	Shifting Cultivation
Poramboku	:	Government wastelands
Pucca	:	Firm or permanent
Ragi	:	Small Millet
Ramayana	:	Hindu Mythological Epic
Sahukars	:	Moneylenders
Sal	:	*Shorea robusta*, a species of tree found in southern Asia
Sarpanch	:	Village headman
Seethaphal	:	Custard apple
Shamianas	:	Tents used in big functions or meetings
Shamisen	:	Japanese musical instrument
Shekakai	:	Soap Acacia
Shramadanam	:	Offering voluntary labour
Thatmokkalu	:	Palm leaves
Tumma	:	Acacia
Tunuka/Beedi	:	Abnus/*Diospyros Melanoxylon*
Usiri/Amla	:	Indian Gooseberry/*Emblica Officinalis*
Vippa/Ippapuvvu Mahuava	:	*Madbuca Indica* (flower used to distil a liquor served among tribal households)
Vyapa/Neem	:	Margo/Margosa/*Azadirachtha Indica*
Zamindari	:	Feudal system

Forestry-related Technical Terms

Afforestation : The establishment of a tree crop in an area where it has always been or for very long been absent.

Agency Area : North coastal districts of Madras Presidency during British regime were called 'agency tracts' denoting agent of the governor in charge of the administration. These areas were brought under the V Schedule of the Constitution after the independence and continued to remain in force with some changes by bringing in special laws to protect them from the exploitative moneylenders and other non-tribals.

The Scheduled Areas in AP are Adilabad, East Godavari, Mahboobnagar, Prakasam (few Mandals), Srikakulam, Visakhapatnam, Vizainagaram and West Godavari.

Biodiversity : A biological diversity, which includes diversity of species, genes and ecosystems, and the evolutionary and functional processes which link them.

Community forestry (or community forest management) : A term used as an all-encompassing operational term. The common denominator in community forestry is the focus on the role of local communities (usually forest-dependent) in managing neighbouring forests and sharing the benefits from those forests. An important role is to foster productive relationships between communities, government agencies and NGOs.

Coppice : Regular trimming of stumps/trees/poles or firewood for continual supply.

Deciduous	:	A forest exhibiting discontinuous, often seasoned tree leaf cover (opposite of evergreen).
Deforestation	:	Clearing an area of forest for another long-term use. Technically, a semi-permanent depletion of tree crown cover to less than 10 per cent.
Degradation	:	Forest degradation is a reduction in the biomass, productivity of forests and alterations in ecological functions such as habitat, climate regulation and soil and water protection. Sometimes, this is also referred to as a lowering in the quality or integrity of the forest ecosystem. One example is a change in forest class, say from closed to open forest, which negatively affects the stand or site, or lowers the production capacity.
Desertification	:	A degradation of land that ultimately leads to desert-like land features.
Designated Forest	:	A forest area legally set aside for protection, production or some other specified use.
Ecosystem	:	A dynamic and interrelated community of biological organisms and the surrounding environment, linked through nutrient cycling and energy flows.
Evergreen Forests	:	Forests which exhibit continuous tree leaf cover (opposite of deciduous).
Farm Forestry	:	A broad definition of farm forestry includes any trees on farm land which are managed to produce saleable products such as timber, oil, tannin, charcoal or carbon credits.
Forest	:	An area characterised by predominance of woody vegetation growing more or less closely together; whether 'closed' or 'open' in canopy, and whether fully intact

		ecologically or modified, fragmented or planted by humankind. Technically, forests are usually defined as ecosystems with a minimum of 10 per cent tree canopy cover.
Forest Sector	:	The group comprising all direct stake-holders in the forest resources.
Forestry	:	The science and vocation of forest management. Traditionally regarded as technical endeavour, forestry is now broadening to include more political elements.
Joint Forest Management	:	JFM is a variant of community forestry widely adopted in India for managing government-owned forests in which responsibility and benefits are shared between local user groups and government forestry department.
Landscape	:	The geographical and ecological integrity and resilience of a particular land area, not merely its aesthetic qualities. Landscape is not just a geographical concept, but includes human, cultural and traditional values that are associated with land.
Logging	:	Felling and extraction of wood, especially as logs (excludes fuelwood harvested non-commercially).
Non-Timber Forest Produce	:	NTFP are medicinal plants, resins, mushrooms, rattans, wildlife and other non-wood goods obtained from forests.
Participatory Forest Management	:	A forest management system in which the decision-making follows from a process of broad public involvement.
Plantation	:	Tree crop of one or a few species, usually planted and managed intensively for industrial wood production, whether timber or fibre. Sometimes, plantations are also managed to produce fuelwood.

Policy	:	A rule or norm usually prescribed by governments to help direct behaviour or decision-making.
Protected Forest	:	Any forest land or wasteland or any other land, which is not included in a reserved forest, but which is the property of the government, or over which the government has proprietary rights, or to the whole or any part of the forest-produce of which the government is entitled, and which is notified in government gazette as 'protected forest' under relevant sections of Indian Forest Act. Explanation: In such forest, most of the activities are allowed unless prohibited.
Reforestation	:	The re-establishment of forests on land which was previously forested.
Reserved Forest	:	Any forest land or wasteland or any other land, not being land for the time being comprised in any holding or in any village *abadi* (population), which is the property of government or over which the government has proprietary rights, or to the whole or any part of the forest produce of which the government is entitled, and which is notified in government gazette as 'reserve forest' under relevant section of Indian Forest Act. In such forest, most of the activities are prohibited unless allowed.
Scheduled Areas	:	Article 244(1) of Constitution of India defines V Schedule Areas. Although it does not provide for a clear definition of Scheduled Areas, but, it denotes to those areas where the tribal population is predominant.

Shifting Cultivation	:	Farming system in which land is periodically cleared, burned, farmed and then returned to fallow.
Silviculture	:	Silviculture is the science and practice of cultivating forest crops.
Social Forestry	:	Social forestry is defined as forestry outside the conventional forests which primarily aim at production of forest goods. In other words it is growing forests of the choice such as fuel, fodder, etc., to meet the needs of the local community, particularly underprivileged section of the local population.
Tenure	:	Ownership or use rights.
Usufruct	:	Usufruct is the legal right to use and derive profit or benefit from property that belongs to another person, as long as the property is not damaged. In tribal cultures usufruct means the land is owned in common by the tribe, but families and individuals have the right to use certain plots of land. Most Indian tribes owned things like land as a group and not as individuals. The family never owned the land, they just farmed it. This is called usufruct land ownership. A person must make (more or less) continuous use of the item or else he loses ownership rights. This is usually referred to as 'possession property' or 'usufruct.' Thus, in this usufruct system, absentee ownership is illegitimate.
Watershed	:	Water catchments area of a river, stream or body of water, and its associated landscape features.

Source: WCFSD, 1999: 168–75.

Local Castes and Ethnic Groups

Aare/Arya/ Maratha	BC	:	Peasantry community migrated from the neighbouring state of Maharashtra inhabiting mainly the Telangana regions in AP.
Adivasi/Girijan	ST	:	Commonly used term for the people living in the forests.
Bagatha	ST	:	Tribe inhabiting the hill tracts of Visakhapatnam district in AP; they consider themselves higher in social hierarchy among other tribes in their region.
Besta/Gundla/ Jalari	BC	:	Community in hereditary occupation of hunting and fishing inhabiting mainly the coastal regions of AP.
Boya	BC	:	Community of hunters and umbrella carriers of royals in the past, also known as Valmikis, inhabit mainly the Rayalaseema region in AP.
Chakali/Rajaka	BC	:	Community of washermen distributed all over AP.
Ediga-Balija	BC	:	Community of toddy-tappers and liquor vendors concentrated in the Rayalaseema region in AP.
Golla	BC	:	Community of cowherds, goatherds and shepherds spread across all the three regions of AP.
Gond/Rajgonds	ST	:	Predominant tribal group in AP (especially in Adilabad) and India.
Goudu	ST	:	Cattle breeding tribe living in the Agency Areas bordering AP and Orissa (now Odisha).

Harijan/Dalits	SC	:	Most oppressed section of the people in Indian society.
Jats	OC	:	Ethnic community of agriculturists and military personals by tradition is spread over the regions of northern India.
Kamma	OC	:	Dominant agricultural community thickly distributed in the Coastal and Rayalaseema regions of AP.
Kammara/Kammari/ Konda Khummari	BC/ST	:	Community of blacksmiths also known as Mettu Kamsali who reside in the hilly tracts in Visakhapatnam district of AP. 'According to the members of this community, their status as ST is often disputed by the authorities'.
Kapu	OC	:	Community of peasants thickly populated in the Coastal and Rayalaseema regions of AP.
Kolam	PTG	:	Tribe concentrated in the Agency Areas of Adilabad district in AP.
Konda Dora	ST	:	Tribe distributed in the Agency Area districts of Visakhapatnam, Vizianagaram, Srikakulam and East Godavari in AP.
Kondh	PTG	:	Important tribal group concentrated in the Agency Area districts of Vizianagaram and Visakhapatnam in AP.
Koppala Velama	BC	:	Community of agriculturists found in the Visakhapatnam district of AP.

Koya/Koya Dora	ST	:	Tribe distributed in the districts of East Godavari, West Godavari, Khammam, Warangal and Adilabad in AP.
Kshatriya/Rajus	OC	:	Community of agriculturists and former zamindars distributed throughout AP.
Kuruba	BC	:	Community residing mainly in hilly areas to rear sheep; they were earlier known as 'Kuruma' in the Telangana region and 'Kuruba' or 'Kurva' in the rest of AP.
Lambada/Sugali	ST	:	Community engaged in agricultural pursuits and also in construction labour works; it is spread across all the districts of AP.
Madiga	SC	:	Major community of Dalits/Harijans in AP.
Mala	SC	:	Prominent community of Dalits/Harijans in AP.
Mali	BC	:	Small community of florists found in the studied village of Lalghad in Adilabad district of AP.
Malis	ST	:	Small tribe living in the Agency Areas of Araku, Paderu and Chintapalli mandals in the Visakhapatnam district of AP.
Mangali	BC	:	Community of barbers found in all parts of AP.
Manne Dora	ST	:	Tribe living in the Agency Area districts of Visakhapatnam, Srikakulam, Vizianagaram and East Godavari in AP.

Manne/Mannevaru	SC	:	Community of agriculturists, agricultural labourers, and village guards found throughout the rural areas of the Telangana region in AP.
Munnuru Kapu	BC	:	Community of cultivators found in the Telangana region of AP.
Muslim/Pathans/ Multani	BC/OC	:	Followers of Islam religion, found in all the three regions of AP.
Naik Pod	ST	:	Agrarian tribe inhabiting the forests in the Agency Area districts of Adilabad, Karimnagar, Warangal and Khammam in AP.
Porja	PTG	:	Hill tribe of shifting cultivators inhabiting the Agency Areas of Visakhapatnam district (they reside mainly in Munchingiput, Anantagiri and Peddabayalu Mandal) in AP and also in adjoining areas of Orissa (Odisha).
Rajput/Thakur	OC	:	Traditionally a warrior community migrated from Bundelkhand in Madhya Pradesh state, now into agriculture and various other sectors; its members are chiefly distributed in the city of Hyderabad and coastal regions of AP.
Reddy	OC	:	Dominant peasant community in AP concentrated in all parts of the state, especially in the Rayalaseema and Telangana regions.

Reddy Dora/ Nooka Dora	ST	:	Tribe taking pride of being second in social hierarchy among other tribes in their region; it is spread over the Agency Areas of Visakhapatnam district in AP.
Relli	SC	:	Community traditionally belonging to grass-cutters mostly found in the coastal regions of AP.
Sali	BC	:	Community of weavers distributed across all the three regions of AP.
Sikh	OC	:	Followers of 'Sikhism' founded by Guru Nanak (1469–1538 AD) predominant in the state of Punjab, while in AP, they have presence only in the city of Hyderabad.
Turupu Kapu	BC	:	Community of peasants concentrated mostly in the north coastal regions of AP.
Vada/ Wada Balija	BC	:	Community of marine fishers spread along the coastal districts of Srikakulam, Visakhapatnam, Kakinada, East Godavari and Krishna in AP.
Valmiki	ST	:	Tribal group inhabiting the Agency Area districts of Srikakulam, Vizianagaram, East Godavari and Visakhapatnam in AP.
Velama	OC	:	Dominant peasant community found in the Telangana region of AP.
Wodlolu	BC	:	Community of carpenters found in all parts of AP.

Yanadi	ST	:	Largest tribe in AP thickly concentrated in the districts of Chittoor, Nellore and Prakasam.

Source: Singh (2003).

Note: SC = Scheduled Castes, according to Indian Constitution is classification of the castes precisely as the criterion of the stigma of untouchables for the affirmative treatment in education, government services and membership in elections at all levels. ST = Scheduled Tribe is constituted of communities following well-established criterion for the affirmative treatment in education, government services and membership in elections at all levels. Unlike SC, criterion for defining ST is not specified in the Constitution, however well-established criterion, viz., communities living in geographical isolation, backwardness (e.g., primitive livelihoods practices, low level of literacy and health), distinct culture, language and shyness of contact are considered while identifying this group. PTG = Primitive Tribal Groups are those who use pre-agricultural level of technology, have low level of literacy and also indulge in food collection and shifting cultivation (Rao, 1990). Following the revised National Tribal Policy, the terminology of 'Particularly Vulnerable Tribal Groups' is now being used for the PTGs by the Government of India. BC = Backward Class is a cluster of castes or classes identified by the Andhra Pradesh Commission for Backward Classes based on their economic and social backwardness for affirmative benefits in education and government services. OC = Other Castes are the remaining section of communities who do not qualify for the above-mentioned groups due to their better economic and social position in the Indian society.

1

Introduction

The pattern of deforestation everywhere in the world is found to be more or less similar. The major reasons for deforestation have been cited as extensive logging and development activities (Rajpraveen, 2000). The pressure of growing population, expanding agriculture and livestock grazing necessitated the setting up of new villages on the fringe of forests; besides, more land going under cultivation also contributed to the erosion of forests (Harrison and Ghose, 2000). Kashyap (1990) identifies organised exploitation of forests for industrial raw materials, railway sleepers, timber for naval stores, military equipment and free arms, and non-industrial uses as the causes of deforestation. Development projects like water reservoirs, industrial estates, roads, airstrips and railway tracks also contributed to the destruction of the forests. Continued legal and illicit felling of trees by Forest Department (FD), contractors and local people (Reddy et al., 2001) and 'shifting cultivation' in tribal areas too are seen as the causes of forest destruction. There are also forest fires and attacks by pests and insects which further deplete forests (Kashyap, 1990). To add on, there is the recklessness on the part of human beings towards natural resources, resulting out of need and greed, that went unnoticed until the importance of maintaining the balance was realised during recent times, following the environmental changes at the local and global level (Hajer, 1995).

Experiences from the past suggest that governments elsewhere in the world have failed in enforcing natural resource policies satisfactorily. Besides, bureaucracy, as their agent, with its rigid approach, is believed to have contributed to faster degradation of forests (Becker et al., 1995). This happens because state bureaucracies initiate and implement projects or policies in the name of modernisation and impose simplified procedures deemed as scientific and universally valid, at the expense of local knowledge, ignoring the resistance and actual effects on ground (Scott, 1998). The story about Indian forest administration is no different.

Describing the theory of 'policing' by the state, Rajpraveen (2000) identifies it as a failure and counterproductive. Iyengar and Shukla (1999) also acknowledge breakdowns of 'centralised regulation policy' because the ethical codes evolved by the communities over a long period for the use of collectively-owned 'common property resources' (CPRs) were far more binding on the members in regulating their use. In such milieu, public demand for 'people-oriented' forestry has emerged in opposition to top-down forestry conceived and controlled by governments (Harrison et al., 2000). Thus, involving people in the protection of forests on a large scale became imminent (Rajpraveen, 2000). The communities, on their own and through voluntary organisations, brought pressure on policy makers to recognise their interest in conservation and to involve them in forest management (Bhatt, 1990). There are numerous case studies of people showing their willingness to participate in forest management (Hague, 1985; Malhotra and Poffenberger, 1989; Gupta, 1997; Shah, 1997; Upadhyay, 1997). Motivational factor for the people to take up natural resource management (NRM) on their own has been either self-initiated, or aroused by external success stories like '*chipko andolans* (movements)' in the Himalayan ranges and the '*arabari*' experiment in Midnapore district in West Bengal of India, led by committed forest officials (Roy, 1997). This was expected to pave the way for local people, especially the more marginalised sections, to engage themselves as more equal partners in implementation, monitoring and enforcement of forest conservation (Nygren, 2005).

National- and state-level policies over the past few years reciprocated by supporting the rights and needs of the rural communities to forest resources in leading the reversal of century-old trends (Poffenberger and McGean, 1996). The arrangement is mutually beneficial because the concept of participatory forest management (PFM) or more popularly known as joint forest management (JFM) holds scope for the much needed interaction between the people and the FD (Rajpraveen, 2000), that is crucial for the conservation of the forests. Above all, popular view is that the local communities which live in the forests are the primary users of forest produce and determinant to its state of condition, so they must be included in the schemes of forest management to make their own rules (Arnold, 1992). As a result, many of the countries across the world are presently experimenting with community-based forest management.

To maintain this precious resource in a state of ecological balance, the communities depending primarily on forests for their livelihoods need to have an effective institutional mechanism to govern them. This is possible only when the policies of the respective governments of such communities towards 'sustenance of ecosystem' are conducive and proactive. Even then, what kind of institutional set-up would make a foolproof system of governance of conservation, or at least something close to it, is a matter of serious concern.

Tribes are the important and main stakeholders of PFM because they roughly constitute one-third to half of the Forest Protection Committees (FPCs) in India. The tribal population in India are among the most vulnerable and deprived group of people. They face severe exclusions in social, economic and political terms. Majority of the tribes in India live in concentration in the forested areas having less accessibility and limited political and economic significance. The tribes in the past lived on subsistence agriculture (shifting agriculture), hunting and gathering. They traded with non-tribes for salt and iron. Despite rich vegetation, the standard of living of the tribes is worst among all other communities in the country. They face acute food insecurity. This is evident from the fact that 46 per cent of tribal population live below the poverty line against the national average of 27 per cent (Saxena, 2005).

To do justice to such long and continuously neglected section of people, the framers of the Indian Constitution identified them for special treatment through constitutional preference. For this purpose, Article 366 (25) of Indian Constitution defined 'Scheduled Tribes' (STs) as "such tribes or tribal communities or part of or groups within such tribes or tribal communities as are deemed under Article 342". The tribals are declared as such by the President through public notification. However, Article 342 does not contain any criterion for specification of any community as Scheduled Tribe. But, often used criterions are geographical isolation, backwardness, distinctive culture, language and religion and also shyness of contact. Those among the tribes who are identified as more backward are categorised as 'Primitive Tribal Groups' (PTGs) by the union government in 1975. They are identified for more special programmes for their sustainable development.

There are many definitions of tribes propounded by numerous scholars across the world. According to western anthropologists, those communities living in primitive or barbarous conditions under a headman or chief are defined as 'primitive tribes' (Sills, 1972). In the words of Majumdar, an Indian anthropologist, the tribes are "a social group with territorial affiliations, endogamous, with no specialisation of functions, ruled by tribal officers, hereditary or otherwise, united in language or dialect, recognising social distance from (other) tribes or castes but without any stigma attached as in the case of a caste structure, following tribal traditions, beliefs and customs, illiberal of naturalisation of ideas from alien sources; and above all, conscious of a homogeneity of ethnic and territorial integration" (in Majumdar and Madan, 1986: 241).

"In all practical purposes, tribals in India also known as '*girijan*' are the original inhabitants '*adivasi*' of the land who were pushed into isolation of hills through marginalization" (Badgaiyan, 1990). They constitute 8.10 per cent of country's total population. They are concentrated in the Himalayas stretching through Jammu and Kashmir, Himachal Pradesh, and Bihar, Uttar Pradesh and West Bengal in the north-west, to Assam, Meghalaya, Tripura, Arunachal Pradesh, Mizoram, Manipur, and Nagaland in the north-east. In the central India, they are found in hilly areas of Madhya Pradesh, Orissa (Odisha), and in some parts of Andhra Pradesh (AP). Comparatively, a small number of tribals also live in the states of Karnataka, Tamil Nadu, Kerala, Gujarat and Rajasthan, and in the union territories of Lakshadweep and the Andaman and Nicobar Islands (Census of India, 2001).

Historical Account of Forest Governance and Policy in India

It is hard to consider that unprecedented destruction of forests in present India are the same *aranyas* (forests), that were earlier known as *Dandakaranya*, *Nandanavana* and *Khandavan*, because the great Indian epics of Ramayana and Mahabharatha mention the bond between these forests and the origin of Indian (Hindu) culture and civilisation (Thakur, 1984). Incidentally, *Dandakaranya* forest is believed to have spread over a great extent of the present-day AP.

Nevertheless, efforts at conservation appear to have also begun simultaneously when the mindless destruction of forests started. Traces of conservation efforts in the Indian context can be found as early as in 300 BC, during the reign of Chandra Gupta Maurya, when a 'superintendent of forests' was appointed to protect forests and wildlife. This is a clear indication of an early administration for forests. Ashoka's (273–232 BC) concern for forests is no less, as seen from his efforts to plant trees along the roads and on camping sites (ibid.). Mauryan kings were also known to have adopted an extremely well-structured system of forest reserves and elephant protection (Trautmann, 1982).

Though most of the Mughals who dominated the medieval period in Indian history showed least interest in upkeeping the forests (Schimmel et al., 2004), Akbar was the lone ruler in the dynasty who could be credited with evincing some interest in the conservation of forest and planting trees (Moreland, 1920). Alam (1991) criticises the rest of the dynasty as being insensitive on this count. He gives an illustration of how from the period of Shah Jahan, the 'woodcutters' and 'ploughmen' were carried along with the army to clear the forests to bring them under cultivation, just to raise more revenue to the royal coffer.

India experienced the heaviest forest destruction and damage to its ecological and social fabric due to decline in traditional conservation and management systems of forests under early British occupation (Gadgil and Guha, 1992). It is also interesting to note that conservation efforts were also initiated by the British when a memorandum was issued in the name of the Government of India in 1855. Lord Dalhousie, the then Governor General of India, proclaimed a forestry policy for the first time, stating that timber in state's forest jurisdiction was its property, and no private individual can have rights or claims over such timber (Chaudhry, 1984). To consolidate and implement this policy, an Indian Forest Service (IFS) was organised; whose primary objective was the conservation and protection of existing forests. Subsequently in 1866, the FD was created in India to halt the fast disappearance of the remaining forests. The conviction was that the people would turn the forest into cultivation land if the forest was left to them to manage on their own. When the FD started working, its chief duties were to preserve and harvest the large timber forests (such as Sal in 'Dudh' and 'Deodar' forests of Himalayas and the forests of the Western Ghats) in a sustainable way (Randhawa, 1984).

In 1864, Dr Dietrich Brandis, was appointed as the first Inspector General of Forests and the rules for the conservation of forests for the whole country were outlined. It was followed by the first Indian Forest Act (IFA), which was drafted in 1865 and later revised in 1878. Soon it was made operational, persisting with the conservation policy in most of the provinces. It was also the occasion, when, for the first time, forests were classified into 'Reserved Forests (RF)' and 'Protected Forests (PF)'. In 1927, the Act of 1878 was consolidated to regulate the law relating to forests – forest produce, forest transport, related duties and penalties. Later in 1910, the Board of Forestry was created at the national level under the chairmanship of the Inspector General of Forests (Rao, 1979).

After independence, the Government of India constituted a Central Board of Forestry (CBF) in 1950 to provide guidance to the government in the formulation of policy and programmes in the field of forestry. The CBF became the supreme advisory body for reviewing, formulating and implementing the national forest policy. Some of the more important recommendations of the CBF on forest policy and its implementation were, paying compensatory fund by the concerned state governments for planting in the mined areas, setting up of high-powered boards by the states to regulate the land use policy on the principle of rational land, extension and popularisation of 'farm forestry', elimination of contract system in forestry operations and stoppage of extraction of wood (Kashyap, 1990).

According to Kashyap (1990), when Indian officers assumed their charge immediately after independence, the task of consolidation of forests, unification of forest laws and extension of scientific management on a reasonably uniform basis became the most important preoccupation for the forest administration at the 'central' and 'state' levels. He further describes, how in the early fifties, most of the states enacted new legislations affecting land tenure systems when control of large areas of privately-owned forests came to rest with the FDs of the states. The introduction of *Vanamahotsava* (national festival of tree plantation) in 1951 was a measure, which is considered as a stepping-stone for wildlife and soil conservation on all-India footing, that also resulted in the commencement of a 'national plan of development'. This was followed by five-year plans, when artificial man-made forests were to be created on an unprecedented scale, triggering increased forest productivity.

Later, the status of forest resources, as well as policies towards management of forest resources underwent significant changes. There have been three forest policy pronouncements in India since then: the 1952 Forest Policy, the National Commission on Agriculture (NCA), 1976, and the 1988 Forest Policy (Saxena, 1999). The 1952 policy affirmed forestry as an important land use category and insisted on one-third of the country's land area to remain as forest. The policy further elaborated the tenets on protecting hill slopes and land from degradation and desertification. There was also a mention for earning revenue from forests on sustainable basis. Here again commercial exploitation of forests received preference, while the needs of the local communities remained in the back seat. This policy continued till 1976, with heavily subsidised forest land given to industries and businessmen in the name of 'national interest' in pursuit of developing the country by industrialisation, which had significant negative impacts on forest and forest dwellers.

The NCA, 1976 differed from the earlier forest policy for adding the concept of 'social forestry'. This policy was all for promotion and continuance of commercial forestry with greater vigour on forest land; but at the same time, more funds were provided for social and farm forestry on non-forest and private land to meet people's demand for timber. It is widely argued that the four decades of forest policy, preceding 1988 were mainly concerned with timber production for commercial purposes, and have neither been sustainable in terms of checking the process of deforestation, nor have they improved people's access to forest for meeting their basic needs.

The Forest Conservation Act (FCA) of 1980 was definitely a historic landmark in the annals of forestry in India for containing the diversion of forest land for non-forestry use. Later the amended 1988, National Forest Policy (NFP) envisaged to balance commercial, conservation and participation issues. The recognition of local people's requisites like fuel, fodder, and other domestic needs was also a significant development. A remarkable step towards checking the depletion of forests was taken when it was made mandatory for the state governments to take central government approval for converting forest land for non-forest use by compensating it with the afforestation of the equivalent land (MoEF, 1998). In sum, switching from commercial management of forests for industrial raw materials and for government revenue to a policy centred on regeneration was praiseworthy.

Box 1.1

Provision for Forest Protection in the Constitution

Although in the 1950 proclamation of the Constitution, commitment to environmental protection and improvement was enshrined, a direct reference to forest protection and improvement found place only in 1977, with the 42nd Constitutional Amendment Act. The inserted Article 48A states, 'The state shall endeavour to protect and improve the environment and to safeguard the forests and wildlife of the country'. Constitutionally, it has been enjoined upon every citizen of India as a fundamental duty: 'to protect and improve the natural environment including forests, lakes, rivers and wildlife, and to have compassion for living creatures' (Article 51A (G), Constitution of India). Another aspect of the amendment was that, the forestry 'subject' was placed under the 'concurrent list', picking it from the 'state subject', which meant that both state and union governments share the forestry sector. However, the management of forests remained the responsibility of the states and it was up to them to decide on the strength and deployment of the staff and other resources for implementation of the NFP. The investments for the forestry development were to be financed by both the state and union governments, while forest maintenance and protection, including staff costs were to be borne by the state governments (GoI, 1980).

Source: As referred.

Traces of PFM in India

In the past, it was natural for the people, to use the resources 'more or less in a sustainable way' when their religious, social and economic life revolved around the forests (Rajpraveen, 2000). The usage of the common resources like food, fodder, fuel, or timber was dictated by their own unwritten rules that had no scope for free access or abuse (O'Riordan and Jordan, 2000). But this was not the case with all the communities that lived or were dependent on forests; only few tribes or communities practised it (Rajpraveen, 2000). Hence, administrations of their times in some of the regions in India made efforts to bring in conservation norms to conserve the natural resources, especially forests with the participation of 'local users' or forest dependent people, much before the formal introduction of participatory conservation institutions as a policy in India in 1990s.

Box 1.2

Traditional Institutions of NRM in India

NRM Institutions in India experienced significant changes with the passage of time. In the pre-colonial era, the institutions were locally managed with the in-built skills and knowledge of the people, who in return, enjoyed rights over the resources as a community's subordinate member. The conflicts and cess collection was resolved within the community. Biodiversity was conserved on a caste-based approach, and the forests were developed and governed by the community by following the sacred and secular constraints. During the colonial time, the institutions were completely substituted with centralised control. Production approach was turned market oriented from subsistence mode. Besides, state rights were replaced with that of community, resulting in the enclosure of 'commons' barring tribals and other forest-dependent communities into forests. Moreover, the FD created during this period aimed at uprooting the shifting cultivation and declaring activities such as grazing and cutting wood for making agricultural equipments like ploughs very difficult. This resulted in the disappearance of a protective ring created by the local community. All these developments led to uneasiness between the locals and the government, resulting in conflicts and rebellions in many places. Even after India's independence, the story was not much different. Instead, issues like biodiversity were now dictated by international rules. Restoration of community rights remained a far cry; while the powerful and wealthy were filling their coffers, a large chunk of the poor in the society suffered.

Source: Rangachari and Mukherji (2000).

In 1931, the Kumaun forests in the Uttaranchal region in India were brought under *Vana Panchayats* (Sharma, 1997). While in Tamil Nadu, it was with an intention of generating employment, that a programme in 1956 was started to plant trees in village wastelands and to extend fodder collection rights from the plantation area to the local people. By 1973, half of the proceeds from such plantations were also shared with the local Panchayats. By then, Gujarat too had set up a 'community forestry wing' in its FD (Wiersum, 1986). Between 1958 and 1959, a huge amount of forests in Bihar were transferred to the people for management and protection (Gupta, 1997). This shows that participatory forestry is not alien to the Indian setting; rather, the so-called new approaches are only a reproduction of the indigenous management of forests (Fisher, 1991; Bartlett and Malla, 1992; Hobley et al., 1994).

In India, as a national policy, the National Commission on Agriculture (NCA) introduced 'social forestry' in 1975, to develop forestry on the underproductive non-forest government and community land, after realising the importance of the local people's support in the protection of the forests (Nath, 1996). At the same time, the farmers were also encouraged to plant trees in their private lands; this resulted in the overlapping of the terms 'social' and 'on-farm' forestry (Shen and Contreras-Hermosilla, 1995).

Australian eucalyptus was the species adopted for plantation in many states of India, especially in the fertile north-western states. The peak in plantation reached between 1981 and 1988, when 8.6 billion (860 crore) trees were planted on private lands supported by the government and assisted by the World Bank and Canadian and Swiss donor agencies. However, most of the farmers were rich and could afford to wait for the six years for the poles to be ready for harvesting (Dewees and Saxena, 1997). However, social forestry helped little in bettering the lot of the poor, as the timber was directed to the markets and pressure on native forests remained the same. Moreover, social or farm forestry faced reversals following the price collapse in the wake of supply exceeding the market demand for eucalyptus timber, due to lack of marketing infrastructure (Harrison and Ghose, 2000). Another reason for failure is attributed to the absence of people's participation in planning and management, and also reluctance on their part to take up the plantation responsibility as a community institution. However, social forestry and farm forestry that started in recent times have, for sure, paved the way for new community forestry programmes for recognising the role of the users in the management of natural resources (Hobley, 1996). The JFM concept, a radical shift from the earlier revenue orientation to that of conservation as a priority was also a result of the efforts of few activists and non-government organisations (NGOs) voicing the concerns of the local people in the backdrop of the intensified forestry debate in the late 1980s, thus ending the bias of favouring commercial and industrial exploitation that was in practice at the cost of social justice from 1864 to 1988.

Emergence of Modern PFM

In accordance with the provisions of NFP of 1988, the Government of India, vide its letter of 1 June 1990, conveyed to state governments a framework for creating massive people's movement through involvement of village committees for the protection, regeneration and development of degraded forest lands (GoI, 1990). This gave impetus to the participation of stakeholders in the management of degraded forests situated near villages. The guidelines suggested that state governments could devolve everyday forest protection, management and development responsibilities to local community institutions at village level, and prescribe benefit-sharing arrangements following regeneration. Accordingly, all the Indian states formally resolved to implement JFM, making it one of the largest of such programmes in the world.

Initially, the state governments were given certain criteria for initiating the PFM/JFM programme; however, after consultation with other stakeholders and NGOs, these criterions were revised and formulated, and re-sent to the state governments. The criteria were: (a) providing legal back-up to the JFM committees; (b) extension of JFM to both degraded as well as good forests within two kms of village boundary, leaving aside the wildlife area network; (c) enhancement of women participation, with a minimum of 50 and 33 per cent of membership in the General Bodies (GBs) and Managing Committees (MCs) respectively, besides a reservation for an office bearer post for them; (d) recognition of the self-initiated groups; (e) measures to contribute to the regeneration of forest resources; (f) resolve conflicts; (g) integrate micro-plan with the working plan; and (h) monitor and evaluate the JFM programme (GoI, 2000).

After the national JFM guidelines were issued in 1990, twenty-eight state governments started implementing the JFM programme in their respective states after adopting resolutions (Bahuguna et al., 2004). The states of West Bengal, Haryana and Odisha have already completed two decades of JFM initiation (as they had initiated this programme on their own much before the national guidelines), while others like Assam, Sikkim and Mizoram issued enabling orders in 1998. As on March, 2006, there were 1,06,482 JFM committees in 28 states in India. The area co-managed by these committees is 220,17,583 ha (State Forest Departments, 2006). About 83,00,000 families are involved in these efforts, while the number of families indirectly benefited due to the process would be much more than actual number of families involved (Bahuguna et al., 2004).

Contemporary Context

AP is one of the states in India, which has been in the forefront in the implementation of PFM programme since early 1990s. The sheer magnitude of the project in AP places it at the 6th position among other states as far as the number of committees is concerned (Table 1.1).

Table 1.1

Number of JFM Committees and the Area under them in Different States of India

Name of the State	*No. of J/CFM Committees*	*Area under J/CFM (ha)*
Andhra Pradesh	8,498	25,66,343
Arunachal Pradesh	362	21,416
Assam	700	1,00,000
Bihar	615	3,85,080
Chhattisgarh	7,820	32,76,000
Goa	26	10,000
Gujarat	2,124	2,72,801

Cont'd...

...Cont'd

Haryana	1,075	60,000
Himachal Pradesh	1749	4,24,649
Jammu & Kashmir	4,861	40,000
Jharkhand	10,903	21,90,000
Karnataka	2,254	3,03,425
Kerala	561	1,73,235
Madhya Pradesh	14,428	59,46,800
Maharashtra	11,799	26,85,000
Manipur	283	60,307
Meghalaya	73	7,400
Mizoram	505	97,981
Nagaland	335	25,528
Odisha	9,905	8,80,187
Punjab	1,378	1,98,466
Rajasthan	4,691	7,69,895
Sikkim	204	88,518
Tamil Nadu	2,642	58,403
Tripura	399	1,12,328
Uttar Pradesh	2,096	93,857
Uttarakhand	12,089	5,44,964
West Bengal	4,107	6,25,000
Total	1,06,482	2,20,17,583

Key: J/CFM = Joint/Community Forest Management; ha = Hectares.

Source: State Forest Departments (2006).

A number of poor people, especially disadvantaged sections such as Scheduled Castes (SCs), Scheduled Tribes (STs) and Other Backward Classes (OBCs or simply BCs as is used by the government in AP) have their fortunes attached to this programme for their economic, social and political emancipation. However, success of any policy depends upon the institutional competency of a particular legislation, and also on how well the stakeholders receive it. Even the best of the legislations fail, if not implemented in word and spirit. This study is necessitated following the reports on the Andhra Pradesh Community Forest Management (APCFM) policy and its falling short in soaring to its own envisaged objectives of regeneration of forests, and also in the enhancement of the livelihoods of the communities depending on it (FPP and Samata, 2005; Reddy et al., 2007). There are also allegations of FD's attitude of continuing with the colonial legacy of dominance over the people living in the proximity of forests, in spite of their relegated role under the community forest management (CFM) (Springate-Baginski and Blaikie, 2007). At the same time, people's response too is questioned, as they are blamed to have received this policy only as another poverty alleviation programme and not as an opportunity to enhance their livelihoods in a sustainable manner through forests (Reddy et al., 2007). Besides, APCFM, or its earlier version of JFM, has been receiving flak from its critics ever since its inception for not addressing the vital concerns such as people's customary rights and land rights (Sarin, 2003). Against this background, this research is intended to understand how CFM is performing with its own idealistic goal of developing forests with the participation of the community that was supposedly better placed (after CFM, in terms of power share between them and FD) at ground level. Against this backdrop, the research specifically questions whether the APCFM, as a policy, has adequate governance and institutional arrangements to face the challenges of the community-based natural resources management (CBNRM) that has direct implication on the lives of the forest-depending people.

The overall objective of this research is to understand the working of the *Vana Samrakhana Samithi* (VSS) institutions in practice under different community inhabitations, and also to find out where the lacunas are in the successful implementation of CFM. The research also probes to unravel the causes that are holding back community participation to its full potential. The specific objectives of this research are as follows:

- To examine the feasibility of the forest-dependent communities, particularly tribals, to govern themselves under the existing institutional and organisational structure of CFM.

- To look into the transparency and accountability levels of the delivery mechanisms of the VSS institutions.
- To find out the power relations between the FD and user community in practice, in tribal and non-tribal areas.
- To understand the factors that determine institutional sustenance and the CFM programme as a whole.

Reflections on the Concepts of PFM on this Research

The role of 'community' or for that matter the 'local people', in the management of 'common property resources' remains nucleus to the institutions of NRM (Ostrom, 1990; Hecht and Cockburn, 1990; Marks, 1984; Blockhus et al., 1992; Poffenberger, 1990; Bromley et al., 1992; McCay and Acheson, 1987; UNFAO, 1990; Ascher, 1995) despite the importance of physical and natural factors. In the context of APCFM also, 'community' is expected to play a vital role, especially after Government Order (GO) 13 (2002), when the JFM was modified into CFM. However, for better governance of the APCFM institutions, retrenchment of the government as recommended by Chandhoke (2003) seems imperative. Institutions are rule-making bodies (Leach, Mearns and Scoones, 1997; Ostrom, 1992; Gupta, 1985) and so are the VSS, to guide their day-to-day affairs of managing forests. They need to be independent from undue influence of any other stakeholder, including FD, in order to be autonomous, especially while preparing micro-plans and annual plans (for details see Chapter 4) that determine their performance. Access to use, and excluding others from common property rights (Libecap, 1989; Ascher, 1995) are few of the common rights that need rules for the users. VSS also have such rules. It would be interesting to find out the significance they have in their day-to-day management of forests.

Fabricius (2004) found defining 'community' difficult. In a dynamic society like AP (India), defining the term 'community' in the context of NRM is equally difficult because the conditions (physical, natural, social, political and financial) and needs of the community are different not only from one place to another, but also from region to region.

Olson's (1965) view on collective action is that those who are already benefiting from the incentives find themselves trapped in a rigid situation – they have to forgo their individual benefits to cooperate towards collective action. Which in some way, benefits the 'shifting cultivators' inhabiting the Visakhapatnam agency areas. Their position quite matches with the description of Olson's logic of collective action.

Stern et al. (2003) highlighted the importance of institutions providing additional incentives in the guise of job provision and scope for wealth creation for better performance. APCFM indeed, has provision for such clause in the form of wage-employment to the VSS members to keep their interest until they start reaping sustainable resources for their forests. It is of research interest to find its implications on the programme.

According to Baland and Platteau (2000), achieving cooperation between the users in a 'location' close to the resource is notably high. The degree of its influence can be compared with the forest users in sample villages in Visakhapatnam with their counterparts in Adilabad and Chittoor, because the forest user communities in Visakhapatnam come close to the description of what Baland and Platteau surmised about relationship between forest users and the location of their forests.

There are more than 8,000 VSS in AP, which reflect the high number of user communities of forest; this in turn, means huge participation of the communities in the affairs of managing community forests. But it is a challenge for research to gauge their actual level of participation as pointed out by Arora (1994) and Vira et al. (1999). According to them, token participation cannot qualify to measure the level of participation.

Effective decision-making in common pool resource management institutions is a vital ingredient and this in turn, is determined by the presence of accountability for its users (Crook and Manor, 1998; Agrawal and Ribot, 1999; de Oliveira, 2002; Ribot, 2002). APCFM also has measures for accountability in its institutional set-up for its members in the form of periodic meetings to voice their concerns at GB and executive levels (MC). This aspect would be interesting to test the potency of the

VSS in actual practice, because this is an important step in the democratisation of the institutions.

Leaders are those who hold a sway over others resulting in mutual rise in motivation and morality (Burns, 1979). In VSS, there is immense scope for leadership to emerge and make difference to their forest vegetation and the lives of their communities by their dynamism. Such potential individuals get a chance to be the 'chairperson' or 'vice-chairperson' through election. Assessment from field will throw light on whether the provisions are utilised by the leaders of the institutions in enhancing their communities through the CFM.

Fiszbein (1997), Kaimowitz et al. (1998) and de Mello (2000) pointed out the importance of funding for natural resource governance at the local level. There is no denying its importance. Even the APCFM project is run on external funding. Other programmes like Forest Development Agency (FDA) and National Bank for Agriculture and Rural Development (NABARD) are also sponsored schemes under the central government budgetary allocation. How far such funding is utilised in a constructive manner is interesting to comprehend from field investigation.

Sharing benefits from resources is what community primarily looks forward to in NRM institutions. Rangachari and Mukherji (2000) emphasised on secure tenure and assured access to resources, benefits and more voice with regard to resources for better protection of common resources. There are provisions for such benefits notified in the GO 13 (2002) governing the APCFM, but how effective these provisions are in action, and to what extent they have been able to motivate the community in the protection of their forests remains to be seen.

Fabricius and de Wet (2002) described corrupt practices in NRM as an ill-treatment of the communities and indulging in dishonest financial dealings. Such practices have the potential to dismantle the very objective of effective 'community participation'. Looking from this aspect would help the research to bring in necessary amendments to the document implementing APCFM on reports of such happenings.

History of collective action in the village is seen as one of the vital characteristics of the successful management of resources (Baland and Platteau, 2000). Most of the communities in AP are new to the concept of 'PFM', hence probing them on their handicaps, if any, in not having 'formal institutions' influencing them in the management of their VSS.

Baland and Platteau (2000) believe that small groups are good for managing NRMs, while Agrawal (2000) sees advantage in bigger groups; yet, he also settles for moderate groups for ideal management of NRMs. In APCFM, there are varying sizes of VSS managing their forests. In such cases, investigating the impact of group size on the management of VSS is sure to help in understanding the benefits and difficulties encountered by them. Even while conceding homogenous institutions as a better prospect in managing NRM, Baland and Platteau (2000) do not see serious handicaps in having heterogeneous institutions managing natural resources, provided their 'economic interests' are protected. With AP being a dynamic society, the effects of social dynamism are expected to have definite bearing on the performance of the VSS institutions. Hence, they are important for a research on governance like this. WCFSD (1999) described the importance of the role women play across the world in the forestry sector. AP is no different; hence, APCFM has provided for a special provision for women by reserving half of the membership at all levels in the VSS institutions. This research tries to evaluate as to how effective such provisions have been to women in their emancipation.

The possibilities of the elite squeezing resources disproportionately as illustrated by Fabricius (2004) has relevance in APCFM context, given the economic disparities prevalent among the various groups in the Indian society. However, Bandyopadhyay et al. (1983), maintain that class system was never a hurdle in the NRM because of the self-sufficient nature of the traditional Indian village economy. But class discrimination prevalent in the Indian society (Beteille, 1965) cannot be simply wished away as inconsequential; it may harm the performance of the members in the VSS managing their forests. Conflicts are a common feature within or among the groups, but what matters is a low-cost resolution mechanism (Ostrom, 1990), to achieve long-run objectives (Rangachari and Mukherji, 2000). APCFM designated this power to the 'MC' of VSS at the local level, and also at each level in the hierarchy. It will be of interest to see the effectiveness of these institutions in resolving conflicts, and also the cost and its resultant effect on the efficiency of the VSS as a whole.

Features of Sustainable Management of Natural Resources Institutions

Many factors determine sustainable management of NRM institutions, one essentially being the availability of 'enough resource' for the users to invest their energy and time to create new institutions (Gibson, 2001). Bromley et al. (1992), McCay and Acheson (1987) and Ostrom (1990), emphasise on certain preconditions that yield positive results to manage common pool resources. They put forth preconditions such as locals valuing resources with a provision to enjoy some individual property rights, while simultaneously constructing local-level collective institutions that control the use of resources. Importantly, it has to be followed by an 'inclination' of the 'village group' to manage the natural resources (Saxena, 2001). This inclination comes from the people when they think the protection of the resources is 'vital for their survival'. At the same time, the interest may dwindle when the degradation is too extreme to reverse. Another important factor is that the different sections in the society· especially, the rich and the poor, have to be equally dependent on the forests for their survival needs of fodder and fuelwood to maintain interest in the collaborative action (ibid.).

Stern et al. (2003) believe economic dependence on forests, past practice of equitable costs and benefits-sharing mechanism among the tribals, added by their socio-cultural habits in bonding with forests makes such groups easy to initiate for the newer concept of institution to manage forests. Durability of institutions is important for effective 'ecosystem resilience', and this is provided by its flexibility and level of diversity to adapt to changing situations (Holling, 1986). In order to nurture flexibility in the institutions, Berkes (1996) stresses on more interaction, and openness towards feedback. Agrawal and Gibson (1999) and Robbins (1998), insist not only on focusing on the entire spectrum of actors with divergent interests but also on the social and political process through which these actors interrelate to shape interactions in the institutional mechanisms. For that matter, 'a complete institution managing "commons" means controlling access, defining property rights, establishing codes of procedure that are accepted by all, enforcing compliance, and ensuring that the whole management process operates on the practice of accountable consent' (O'Riordan and Jordan, 2000: 488). On a similar pattern, Rangachari and Mukherji (2000: 77) recommend efforts to treat different situations in accordance to their needs, 'if the institution has socio-cultural origins, it should be supported by strong social sanctions (as in the case of traditional institutions); if it is state-sponsored, appropriate policy, and fiscal and legal instruments would need to be adopted that support and strengthen such institutions'. Hence, Thompson and Schoonmaker (1997) and Ostrom (2005, 2007) strongly advocate 'crafting' 'resource management institutions', rather than simply coming up with universal 'blueprints', because it is often seen that 'one size doesn't fit all'. Similarly, Poteete and Ostrom (2004) question the possibility of 'simple recipes' for all types of collective action because of the existence of socio-economically diverse groups in addition to the diverse ecological conditions they encounter.

However, there is no simple recipe for successful collective action (ibid.). But, keeping 'free-riders' ratio low would certainly help the survival of institutions (Gupta, 1990). Nevertheless, institutions that provide additional incentives in guise of job provision and scope for wealth creation can do better (Stern et al., 2003) as it has happened in the AP's, PFM programme; however, such temporary provisions in the form of 'wage-employment' and 'entry point programmes' have left much to be desired following loss of interest by the 'communities', once the funding for such incentives were stopped briefly between the two phases of JFM and CFM (Reddy et al., 2007). In such scenario, international donors and political elites have their own share of making difference by taking local users into confidence towards organising them more effectively (Silva, 1994; Blair, 1996).

Then again, there are situations in NRM, wherein it is difficult for institutions to flourish; especially where demographic changes are rapid, the local community is not dependent on the resources in question, substantial heterogeneities of interest exists, there is no local autonomy to make or enforce, and when the resource system itself is very large (Acheson, 1989; Feeny et al., 1990). Even the role of 'community' itself, especially in NRM, is seriously contended by some of the scholars (Ghai, 1992; Sivaramakrishnan, 1999). According to them, this concept has been 'romanticised' because they do not see the 'state' always acting as a 'predator' ready to pounce on natural resources, and the village imbued with 'conservation ethics' with no internal conflicts. In fact, these are the sort of situations that provide for the real challenge to the researchers.

Approach

To optimise the chances of everyone standing up and taking notice of degrading environment, Hajer (1995) sees no harm in presenting effective storylines over environmental issues, whether or not they are anomalies to the existing institutional arrangements that influence the formulation of the public policies, sub-politics (politics played in non-conventional form by non-political players through well-articulated presentations) are typically as important or more important than formal parliamentary politics. He also observes that seeing scientific knowledge formation as being, in the past, a sub-political process, helps to overcome the laboratory boundaries of sociology of science research on environmental knowledge. His observation on the emergence of newer discourses leads one to think that no discourse is an end in itself as far as new ideas are concerned, because there is movement and with changing times, the theory also could be put to test and rejected if found to be not meeting to the demands of the situation.

With regard to specific approach to this study, the fact is that 'India never had and will never have common single problem... any effort to reduce India to a single micro- or macro-problem will always be a disaster' (Yumnum, 1996: 99). In the background of this statement, any approach adopted for any kind of social science research in the Indian context could prove misleading. Hence, a pragmatic approach arising from critical realism is adopted for this research. For this purpose, an interdisciplinary multi-scale theoretical approach aimed at understanding relationships between the people and their forests within the broader governance and institutional context is adopted. For a wider generalisation of the policy analysis, a number of CFMs spread across the three different regions of AP are selected. These CFMs were clubbed in two streams of only tribals including PTGs and mixed-caste members respectively, in order to examine the dichotomy between the implementation in these two different settings. The characteristics of the sample CFM and their profiles are discussed in detail in the Chapter 3.

About the Book

This book is organised into eight chapters.

The history of forest governance and policy in India is presented in Chapter 1. It gives an interesting blend of conservation and exploitation of the forest-depending people. This is evident since the ancient times, when fitting measures were considered to combat the destructing menace. During the Mauryan period, forest superintendents were appointed for protection of forests, while few Mughal rulers in medieval times were eager to generate revenues for the royal treasury by clearing forests, others made efforts to conserve them. The colonial phase can be remembered not only for immeasurable destruction, but also for bringing into force the modern system of forest administration into Indian forestry. This was also the time when many of the traditional institutions managing forests were disturbed, contributing to imbalance in their ecology and customs of managing forests. In independent India, forest policy was just a continuation of the legacy left by the British administration. Though there were a few half-hearted steps towards revegetation of the forests through experiments like 'social forestry', involving the local people, the main thrust remained on the exploitation of forest in the name of 'industrialisation'. Moreover, forest-depending people's rights remained ignored; rather, their livelihoods hinged on suspicion for the unofficial policy of treating them as destroyers of forests. The chapter also traces the PFM in India much before the emergence of its modern concept. Further touching upon the features of sustainable management of NRM institutions, the chapter also reflects on the concepts and theories on the study in context.

Chapter 2 looks into the evolution of forest policy in AP, the context of the study, and discusses the forest acts that came into force. It discusses experiments that were tried earlier in AP on conserving forests with the help of people. It is a different matter though, that the objectives were not entirely conservation. The chapter also presents as to how the forest policies were being implemented in the Nizam and Madras Presidency before the Indian independence and after AP became a united state with the merger of two regions. It also gives an account of how a major shift towards forest protection and concern for people depending on it received consideration, after the issue of national guidelines on JFM in the state of AP. The emergence and implementation of 'PFM' in AP is reviewed on its statutory position (rules governing the functioning of CFM in AP) and also in operation, focusing on its ecological impact, governance and institutional challenges. Elaborating about the context of the study, Chapter 3 discusses the particulars and background of the area and the communities studied. Besides presenting the operationalisation of the study, the chapter also helps in understanding many of the factors that set the communities with pre-existing conditions that lead them into success or failure in the management of community forests.

Participation and decision-making is an important activity in the CFM for the impact it will have on the outcome of the programme like this. But, the ground realities suggest that there has been very less freedom extended to the communities involved, especially tribals, to voice their opinion on how their forests should be managed, especially when it comes to species selection for plantation. This is all discussed in Chapter 4.

Acute dearth of awareness among the community, especially those in tribal areas is found to be the cause for lack of transparency and accountability in the management of community forests. FDs conceal about the financial aspects and other issues from the members, sometimes in collusion with those in elected executive positions. In other words, it could be said that the democratic tenets of CFM were not subjected to test to its fullest. Yet, the community members found to be of the view that FD is necessary to protect forests as it is a professional outfit. For a balanced understanding of the situation, FD's point of view explaining about their handicaps in its management of CFM is presented in Chapter 5.

Chapter 6 gives an insight into the determinants of CFM that have a direct bearing on the performance of any particular CFM. When such determinants boost motivation, there tends to be chances of better showing. In the same way it is in adverse, the results could be opposite. The motivational factors in the positive are found to be extension of monetary benefits for community welfare or wage employment, share in forest produce and harvest. There can be issues like persistent forest theft, threat from smugglers and hostilities from FD or encroachment on the CFM forest land that determine in negative on the outcome of the programme. Chapter 7 provides a theoretical discussion locating the empirical material of Chapters 4–6 within a wider theoretical context. The idea to have theoretical discussion after the empirical chapters is only to present the reader a triangulation of already existing knowledge with the findings from this research. Besides, it theorises the factors that determine towards the better management of community forests emphasising on certain preconditions. Finally, Chapter 8 in the conclusion briefly outlines the policy and research implications with the specific suggestions for APCFM. It discusses the FD official's attitude in shedding the colonial hegemony and the need on part of them to work in cohesion with the communities in the participatory forest magnet in letter and spirit. Besides, highlighting the fact that this concept has come to stay irrespective of any individual FD officer's whims of acknowledging it.

2

Forest Policy from State Control to Community Participation

AP's share of experience in PFM started in 1983. It was in Olgapur, a village in Karimnagar district, where the Government of AP leased degraded lands on 'tree *pattas*' to the poor people for raising fuelwood under 'social forestry project' with Canada India Development Assistance (CIDA) (Madari, 1997). The planting material was supplied through nurseries set up exclusively for this purpose (Venkatraman and Falconer, 1998; Gopal and Upadhyay, 2001).

However, this scheme did not see much success due to various reasons, though in terms of legalities, it attracted the provisions of FCA, 1980. Therefore, in 1986, the same was examined in the light of the FCA, 1980, and was modified as 'Reforestation of Degraded Forests' with 'Family Assistance Method', which was apprised in GO No. 445 (1986). Yet, there were apprehensions about this GO also getting attracted to the provisions of the FCA, 1980. Hence, the Government of India was pleaded to clarify this matter and it then asked the state to abandon the scheme with a suggestion to take up any other scheme, wherein community participation could be sought or attached in place of the existing 'tree *patta* scheme' for the protection and development of degraded forests. 'Social forestry' did not yield the desired results. Nevertheless, the experiences of the project established the fact that neither regeneration nor prevention of the degradation of forests could be achieved without involvement of the local people who depend on the forests for usufruct and cattle grazing.

Forest Policy in AP

Before the state of AP was formally formed on 1 November 1956, Hyderabad Forest Act, 1355 *Fasli* and The Madras Forest Act of 1882 were in force in their respective regions. Eight districts of Telangana (Adilabad, Karimnagar, Khammam, Mahbubnagar, Medak, Nalgonda, Nizamabad and Warangal) were governed by the Hyderabad Forest Act, 1915, while the Madras Forest Act of 1882 governed 14 of the Coastal Andhra and Rayalaseema districts (Anantapur, Chittoor, Eluru, Godavari, Guntur, Kadapa, Kakinada, Kurnool, Krishna, Machilipatanam, Nellore, Ongole, Srikakulam and Visakhapatnam).

When a separate department was created during the premiership of Sir Salar Jung (before 1277 Fasli (1867 AD)), the forests in Hyderabad state (Telangana was under the Nizam Rule) were considered subordinate to the interest of agriculture and were thus administered by the district officials. The department's work was only to protect and sell around nine valuable species of trees, designated as 'reserved' or 'irsali' timber, under a set of simple rules, while the rest of the produce and administration remained in the hands of the district officials. This dual control over the management of the forests proved to be a failure. On the other hand, there was scant regard for environmental balance, because forests were cleared by the revenue officers for cultivation, thus wiping out valuable timber in the process. During the same time, schemes for rehabilitating deserted villages by expanding cultivation were initiated, resulting in the loss of lakhs of acres of forests (Gogia, 2002).

In 1887, the government secured the services of Mr Ballantine, a European officer trained as an IFS from Berar. He served in the domain of Nizam till 1893; during this period, he managed to arrest forest abuses of unrestricted felling and selected several tracts for 'reserves'. By the year 1303 Fasli (1893 AD), the government declared vast tracts covered by forest growth as protected forests and placed them under the singular charge of the FD. Clear circulars of instruction were issued by the government for the administration of these protected areas. The Forest Act was enacted to obtain a legal control over the forests in 1310 Fasli (1900 AD) to consolidate the instructions embodied in government circulars. The number of reserved timber species was increased in the areas other than the protected ones. The efforts of the department was directed mainly towards the survey and reservation of forest areas, introduction of felling schemes and works of improvement, systematic exploitation of forest produce, development of a sustained revenue, plus the consolidation and conservation of big valuable forest estates. Yet, the Forest Act of 1310 Fasli (1900 AD) was found inadequate for the growing requirements of the FD. It was, therefore, superseded by a revised Forest Act of 1326 Fasli (1916 AD). This Act was again repealed by Hyderabad Forest Act of 1355 Fasli (1945 AD), which was modelled on the lines of Indian Forest Act of 1878 (Gogia, 2002).

With the decline of Mughal Empire, the Coastal Andhra and Rayalaseema regions fell into the hands of British administration as Madras Presidency (Coastal Andhra and Rayalaseema Region). Within no time, it started asserting its control which is evident from the proclamation of royal rights over teak and tree-felling. This was followed by National Indian Forest Act, 1865 that facilitated the creation of Imperial Forest Service to survey, reserve and monitor the forest under its domain. Later, through 1878 Act, FD acquired absolute control over the forest resources. In 1882, a separate Madras Forest Act was legislated for application in the districts of these two regions. In brief, the British regime observed massive expansion of agriculture in the forested areas in Coastal Andhra and Rayalaseema regions (Rao, 1958). Besides, the demand for timber for ship building and railway expansion in a way brought administration in conflict with the local tribals as it disturbed their livelihoods (Cleghorn, 1964).

Following the formation of AP, the AP Forest Act, 1967, was drafted after the Law Commission of AP examined the two forest acts existing in the respective regions of Madras Province and Nizams. The draft was passed by the Legislature, and it is in force since 15 April 1967 (Gogia, 2002; Sunder et al., 2001). The 1967 Act was followed by various legislations. The first one was Forest Offence Rules of 1969, which was enacted to describe compounding prosecution when officers combat the offence and also to fix the penalty to the offenders. This was immediately followed by the AP Forest Produce Transit Rules, 1970. This legislation was aimed at halting illegal movement of forest produce within the state unless accompanied by a permit issued by a competent authority (official of the state government). The following year, AP Minor Forest Produce (Regulation of Trade) Act of 1971 was passed. This Act was made to prevent the loss of revenue to the government from 'abnus' (beedi) leaves trade. In the absence of any statutory control over the minor forest produce (MFP), the contractors had a scope of manipulating their contract, but the act created a state monopoly, wherein the government appointed officer or agent for a unit, sells, purchases, processes, collects, stores or transports such minor produce (mainly the beedi leaves).

AP Scheduled Areas MFP (Regulation of Trade) Regulations, 1979 were introduced in public interest to create state monopoly over the trade of certain MFP in the Scheduled Areas in the state. It contained restrictions on the sale, purchase, curing, processing or transportation of the minor produce other than by the state corporation. In recent times, the AP Scheduled Areas MFP (Regulation of Trade) Rules, 1990 were introduced. The nucleus of these rules was the definition of who is 'accused' and when it is an offence to procure any MFP in the Scheduled Areas. The regulation referred is made under the guidelines of the V Schedule of the Constitution of India. The state government appointed Girijan Cooperative Corporation Ltd. (GCC) (a body of officials and tribal representatives) Visakhapatnam, as an agent for scheduled areas for purchasing and trading any MFP (Gogia, 2002).

Implementation of PFM in AP

The World Bank started negotiations to sponsor the AP forestry project in 1991, when Andhra Pradesh Forest Department

(APFD) wanted guns and ammunition, more staff, and subsidised distribution of seedlings for farm forestry and research. However, World Bank introduced new ideas into APFD on the lines of West Bengal, after holding a workshop in 1992 and attended by FD staff and NGOs. This was followed-up by an understanding signed between World Bank and the AP government for the implementation of JFM to protect, improve and develop forests with the involvement of local forest-dependent people by forming 'FPCs' called *Vana Samrakshana Samithies* (VSS) (Sunder et al., 2001).

By the year 1993, the Government of AP issued a state forest policy GO 237 (1993) in consonance with the national policy. This forest policy of AP laid down broad guidelines for future management perspectives by identifying immediate forest concerns, by encouraging participation of local village communities in its management through JFM, by organising them into VSS. The objectives of the policy were: (a) abolition of forest contracts by encouraging departmental working; (b) establishment of forest development corporations to attract investments; (c) encouragement to social forestry, agro forestry and farm forestry; (d) biodiversity conservation and enactment of a special act for such purpose; and (e) widening the scope of forest laws to cover specific issues such as timber in transit, regulation of tree felling in private lands, regulating saw mills and timber depots in the private sector (GoAP, 2002). Determining the policies and procedures for the joint action, the GO laid down certain canons for the VSS formation, its role, and responsibilities along with FD, and elucidated the benefit-sharing policies.

Then, in 2002, the Government of AP issued a vision statement titled 'Vision 2020', which had special mention for forestry sector (ibid.). The focal theme of the vision on state forest sector was sustainable management of forest resources through participatory approach, with emphasis on the protection and regeneration of forests and forest land to ensure a green and healthy AP for future generations. The strategies evolved were in tune with the National Forestry Action Plan

(NFAP), and the vision of the state of AP. They specifically address various focused areas of forestry and provide direction for future planning and development, namely: (a) conservation and improvement of the quality of existing forests; (b) strengthening social forestry activities; (c) streamlining forest management strategies; (d) encouraging people's participation in forest management; and (e) conserving biodiversity and genetic resources.

The most significant concept in this 'vision' was mentioning about 'CFM' because the refined approach was aimed at upgrading the initiatives taken under JFM. While JFM was more of a partnership between the forest-dependent communities and the Government of AP, CFM was expected to be more of a democratic process through delegation of the decision-making process by decentralising the entire process of planning and implementation with APFD and Government of AP. The role of FD was envisaged as facilitators and providers of technical and infrastructural support. CFM is an approach for forest development through a democratised participatory approach, which empowers the forest-dependent local communities. It is aimed to balance the local needs with external and environmental needs through increased productivity of the forest resources, reduced dependence on forests through substitution of demand and alternate livelihood opportunities, upgradation of living standards and inculcating a sense of ownership and pride among the forest-dependent communities. Despite the fact that CFM is claimed to be more democratic than JFM, the structure of the hierarchy above VSS gives the impression of a top-down exercise of authority and power, still resting with the FD.

It is seen that, there are enabling steps in the 'vision' to receive special attention to create an enabling environment for holistic and sustainable development of forests. They are: legal backing for CFM, relaxation under FCA, 1980, for medicinal plants cultivation by VSS, liberalisation of state monopoly of Non-Timber Forest Produce (NTFP), conformity of panchayat laws with CFM regulations, conflict resolution among stakeholders and traditional rights, and maintaining consistency of micro-plans with working plans.

Table 2.1
Difference between JFM and CFM Policy

Policy Particulars	*JFM*	*CFM*
Implemented Through	GO MS.No.173	GO MS.No.13
Year	1996	2002
Member Secretary of VSS MC	FD Official	MC Member
Executive Position in the VSS MC	One (President)	Two Positions (Chairperson and Vice-Chairperson)
Bank Transactions	One Account	Two Accounts
Signatories	FD Official and President	Chairperson and Vice-Chairperson for both the accounts, while FD official is the third signatory for the project account
Mode of Granting Funds	From DFO to VSS through FRO and FSO	Directly deposited into VSS account
Levying and Collection of Fines	No Provision	Can collect fine up to ₹ 100 from the forest offenders
Role of FD	Project implementer with the help of VSS	Facilitator, while VSS has to prepare and implement plans
Role of Panchayats	No Role	Panchayat President is a member of the Advisory Council
Role of NGOs	No Role	Defined Role

Key: GO = Government Order; MC = Managing Committee; FD = Forest Department; DFO = Divisional Forest Officer; FRO = Forest Range Officer; FSO = Forest Section Officer.

Source: Reddy et al. (2004).

Different Schemes and Projects in Operation under PFM in AP

APCFM

As already mentioned, JFM has now graduated into CFM since 2002 (26 November). APCFM is functional in 15 districts,[1] with 3,26,000 families benefiting from the scheme, which includes

19.5 per cent SC and 30.7 per cent ST population; women account for 48 per cent in the overall composition. By January 2006, ₹ 317.83 crore (48.6%) was already utilised, while treating (mostly degraded patches) 3,24,948 ha of forest area that includes plantation of over 71,080 ha (APFD, 2005).

FDA

FDA is a national afforestation programme formulated by the Government of India by merging four 'Centrally Sponsored Afforestation Schemes under the Ministry of Environment and Forests (MoE&F), which were formerly functioning under the Ninth Plan. This was intended to do away with an array of schemes, besides removing unnecessary delays in availing funds at field level. Above all, it was also an effort for institutionalising people's participation in project formulation and its implementation. The four merged plans were: (1) Integrated Afforestation and Eco-Development Projects (IAEPS); (2) Area Oriented Fuelwood and Fodder Projects Scheme (AOFFPS); (3) Conservation and Development of NTFP including Medicinal Plants Scheme; and (4) Association of Scheduled Tribes and Rural Poor in Regeneration of Degraded Forests (ASTRP). FDA and Joint/Community Forest Management (J/CFM) implement the scheme with an objective of capacity building at the grass-root level and empowering the local people towards participation in the decision-making process. FDA is constituted at the territorial/wildlife forest division level. FDA is a registered society under Societies Registration Act. FDA started operating since 2002, almost simultaneously with APCFM (ibid.).

Forest areas are managed with the involvement of VSS as per Government of India's approval. The activities of FDA are similar to those carried out under APCFM. The Government of India sanctioned 29 FDA Projects in AP. They were sanctioned in phases, i.e., 13 projects during 2002–03, 10 projects during 2003–04, five projects during 2004–05 and the remaining one project was sanctioned in 2005–06. Under FDA, the total number of beneficiaries was 2.89 lakh, of whom 1.04 lakh were tribals. An area of 43,910 ha was proposed to be treated during the project period. By December 2005, an area of 27,547 ha was already treated (ibid.).

NABARD/Rural Infrastructure Development Fund (RIDF)

NABARD-assisted RIDF schemes were started in 2000 by FD, beginning with RIDF V – JFM. Three streams of works were undertaken through RIDF schemes. They are: (1) JFM; (2) Soil and Moisture Conservation (SMC) works; and (3) *Pongamia* (bio-diesel) plantations (ibid.).

Execution of APCFM through Statutory Document

The Government of AP is implementing its CFM programme as per the comprehensive GO issued through MS No. 13 (2002), see Figures 2.1 and 2.2 for institutional structure of VSS, its constitution and functions, and also rights, privileges, duties and responsibilities of its members.

By the end of 2006, there were 8,412 VSS functioning in AP (Table 3.1). Out of these, 5,000 committees are sponsored by World Bank, while the remaining were under centrally sponsored schemes such as FDA, Employment Assurance Schemes (EAS), RIDF and NABARD (APFD, 2006). These projects require funding, in order to undertake various forest regeneration activities such as plantation, labour payment, and also to spend on 'entry point programmes' such as building 'village community halls', buying 'irrigational equipments', or any other activity that helps in village development, to keep the community interested in the programme until their forest reaches the stage of yielding sustained produce to the communities.

A Review of J/CFM Implementation in AP

Evidence suggests that the swift expansion of JFM in AP has led to regeneration of forests, which in turn resulted in economic gain of the local people. Additional benefits were reduction of forest land, conversion for agriculture, reduction of illicit timber felling and improved safety for forestry staff. However, many glowing reports have been presented either by

Figure 2.1

Organisation and Structure of VSS

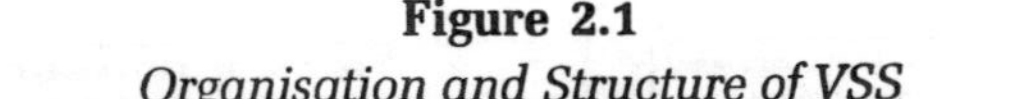

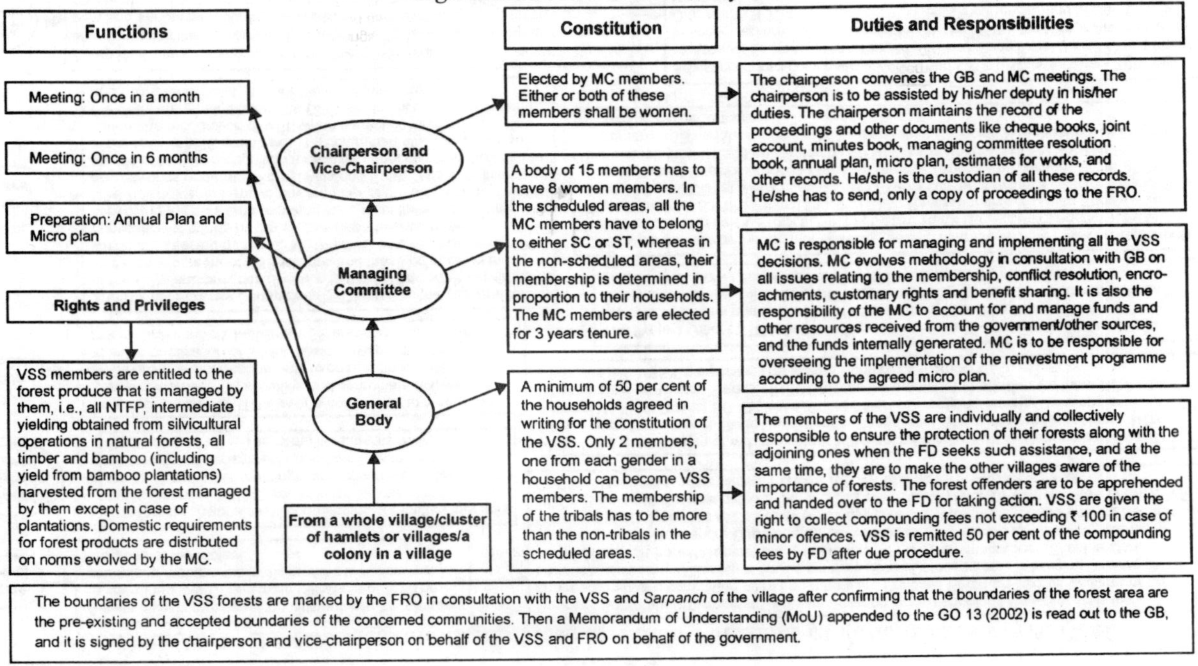

Source: APCFM GO MS. No. 13 (2002).

Figure 2.2

Constitution of the Councils and Committees and their Functions at Various Levels of APCFM

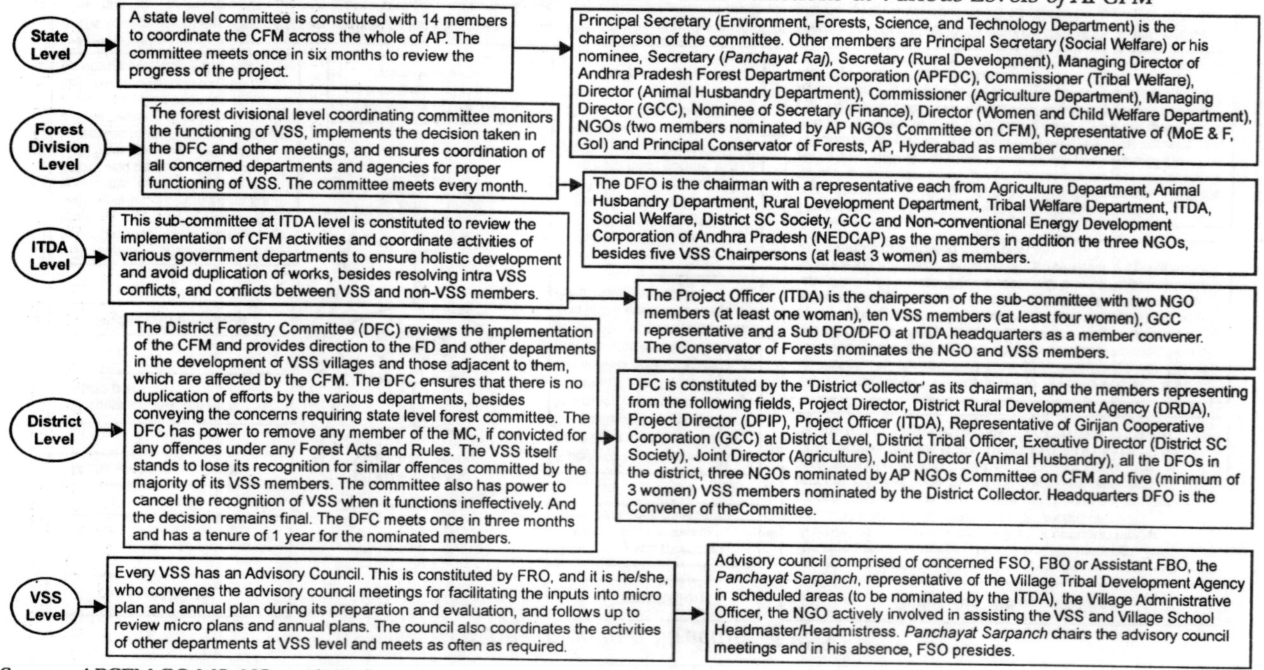

Level	Function	Constitution
State Level	A state level committee is constituted with 14 members to coordinate the CFM across the whole of AP. The committee meets once in six months to review the progress of the project.	Principal Secretary (Environment, Forests, Science, and Technology Department) is the chairperson of the committee. Other members are Principal Secretary (Social Welfare) or his nominee, Secretary (*Panchayat Raj*), Secretary (Rural Development), Managing Director of Andhra Pradesh Forest Department Corporation (APFDC), Commissioner (Tribal Welfare), Director (Animal Husbandry Department), Commissioner (Agriculture Department), Managing Director (GCC), Nominee of Secretary (Finance), Director (Women and Child Welfare Department), NGOs (two members nominated by AP NGOs Committee on CFM), Representative of (MoE & F, GoI) and Principal Conservator of Forests, AP, Hyderabad as member convener.
Forest Division Level	The forest divisional level coordinating committee monitors the functioning of VSS, implements the decision taken in the DFC and other meetings, and ensures coordination of all concerned departments and agencies for proper functioning of VSS. The committee meets every month.	The DFO is the chairman with a representative each from Agriculture Department, Animal Husbandry Department, Rural Development Department, Tribal Welfare Department, ITDA, Social Welfare, District SC Society, GCC and Non-conventional Energy Development Corporation of Andhra Pradesh (NEDCAP) as the members in addition the three NGOs, besides five VSS Chairpersons (at least 3 women) as members.
ITDA Level	This sub-committee at ITDA level is constituted to review the implementation of CFM activities and coordinate activities of various government departments to ensure holistic development and avoid duplication of works, besides resolving intra VSS conflicts, and conflicts between VSS and non-VSS members.	The Project Officer (ITDA) is the chairperson of the sub-committee with two NGO members (at least one woman), ten VSS members (at least four women), GCC representative and a Sub DFO/DFO at ITDA headquarters as a member convener. The Conservator of Forests nominates the NGO and VSS members.
District Level	The District Forestry Committee (DFC) reviews the implementation of the CFM and provides direction to the FD and other departments in the development of VSS villages and those adjacent to them, which are affected by the CFM. The DFC ensures that there is no duplication of efforts by the various departments, besides conveying the concerns requiring state level forest committee. The DFC has power to remove any member of the MC, if convicted for any offences under any Forest Acts and Rules. The VSS itself stands to lose its recognition for similar offences committed by the majority of its VSS members. The committee also has power to cancel the recognition of VSS when it functions ineffectively. And the decision remains final. The DFC meets once in three months and has a tenure of 1 year for the nominated members.	DFC is constituted by the 'District Collector' as its chairman, and the members representing from the following fields, Project Director, District Rural Development Agency (DRDA), Project Director (DPIP), Project Officer (ITDA), Representative of Girijan Cooperative Corporation (GCC) at District Level, District Tribal Officer, Executive Director (District SC Society), Joint Director (Agriculture), Joint Director (Animal Husbandry), all the DFOs in the district, three NGOs nominated by AP NGOs Committee on CFM and five (minimum of 3 women) VSS members nominated by the District Collector. Headquarters DFO is the Convener of theCommittee.
VSS Level	Every VSS has an Advisory Council. This is constituted by FRO, and it is he/she, who convenes the advisory council meetings for facilitating the inputs into micro plan and annual plan during its preparation and evaluation, and follows up to review micro plans and annual plans. The council also coordinates the activities of other departments at VSS level and meets as often as required.	Advisory council comprised of concerned FSO, FBO or Assistant FBO, the *Panchayat Sarpanch*, representative of the Village Tribal Development Agency in scheduled areas (to be nominated by the ITDA), the Village Administrative Officer, the NGO actively involved in assisting the VSS and Village School Headmaster/Headmistress. *Panchayat Sarpanch* chairs the advisory council meetings and in his absence, FSO presides.

Source: APCFM GO MS. NO. 13 (2002).

donor-project staff or by the foresters themselves, and so are not entirely objective. The discussion of a number of different case studies here is illustrative of the sort of benefits possible, rather than attempting a conclusive weighing of positives and negatives.

Positive Impact

The Behroonguda VSS in Adilabad has been used as a model by the FD to present the successful efforts of managing forests with people's participation. It was here that JFM was launched in AP on May 23, 1993. It was also the first village in AP to win official recognition for VSS. The village committee comprised 50 per cent women members in a 97-member body; in fact, it was headed by a woman member. In 1998, Behroongooda also became the first VSS in AP to reap the fruits of forest protection. It generated an income of ₹ 36,000 from the sale of teak poles, the first round of thinning in an 80-year teak management rotation. A number of NTFP also re-emerged due to better protection by the VSS. From the point of employment, the labourers were kept busy in 'coppicing shoots' for which they were paid ₹ 40–50 per day; a better deal than agricultural wage. At the same time, out-migration was reduced. In terms of income, the VSS families earned ₹ 1,000 each per year, apart from the 'usufruct benefits' (D'Silva and Nagnath, 2002).

Ippapenta, a hamlet located in Chintakommadinne Mandal in Kadapa district formed VSS in 1995 with 35 'dalit' families. It was a challenge for them to protect their forest under testing conditions. However, they succeeded through their convincing skills and patience. First, they had to curtail their neighbouring villages from smuggling the wood from their forests; they then persuaded the rich farmers in their village to stop collecting firewood from the VSS forests, and above all, they restricted their cattle from grazing in the forest land. As part of VSS activities, contour trenches were dug; rock-filled-dams and concrete check dams were constructed – to conserve water – by the VSS members with technical and financial support from the FD, which in turn, helped in regeneration of their forests (Gopal and Upadhyay, 2001).

Rangachari and Mukherji (2000) mention the improvement in biodiversity due to VSS protection. They cite examples of the 'RF' in the districts of Adilabad, Nizambad, Kurnool, Khammam, Visakhapatanam and Warangal, where VSS members protected the fringe forests under their control. They observed that this resulted in checking timber smugglers and firewood head loaders from entering into the forests through the routes of VSS forests. Naginayana Cheruvu, a remote area adjoining forests in the district of Ananatapur, experienced a vast improvement in its natural vegetation and an improved forest growth that in turn, led to increase in the 'fauna'. Biswas et al. (1997) credit this to the involvement of the people in the management of the forest. VSS in Anantpur district were seen to be actively controlling forest fire, preventing illegal felling of trees and indiscriminate cattle grazing, leading to 'natural regeneration of the forests' and subsequently, the 'wildlife' in the villages studied by Reddy et al. (2000).

Suryakumari (2001b) observed that the degraded forests that were given to the people under JFM in Adilabad and Visakhapatnam are now crowded with medicinal plants. This was due to the incentives provided under the 'entry point programme'. They were given buffaloes as incentive to refrain from cutting the forests for cultivation. There are many examples of VSS like Sircilla Range of Karimnagar district, Sonapur VSS of Adilabad district and Chengicherla in Rangareddy district, which have earned a good amount of income through the plantations (APFD, 2006).

As far as VSS under NABARD-assisted RIDF Schemes are concerned, there are many good examples of VSS successfully achieving the project objectives of conserving soil moisture, and also planting bio-diesel crops like '*kanuga*'. 'Poolbagh', a VSS village in Vizianagaram district is a good example for arresting degradation from soil erosion after undertaking activities such as digging continuous contour trenches, followed by planting *neem* and *agave* on the mounds. Gully plugging was carried out across the streams, check dams were constructed at appropriate places, in addition to building two percolation tanks. These activities, in turn, led to the opening up of a nursery with 3 lakh seedlings being nursed on an average in the season, which was again possible due to the improvement in the water level (APFD, 2005).

The physical achievements of the FD under APCFM and FDA included forest treatment like plantation of timber (teak, non-teak and bamboo), aided natural regeneration, artificial regeneration, pasture development, mixed plantations and regeneration of herbs. These activities have generated livelihoods for many VSS members (APFD, 2006).

Subdued Impact

The above success stories, however, cannot represent the entire programme; there are reports of degradation of forests even under the VSS. Sometimes, it is believed to have actually worsened the quality of the forests. According to the report of Samata and CRY-Net (2001), the staff of some NGOs witnessed timber smuggling in Srikakulam district. It is an incident of Dommingivalasa where the Mandal Revenue Officer (MRO) and other revenue staff were present when the timber was stacked and transported illegally. On the claim over the 'joint' control over resources and decision-making, the critics have proved that there was nothing like 'joint' in the JFM, nor was there any 'community control' under CFM, rather the FD is said to be wielding undue power over the VSS (FPP and Samata, 2005).

Das (2003) finds relationship between FD and the people to improve in forest seem to be worsening in many instances, FD officials are still reluctant to work with the villagers. However, the high-handedness of the FD in vetoing the people's wishes was also quite apparent everywhere (Samata and CRY-Net, 2001). Complaints of FD keeping VSS members away from 'decision-making' has been a common feature since the inception of J/CFM. Above all, even the existence of important documents such as 'micro-plan' is not known to the VSS members; and they are always in the dark about the budgetary allocation (Farrington and Bauman, 2002; FPP and Samata, 2005). An exclusive discretionary power vested with the APFD in selecting villages for CFM has been a bone of contention in the whole affair, with a disgruntled feeling among the excluded villages to the extent of alleging the FD of indulging in serious corrupt practices (Sunder, 2000).

Arguments over the distribution of benefits are a matter of concern that could be a demotivating factor for people's participation (D'Silva and Nagnath, 2002). Overlooking profit sharing and compounding fees issue by the FD is also not going well with the people (Samata and CRY-Net, 2001). The AP benefit-sharing mechanism is worked out by deducting 'operation costs' (includes basic cost of timber harvesting), which literally brings down the profit of community to less than 50 per cent of the harvest (Upadhyay, 2003).

As far as the socio-economically disadvantaged sections are concerned, it is a common story of the elite dominating the decision-making process (Reddy et al., 2000). Unveiling the mechanism of exploitation of disadvantaged sections, Suryakumari (2001a) describes how BCs, SCs and STs are left alone when the monetary benefits from the forests are not of any consequence; but when the yields are higher, the dominating communities push these disadvantaged sections into the background by whatever means. Regarding women, in many instances they are found to be not even being aware of their membership in the MCs and sometimes, even the GB (Sarin et al., 1998).

The policy on *'podu'* (shifting cultivation) and 'grazing' have been attracting attention from critics since the inception of J/CFM in AP. Sarin (2003) has been one of the most vociferous among them, claiming that the FD has been usurping tribal lands under the garb of J/CFM programme. The claims of FD recovering 24,000 hectares of *podu* land in the districts of Visakhapatanam and Adilabad after the JFM (Rangachari and Mukherji, 2000) is seriously contended by Sarin (2003). She debates that the *'podu* land' on which tribal people depended for their livelihoods were never under the FD, and in reality, they were only in records or paper, and were later declared as encroachments, in complete disrespect to the customary rights of the tribals. Many of these lands are disputed due to inadequacies in the legal processes by which largely tribal lands were declared as state forests, since no proper legal settlement mechanisms were seriously conceived. Sticking to its ground, the FD puts loss of land to encroachments in figures as 29,160 ha, accounting to 12.4 per cent of the total forest land lost in the state by 1991 (APFD, 1999). To address the problem the FD proposed to educate the tribals on the adverse effects of the practice and motivate them to take viable alternate land use practices on such lands. This was to be ensured through close coordination between the agriculture development and tribal welfare initiatives of the Government of AP (GoAP, 2002).

On similar lines, grazing policy is seen as anti-poor, anti-low caste, pro-landowning caste and anti-livestock, in general, and 'anti-goat,' in particular, as many of the households solely depend on goat and sheep rearing for their livelihoods (Ravinder, 2003).

Cooperation from other departments working for tribal welfare and rural development in the same jurisdiction of VSS is not too encouraging (Samata and CRY-Net, 2001). The strife between the Tribal Welfare Department (TWD) and FD – much before the implementation of the JFM – over who gets implementing task is well known (Rangachari and Mukherji, 2000). As far as Integrated Tribal Development Authority (ITDA) is concerned, very little scope is left for coordination among them, with FD taking away most of the role after the inception of JFM (Rao et al., 2000). The coordination between panchayat and VSS remains as elusive as before (Reddy et al., 2007). Ineffective coordination and indifferent relationship between VSS and panchayat exist, subject to the stakes from the forests – if potential returns are high, the conflicts are inevitable, while harmony prevails when the condition of forests is poor (Gopal and Upadhyay, 2001). Another area of contention and unrest between these institutions is allotment of forest to a village outside their Panchayat (Tiwary, 2005).

Panchayats Extension to the Scheduled Areas Act (PESA), 1996, which has wider implications on forest resources in tribal areas (as specified in the V Schedule), was expected to provide far-reaching governance powers to the tribal community, viz., recognising tribals as a traditional community, accepting the validity of their traditional rights, customary law, social and religious practices, and their traditional management of natural resources (Mukul, 1997).

This amendment includes items relating to forests (land improvement, soil conservation, watershed development, social forestry, farm forestry, MFP, fuel and fodder), although the management of state forest lands were not as yet included. Then again, for the tribals to benefit from this act, the state government has to devolve the powers to their panchayats. However, AP is yet to devolve such powers to the panchayats in the state. The Ministry of Environment and Forests that constituted an expert committee thought that the villagers are incapable of managing NTFPs in a sustainable way, and pointed out the inadequate definition of MFP. Nevertheless, it is claimed by the AP government that in terms of returning profits from NTFPs to the village committees, it is following PESA through GO MS No. 66 of 1999 (Sunder et al., 2001); but a draft report by CWS (2003) contradicts such claims by presenting GCC as enjoying 'monopoly rights' for marketing about 25 NTFP items. Now approaching a decade and a half of its implementation, the review from the field on the performance of J/CFM in AP suggests that the programme is a mixed bag of sporadic success and failures on both fronts of ecology and governance.

The historical evaluation of policies and governance, positions this research to weigh how policies are received by the people and the encouraging factors that make them a success or a failure. Besides stressing on the importance of the role played by the FD in the new format of managing forests, wherein they have to share their power with the people when their relationship with the communities is never a smooth one.

Note

1. Adilabad, Karimnagar, Khammam, Mahbubnagar, Medak, Nizamabad and Warangal in Telangana; East Godavari, Srikakulam, Visakhapatnam and Vizaianagaram in Coastal Andhra; and Chittoor, Kadapa and Nellore in Rayalaseema.

3

Contextualising Community Forest Management (CFM)

The study is located in the state of AP. It is the fifth largest Indian state in terms of area and population. It is located in the southern region of India, surrounded by Maharashtra to the north-west and north and Chhattisgarh and Odisha to the north-east. Karnataka is to its west, while Tamil Nadu is to the south. The Bay of Bengal forms a 600-mile (970 km) coastline in the east. Geographically, the northern part of AP is mountainous with 'Mahendragiri' rising 1,500 metres (4,920 feet) above the sea level. AP has 23 districts, which are distributed in the three regions of AP with Coastal Andhra accounting for nine, Rayalaseema four and Telangana 10. Hyderabad is the state's capital city. The distribution of its geographic area between these three different regions is 33.78 per cent (Coastal Andhra), 24.47 per cent (Rayalaseema) and 41.50 per cent (Telangana) (Reddy and Kumar, 2010).

In 2001, the population of AP was 75,727,541 for an area of 275,069 sq. km. It has a ratio of 978 females for every 1,000 males. The density of population was 275 per sq. km. The literacy level in the state stood at 61.11 per cent (males 70.85% and females 51.17%) (Census of India, 2001). The climate is normally hot and humid (maximum being 40°C and minimum 13°C), and the average annual rainfall is about 912 mm (Coastal Andhra 1094 mm; Rayalaseema 680 mm and Telangana 961 mm) (Disaster Management Department, 2008). As per Forest Survey of India (2006), AP has 63,814 sq. km. of forest area out of its total geographic area of 275,069 sq. km., which is 23.2 per cent of its total area.

AP is primarily an economy of agriculture, dominated by food grain production, especially 'rice'. The state also produces four-fifths of the nation's 'Virginia' tobacco. AP has rich mine reserves. The main mineral resources found in AP are asbestos, mica, manganese, barite, high-grade coal and low-grade iron ore. AP produces all of India's barite. The state, in terms of transportation, is well connected with other parts of the country through airways, railways, roadways and waterways.

For the purpose of the study, three districts, viz., Adilabad, Chittoor and Visakhapatnam respectively from the Telangana, Rayalaseema and Coastal Andhra regions were selected. The basic reason for selecting these three districts was that the number of VSS functioning in these districts is the highest among other districts within their respective regions. Furthermore, Chittoor has the highest number of VSS under the FDA scheme. A brief profile of the districts selected for this study is as below.

Adilabad

Adilabad district is one of the 10 districts in the Telangana region of AP. It is situated in the northernmost part of AP. Adilabad has six statutory towns, namely, Adilabad, Bellampalle, Nirmal, Kagaznagar, Mancherial and Bhainsa, along with five census towns, namely, Asifabad, Mandamarri, Kyathampalle, Lakshettipet and Sirpur. The district, which has 52 mandals is organised into five revenue divisions; they are Adilabad, Utnoor, Nirmal, Asifabad and Mancherial. The district headquarters is at Adilabad. The population of Adilabad was 24,79,347 per 16,128 sq. km. of its geographic area. The district encounters 1044.5 mm of average rainfall. The climate of the district is hot, with an exception during the monsoon (Census of India, 2001).

Godavari is a large river that flows through Adilabad, while the other small rivers are Wardha, Pranahita and Penganga, which ultimately join Godavari in Chinnur taluk. The district is rich in minerals and mines; coal, limestone, iron-ore (low-grade), clay and manganese being the most important. About 44.8 per cent of the total land is under forest cover. Six divisions (highest for a district in the state) of forest administer them. Adilabad forests are called 'southern tropical-dry (region with low rainfall) deciduous' and it is abound with a variety of flora and fauna species. Timber, especially teak, rose-wood and bamboo, is the major species besides *beedi* leaves, firewood and charcoal. Adilabad is also a rich house for wildlife sanctuary including 'crocodiles' (Directorate of Census Operations, 1997).

The economy of the district revolves around forest wealth. Agricultural activity in the district is not too encouraging, falling way below the state's average per capita. Millet is the main crop, followed by rice and maize. Cotton is another non-food crop, while sesame is a major oil crop. Under animal husbandry, buffaloes, cows, donkeys, sheep, goats and pigs are reared; poultry and ducks are also raised, and there is a rich potential for fishery. Mining and paper industries are a major support to the state economy in their own way (ibid.). When it comes to railway and road system, the district is well connected to every part of the state with major railway lines passing through it. Good length of *kuccha* and *pucca* roads and the National Highway 7 provide for all types of motor vehicles to ply on (ibid.).

Chittoor

Chittoor district is situated in the southern-most part of the state, falling under the Rayalaseema region; it is one of the four districts in this region. In terms of area, the district ranks 8th in the state, accounting for 5.51 per cent of total state's area. The district has 66 mandals organised into three revenue divisions. The district headquarters is at Chittoor. The population of the district is 37,35,202 spread over 15,152 sq. km. of its geographic area. The average annual rainfall is only 934 mm (Census of India, 2001).

Chittoor has no perennial river, but some important minor rivers like Papaghni, Pincha, Koundinya, Palar, Ponne, Arani, Swarnamukhi, Bahuda, Kalyani and Kausasthali flow through it. With respect to mineral resources, this district has 'pre-Cambrian' granites in a significant quantity. Barites, gold, iron-ore, clay and lead too are found in different areas of the district (Ramesan, 1979). About 29.9 per cent of the total area of Chittoor is covered under forest. The vegetation of the district could be classified into three types of forests – dry tropical south Indian mixed deciduous forests; southern cutch thorn forests; and tropical dry evergreen forests. The Chittoor forest is very famous for a good quality of the species 'red sanders (*pterocarpus santalinus*)'. Commercially, this timber is used for a variety of purposes due to its hardness, from agricultural implements to construction purposes; besides attracting great demand in Japan for making a musical instrument called '*shamisen*', it is also used for making toys. The district is also well known for 'medicinal plants'. Fauna like elephants, tigers, bison, panthers, cheetahs, rabbits and many other creatures, though rarely sighted, inhabit this forest. Birds are comparatively found in better numbers. Parakeets, peacocks, grey jungle fowls and weaver birds are some of the bird species that live in the forest. Reptiles such as boa, Russel's viper and cobra are commonly found, besides a variety of fishes (ibid.).

The economy of Chittoor is mainly based on agriculture. Food grains, sugar cane, mango and tomato are some of the main produce in this district. Vijaya Dairy Farm is one of the biggest industries in Chittoor. Agro-based industries, other small scale industries and sericulture also complement the economy of the district. The district is well connected to other parts of the state by airways, railways and roadways (Census of India, 2001).

Visakhapatnam

Visakhapatnam is one of the nine districts in the region of Coastal Andhra. It is situated in the north-eastern part of the state. The district is featured by two distinct characteristics of ecology and topography. One is plain landscape, extending from seacoast to the foothills of the Eastern Ghats. The other is hilly forests on the north-western part of the district. The district has 43 mandals organised into three revenue divisions; they are Paderu, Narsipatnam and Visakhapatnam. The district headquarters is at Visakhapatnam. In 2001, the population of the district was 37,89,823 per 11,161 sq. km of its geographic area. The annual average rainfall is 950 mm. The temperature in the plains is moderate while the hilly region is relatively cool (ibid.).

The important rivers flowing through the Visakhapatnam district are Sarada, Varaha and Thandava. The district is also rich in minerals, bauxite and apatite being the major ones, along with calcite and crystalline lime stones (Directorate of Census Operations, 1998). About 39.3 per cent of this district is spread under forest cover (mostly degraded) atop the Eastern Ghats, which is notified as Scheduled or Agency Area under the Constitution of India. The forest in Agency Areas is basically rich with minor forest produces like tamarind, *adda* leaves, *shikakai*, honey and soap nuts. There are also timber species like eucalyptus and non-thorny variety of bamboo. Coffee and silver oak have also been found significantly since 1980s. Tigers, jackals, snow bear and wild bear are sighted now and then. Spotted deer and wild buffalos are found in the deep forests. Monkeys are commonly found all over the district. Jungle fowl (*gallus sonneratica*), pea fowl (*pavo cristatus*), pigeon, parrot, mayna (*Acridotheres tristis*) and grey partridge are the species of birds found, along with the migratory ones like ducks and teals. Reptiles and snakes, including pythons, *naga pamu*, *katla pamu* and *penjeri* are also common in the district. *Nach Kundam* (pond) in Paderu Region hosts many kinds of fishes including 'golden coloured fish' (ibid.).

Economy of the district revolves basically around agriculture, with 62 per cent of the population eking a livelihood from this sector. Paddy, *bajra*, groundnut, *ragi*, sugar cane, maize and pulses are the main agricultural products, along with red gram, chillies and cashew. Visakhapatnam Dairy, known as 'Visakha Dairy', is one of the important milk suppliers all over the state. On the other hand, the district lands about 44,640 tons of fish per annum. When it comes to industries, Visakhapatnam is crowded with sugar factories, jute mills, agro and non-agro based small and large scale industries, including a giant steel industry (ibid.). As far as transportation is concerned, the district is well connected not only to other parts of its own state and nation through a good railway system and road system, but is also connected internationally thanks to the airport and shipping port (ibid.).

Operationalising the Study

Total sample size of 30 VSS was selected in proportion (1%) to their number of VSS in the selected districts. Then, 'stratified simple random sampling without replacement scheme' was adopted to select VSS in each district from the categories of different sponsors representing only tribal VSS[1] and the mixed-caste VSS,[2] again in proportion to such VSS villages in each district. The final composition of the sample VSS villages constituted of 11 each from Adilabad and Visakhapatnam districts and eight from Chittoor district. Among these, 20 VSS were under the sponsorship of APCFM and the remaining 10 were non-APCFM sponsored VSS (Table 3.1). Various sponsors under the Central Government schemes are EAS, Eco-Development Committee (EDC), FDA and NABARD.

The deliberate selection of VSS from tribal, mixed-caste and VSS sponsored under different schemes is necessitated to record the differences between these VSS villages. The only tribal VSS (OTV) villages are mostly situated deep in the forest. They had less amenities, and the people were backward, illiterate, and also lacked other social and economic facilities (for details see note on tribals in the following section). The mixed-caste VSS (MCV) villages are mostly those situated in the plains or on the fringe of the forests with better access to roads and other amenities. Multi-caste composition also allows research to record the dynamics of governance having a varied and disparate effect on the physical situation of the forests.

Different methods were used while eliciting quantitative and qualitative information in multiple circumstances in the field. The basic sources through which primary data was obtained for the study were 'Focus Group Discussions' (FGD) at institutional level (one in each VSS) complemented by separate FGDs with the VSS members from OC, disadvantaged sections like SCs, STs, BCs and women on specific issues for their exclusive responses, besides, household (HH) surveys (360 VSS members) with the help of structured schedules.

However, information for the study was also supplemented by direct observation method, informal conversations with the officials and people concerned, individually or in groups. This process has helped in understanding the dynamics present in the VSS in a better way. On a few occasions, the researcher was given an opportunity to participate in the GB meetings held in the VSS villages to discuss issues like wage works[3] and money distribution. The break up of HH schedules for each district is as follows: Adilabad 132, Chittoor 96 and Visakhapatnam 132. From each VSS, 12 HHs were interviewed. To select the 12 VSS HHs for interviewing, the 'Probability Proportionate Sample (PPS)' method was adopted. The resultant sample reflected gender, wealth rank and ethnic/caste composition of the social groups; further, the sample was proportionally distributed between the GB members, MC members including those holding executive positions of chairperson and vice-chairperson.

To record the views of FD, 30 FD officials from village level rank to divisional levels (falling in the jurisdiction of the study villages) were also interviewed in a one-to-one interaction mode on a specific situation existing in the VSS village under their jurisdiction. Similarly, 30 NGO members in various capacities who were working or had worked in the proximity of the study villages were also interviewed for broader understanding of the VSS issues. In all, seven months were spent in the field for the study; the main research was carried out between 1 March 2006 and 31 August 2006.

Secondary data of information was collected from all the possible sources. Secondary materials included policy documents, scholarly writings (from various books, periodicals, journals, and daily newspapers) and statistical data from government and semi-government organisations, governmental reports, GOs, appraisals and evaluation documents of the FD and World Bank.

Table 3.1
Total Number of VSS in the Selected Districts under each Stratum (OTV and MCV)

Regions	*Districts*	*Sponsors*	*Total No. of VSS*	*No. of VSS Selected*		
				Total	*OTV*	*MCV*
Telangana	Adilabad	APCFM VSS	988	8	4	4
		Non-APCFM	151	3	2	1
			1,139	11	6	5
Rayalaseema	Chittoor	APCFM VSS	237	4	2	2
		Non-APCFM	365	4	1	3
			602	8	3	5
Coastal Andhra	Visakhapatnam	APCFM VSS	870	8	4	4
		Non-APCFM	414	3	2	1
			1,284	11	6	5
Total Andhra Pradesh	5,000	APCFM VSS	2,095	20	10	10
	3,412	Non-APCFM	930	10	5	5
	8,412		3,025	30	15	15

Key: APCFM = World Bank sponsored VSS; Non-World Bank VSS = FDA under centrally sponsored afforestation schemes of MoEF (1357 VSS) and RIDF assisted by NABARD (2055 VSS); OTV = Only Tribal VSS; MCV = Mixed-Caste VSS.

Source: APFD (2006).

The information gathered through FGD and HH surveys are presented separately depending on the content of the particular enquiry in the field. Hence, the analysis depicts two levels of aggregates, i.e., 30 and 360 for the information drawn from FGD and HH levels respectively. Presentation of analysis through two stratums of OTV and MCV and also districts is worked out to cover the possible differences between the inhabitants of the two diverse groups and regional disparities respectively, even while presenting a generalised picture of the state as a whole and their approach towards forests. The narration for all the HH data presented in the analysis is complemented by the information collected through other lead and substitute questions enquired from the respondents at FGD level. Similarly, for the all FGD-based data, the narration analysed is a blend of information gathered from the respondents through relevant lead questions enquired at HH level. In some places the report, VSS and their respective villages are either mentioned jointly or interchangeably to maintain the flow.

Figure 3.1

Map of Andhra Pradesh (inset Map of India) Depicting the Three Study Districts in the State

Figure 3.2

Map of Adilabad Depicting the Study Villages in the District

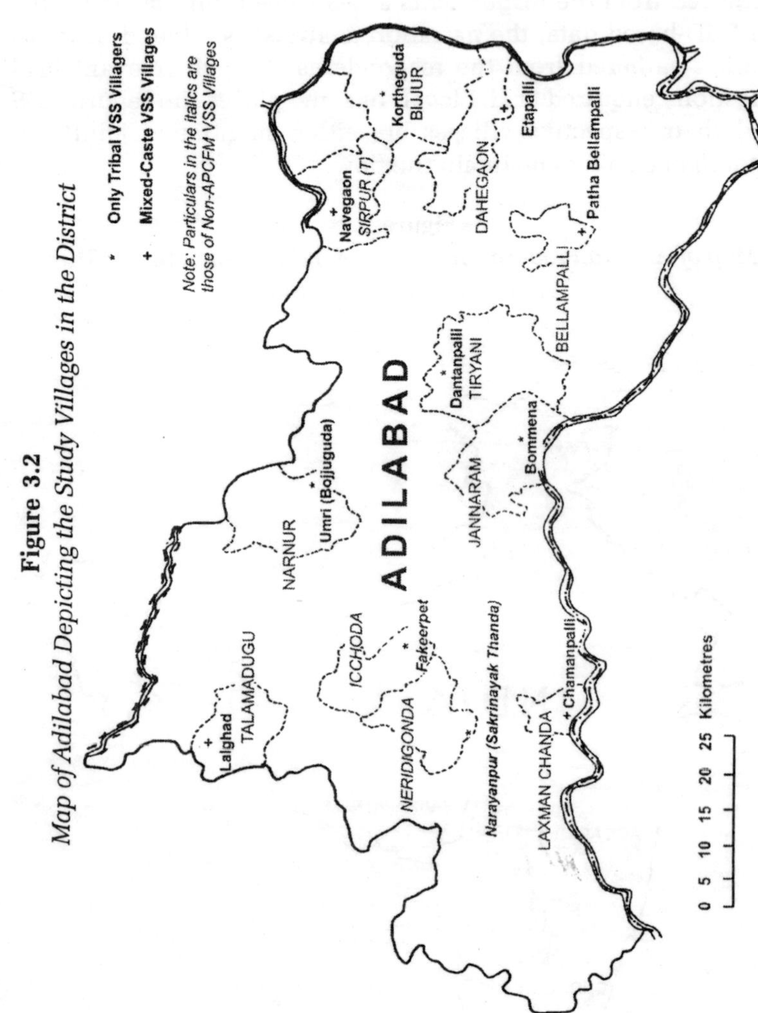

Figure 3.3

Map of Chittoor Depicting the Study Villages in the District

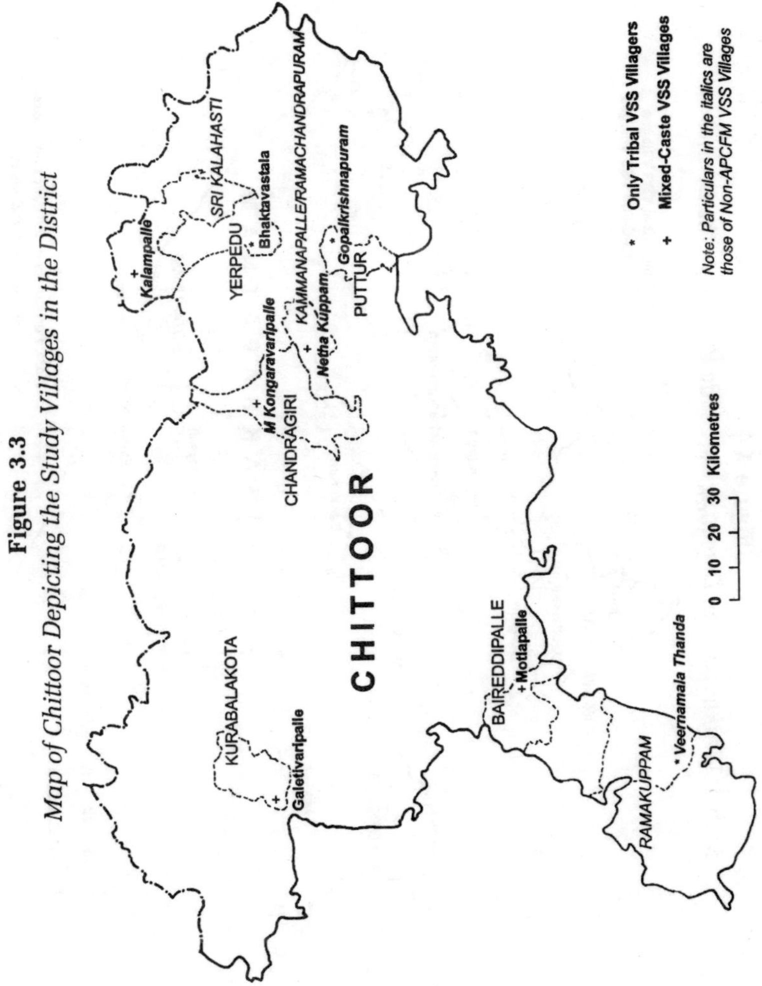

Figure 3.4

Map of Visakhapatnam Depicting the Study Villages in the District

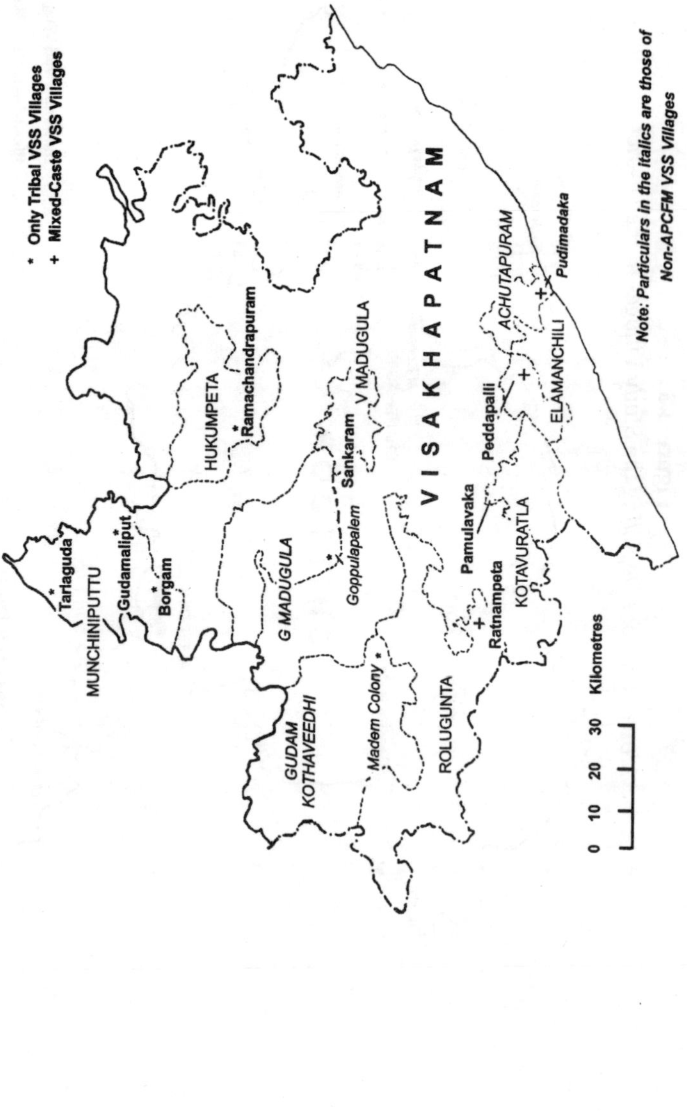

***Note:** Particulars in the italics are those of Non-APCFM VSS Villages*

A Note on Tribes of AP

The tribals in AP belong to different ethnic background with separate culture and linguistic traits from their other counterparts in the country. They are 35 communities officially notified as tribes (including eight other groups as PTGs) in the state (for details see Appendix IV). The population of tribes in AP forms 6.59 per cent (50.24 lakhs) of total population. They live mostly in the hilly regions especially in the north-eastern ghats of the state. Among the 23 districts in the state, five districts, viz., Khammam (26.47%), Adilabad (16.74%), Visakhapatnam (14.55%), Warangal (14.10%) and Nalgonda (10.55%) account

Box 3.1

Plight of Tribals

The history of tribals in India, in general and AP in particular, can be summed up as an unending struggle to shed shackles from the coercive and intimidating oppressors, be it the British or the present-day government (Das, Vidhya, 2003). Poorest of the poor are found to be those depending on forests for NTFP (Neumann and Hirsch, 2000), since NTFP collection is their last resort income source (Angelsen and Wunder, 2003). It is because of this, tribals in APCFM are the important stakeholders constituting 30.7 per cent (APFD, 2005). Some of the events which are testimonials to the sufferings of the tribals are mentioned here: holding tribals back from entering the forests led the to Rampa Rebellion in Godavari district; forcing tribals to lay roads for free led to an uprising under Alluri Sitaram Raju during 1922–24; the Gonds revolted in 1940 in Adilabad district following notification of 'lambadas' as ST that resulted in their influx from the neighbouring state of Maharashtra, putting pressure on the land in their areas; and as recently as in 1968–70, the tribals rising-up in arms against the exploitation by the Sahukars in Srikakulam district under the banner of Naxalites (Rao, Manohar and Rao, 1982; Arnold, 1982). Ironically, tribal areas appear peaceful to outsiders, but in reality, it is nothing but an eerie silence of the poor tribals 'subdued' by the 'brutal force' borne out of the nexus between vested interests and the local administration established over the years (Das, Vidhya, 2003).

Source: As referred.

for more than 50 per cent of state's total tribal population. Sugalis are numerically single largest tribes among other tribes in the state with 41.4 per cent (Census of India, 2001).

Like their brethren elsewhere in the country, the tribals in AP are also most deprived and vulnerable despite constitutional safeguards extended to them. Their economy could be termed as 'consumption sustenance economy'. They are engaged in settled agriculture, shifting cultivation and collection of forest produce. Although, their economy is not in complete isolation as it was once in the past but its level is influenced by their habitat, tradition, possession of ancient knowledge and the skills they posses in using the available resources (Reddy and Kumar, 2010).

On social front, the sex ratio of tribals in AP is skewed against female with 972. Equally poor is literacy rate with only 37 per cent compared to state's overall figures of 61.11 per cent (ibid.).

Administrative, Natural and Physical Profile of the Study VSS Villages and its Members

Social science research revolves more or less around human behaviour. Their behaviour is more often influenced consciously and sometimes subconsciously by several factors in their surroundings. In the context of 'CFM' also such factors in the form of traditional practices, socio-economic background and topographical habitation of the members in the community has a serious bearing on their performance; more so when the differences are at intra- and inter-community levels. Hence, this section is focused on understanding such features existing in the study villages and the respondents interviewed, for the potential influence they have had on the outcome of the objectives of CFM.

From the point of administrative jurisdiction, all the 30 study VSS villages are scattered in 30 different mandals and panchayats falling under the three selected districts of Adilabad, Chittoor and Visakhapatnam in their respective regions of Telangana, Rayalaseema and Coastal Andhra. As already mentioned in the introduction, the OTV villages are more or less remotely situated in all the three districts, compared to the MCV villages; however, the villages in the

Visakhapatnam district are too remote in comparison to the other two districts. When it comes to forest jurisdiction, the selected 30 villages belong to four different circles (Anantapur, Tirupathi (Wildlife), Adilabad and Visakhapatnam) out of the state's 29. These 30 villages further fall under 12 separate divisions under 23 different ranges. The total number of divisions and ranges in the state are 95 and 432, respectively. With regard to sections and beats, each village has a different one for its control. There are 1,627 sections and 2,861 beats in the entire state (APFD, 2003).

Table 3.2

VSS Particulars of the Selected Villages

D	*T*	*N*	*Mandal*	*Panchayat*	*Village/ Hamlet*	*Sponsor*	*Year*	*Area (ha)*
Adilabad/Telangana	OTV	1	Jannaram	Malyal	Bommena	APCFM	1997	247.00
		2	Tiryani	Ullipitta Dorli	Dantanpalli	APCFM	1998	240.00
		3	*Icchoda*	*Nerangonda K*	*Fakeerpet*	*FDA*	*2004*	—
		4	Bijjur	Pothapalli	Kortheguda	APCFM	1995	550.00
		5	*Neridi-gonda*	*Rajura*	*Narayanpur Sakrinayak Thanda*	*FDA*	*2003*	*250.00*
		6	Narnur	Umri	Umri (Bojjuguda)	APCFM	1996	404.27
	MCV	1	Laxman Chanda	Chamanpalli	Chamanpalli	APCFM	1997	75.00
		2	Dahegaon	Girvelli	Etapalli	APCFM	1996	85.00
		3	Talama-dugu	Kuchalapur	Lalghad	APCFM	1995	318.22
		4	*Sirpur*	*Venkatarao-peta*	*Navegaon*	*FDA*	*1998*	*282.00*
		5	Bellam-palli	Patha Bellampalli	Patha Bellampalli SC/BC Colony	APCFM	1997	250.00

Cont'd...

...Cont'd

Chittoor/Rayalaseema	OTV	1	Yerpedu	Ravillavari-kandriga	Bhaktavatsala Colony	APCFM	2003	200.00
		2	Puttur	Gopalkrish-napuram	Gopalkrish-napuram	APCFM	1993	500.00
		3	*Ramakup pam*	*Veernamala*	*Veernamala Thanda*	*EDC*	*1997*	*1020.00*
	MCV	1	Kura-balkota	Thettu	Galetivari-palle/ Nagalapuram	APCFM	1996	250.00
		2	*Srikala-hasti*	*Kalavagunta*	*Kalampalle*	*EAS*	*1998*	*125.00*
		3	*Chand-ragiri*	*M Kongara-varipalle*	*M Kongarava-ripalle BC Colony*	*NABARD*	*1997*	—
		4	Baireddi-palle	Chappidipalli	Motlapalle	APCFM	1998	270.00
		5	*Rama-chandra-puram*	*Netha Kuppam*	*Netha Kuppam*	*NABARD*	*1998*	—
Visakhapatnam/Coastal Andhra	OTV	1	Munchin giputtu	Babusal	Borgam	APCFM	—	200.00
		2	*G Madu-gula*	*Vanjara*	*Goppulapalem*	*NABARD*	*1999*	*100.00*
		3	Munchin giputtu	Pathapalli	Gudamaliput	APCFM	1996	250.00
		4	*Gudem Kotha Veedhi*	*Damanapalli*	*Madem Colony*	*NABARD*	*1996*	*80.00*
		5	Hukum-peta	Bhimavaram	Ramachandra puram	APCFM	1996	250.00
		6	Munchin giputtu	Vanagumma	Tarlaguda	APCFM	1998	110.00

Cont'd...

...Cont'd

MCV	1 Kotavu-ratla	Pamulavaka	Pamulavaka	APCFM	1999	50.00
	2 Elaman-chili	Pedaguda	Peddapalli	APCFM	—	250.00
	3 Achuta-puram	*Pudimadaka*	*Pudimadaka*	*NABARD*	*1996*	*90.00*
	4 Rolu-gunta	Ratnampeta	Ratnampeta SC Colony	APCFM	1996	—
	5 V Madu-gula	Sankaram	Sankaram	APCFM	1998	150.00

Key: D = District and Region; T = Type of Community in the Village; OTV = Only Tribal VSS; MCV = Mixed-Caste VSS; Year = VSS formation year; Area (ha) = Area allotted to the VSS in hactares; Particulars in the italics are those of non-APCFM VSS Villages.

Source: Field data.

Box 3.2

Chilling Experience!

Kortheguda and Umri Bojjuguda in Adilabad are the two villages, which will ever be remembered by the researcher and his assistant. Kortheguda because, the spot in a room where the former chairperson and his well-informed cousin were interviewed for hours was later learnt to be the very place, where just a couple of days ago, the chairperson of the VSS had murdered his uncle on suspicion of practising 'sorcery'.

The day the researcher and his assistant visited Umri Bojjuguda would probably have been their last, if they were not forcibly asked to get down by the driver of the 'ferry-auto' that was to take them to the village. They had to get down because they were taking time to make sure that the village they were going was indeed Umri Bojjuguda, as the particulars of the village they were carrying were not corresponding with the information given by the locals about that village, although its location on the map was matching.

Cont'd...

...Cont'd

Soon after ascertaining that Umri Bojjuguda was indeed the village they had to visit, they boarded another vehicle. At about a distance of a kilometre and half from the place of their boarding the transportation, the researcher spotted their earlier 'ferry-auto' in the middle of the road lying upside-down, and people removing the bodies of passengers from it. It was clear that the vehicle had met with an accident. By the time the duo reached the village, they learnt that all the passengers in the ill-fated 'ferry-auto' were seriously injured and one person had died on the spot. More shock was in store in the evening, when some men narrated about how strangers had been missing from the secluded 'ghat' through which researcher passed, only to be found murdered sometime later. However, they were delighted that the researcher was back and safe. So were the researcher and his assistant for coming out unscathed twice on the same day after being so close to danger.

Source: Field experience.

Box 3.3

Scenic Villages

Galetivaripalle in Chittoor is situated just downhill of the famous 'Horsely Hills', a serene and beautiful place, which is also a hill station and summer resort. The Boarding school situated near the hill is equated with the famous Dehradun school in Uttarakhand in northern India. An equally pleasant and spiritually inspiring village that we came across during the study was Pudimadaka in Visakhapatnam. This village has a rare setting of forest on the seashore.

Source: Field observation.

Better infrastructure is an obvious indicator of development; this applies not only to a small unit of village, but also to any big country. Before understanding the nature of infrastructure, it is to be considered that the parameters used to describe infrastructure here for the sample villages are based on availability of minimum infrastructure such as road accessibility, availability of transportation options and availability of very basic needs like safe drinking water, grocery shop, electricity and Auxiliary Nurse and Midwife's (ANM) regular visit for treating patients. Based on these criteria, the VSS villages were clubbed into suitable categories.

The findings from the field suggest that 10 of the 30 study villages have good infrastructure, while six are reasonable, and six are bad. The remaining eight villages have no form of infrastructure at all; hence they are classified as worst. Only one village (Gopalkrishnapuram, OTV, Chittoor) has good infrastructure. If the data is looked from the stratum (OTV and MCV) angle, a clear picture can be noticed, wherein the MCV villages in all the three districts have comparatively better infrastructure. The OTV villages, particularly in Visakhapatnam Scheduled Areas are so bad that they are devoid of even basic amenities like safe drinking water, and are literally cut-off from the rest of the world during monsoons.

The condition of four villages is very pitiable. They are Borgam (OTV, Visakhapatnam), Tarlaguda (OTV, Visakhapatnam), Etapalli (MCV, Adilabad) and Umri (Bojjuguda) (OTV, Adilabad). Borgam villagers have only a pond to drink water from, and they claim it is contaminated, because of which, the habitants keep falling sick. Tarlaguda villagers face similar water problem. They have only an *'oota'* (water source from spring) to depend upon for their water needs. Even this source was recently spoiled by an NGO (funded by a European Organisation), which constructed a storage tank around the outlet, claiming to provide safe drinkable water, only to end up with a faulty tank, which is now in an unusable state.

Tarlaguda (OTV, Visakhapatnam), Etapalli (MCV, Adilabad) and Umri (Bojjuguda) (OTV, Adilabad) suffer in monsoons as they get severed from the main land by a gushing stream. During this period, children cannot go to schools and the villagers fail to receive emergency medical attention. It is a different matter that all the three villages have alternate routes, as insensitively argued by the local authorities on drawing their attention towards the plight of these villages. However, the authorities forget that those are round about routes comprising many kilometres, for a destination which could be simply reached by walking a few yards through the usual path. Borgam (OTV, Visakhapatnam) villagers have to walk more than 5 kms to collect their ration from the public distribution system (PDS) outlet. Then again, it is quite normal for many such villagers, especially under OTV in the Scheduled Areas, to walk such distances if not more.

The distance between the village and forest is very vital for efficient management of forests and except for eight VSS villages in a sample of 30, the remaining are all in the forest backyard. This means 22 VSS villages should have no major problems in protecting their forests. Among the villages which are away from the forest, are in a range of one km to five kms, one village, Bhaktavatsala Colony in Chittoor district is the only OTV village, while the remaining seven are MCV villages.

Area of the forest, protected by the 'community' is vital because it has to be in proportion with the number of HHs protecting it for a proper balance. However, the average area of forest managed by the sample VSS is 203 ha (Table 3.2). This sum is arrived at by excluding the 1020 ha of Veernamala Thanda (OTV, Chittoor) for its abnormal allotment that is shared between 12 other hamlets. Anyhow, for the remaining VSS, it is 162 members effectively looking after their community forest. Since there is clear-cut proportion available, there remains an unending debate over the ideal area of the forest and the size of the community.

Community-oriented effort of any kind requires a spirit of teamwork. The same is true for institutions like CFM, which demand commitment from each member to work towards making the programme a success. When an entire village as a single community comes forward to protect forests, the chances of success are expected to be more, as far as common pool resources management theories are concerned. In the same way, there tends to be hostilities in a village over the use of common pool resources, where some HHs stay away from being members of the institutions involved. This condition sometimes leads to conflicts, affecting the natural resources and the members as well (for details, see Chapter 6). Among the sample VSS, 15 villages have total membership in the VSS, out of which 11 villages, i.e., 73.3 per cent of the sample are OTV (all tribal villages). Barring two OTV (one each in Adilabad and Visakhapatnam districts), all the other villages have formed VSS with the involvement of the entire HHs. Kortheguda (OTV,

Adilabad) is devoid of the 100 per cent mark, because of one family's rebellion against the former chairperson, who still holds influence in the present VSS. Madem colony (OTV, Visakhapatnam) could not make it to this club because the numerically strong *Kondhs* (PTG) opted to not invite 10 HHs belonging to *Konda Doras* to join VSS due to inter-caste differences. However, it was a positive development to see four villages from MCV in the 100 per cent village involvement club. Less proportion of village HHs in VSS is observed in Chittoor OTV (33.3%) because the tribal villages in Chittoor are not classical hamlets that are found mostly in the Adilabad and Visakhapatnam agency areas.

The case of Peddapalli and Pudimadaka (MCV, Visakhapatnam) is interesting in regard to the formation of VSS. Members of these two VSS narrated, as to how some HH members in their villages ignored their call for a village meeting to discuss the formation of VSS. They refused to be its members for different reasons; if some thought that it was not their community profession to protect forests, others saw it as useless and impractical; some feared for their lives from smugglers and thieves, while many others had no faith in the FD's promises. However, after a decade or so, the same people are now trying hard to be its members; the existing members, though, vehemently oppose to share the fruit of their hard work with such new members. There were also some people, especially belonging to SC HHs, like in M. Kongaravaripalle (MCV, Chittoor), who refused to join VSS citing bitter experiences of their counterparts in their neighbouring VSS. The reasons ranged from fewer wages to non-payment of wages in time.

It is very striking to find as many as nine villages forming VSS in spite of having members less than 50 per cent of their village's total population. As per GO MS. No. 13 (2002), a minimum of 50 per cent of the village HHs have to agree in writing for the constitution of the VSS, before the proposal is sent for approval to the Divisional Forest Officer (DFO). However, on probing the reason with the local forest officials, it was learnt that since most of these villages are MCV that have multi-community background, and many dominant community HHs do not depend on the forests and logically would not be interested to join the

VSS, so the FD classified the poor, especially the SCs or STs, separately and created a colony comprising of them and allotted the VSS to them. There are other instances where, for example, a big village like Patha Bellampalli (MCV, Adilabad), which has more forest, allotted VSS to another colony belonging to a different community from the same village. But many such VSS are not born out of creation of a new colony as in the instance of Netha Kuppam (MCV, Chittoor). It appeared that the FD just wanted to meet the target of forming VSS, only to satisfy the higher authorities, while ignoring the importance of consensus in forming such important committees; to keep it conflict-free and attract cooperation from one and all.

In regard to composition and type of membership, 360 samples were distributed equally among female and male VSS members. This was to reflect equal gender representation necessitated by the CFM guiding GO MS. No. 13 (2002). The reservation provision for women is extended to GB, MC and for a post of either chairperson or vice-chairperson or both, in favour of women. Out of the total sample composition, 66.7 per cent were GB members while the remaining 33.3 per cent were MC members. This proportion between GB and MC members was maintained in each village. Pudimadaka (MCV, Visakhapatnam) presented a unique situation, where only one male VSS member's name from each HH was documented in records, though women members from these HHs participate in all VSS activities as the female members do in any other VSS. Such women who are active in the VSS affairs along with their male HH member have been interviewed. There was no problem in finding women MC or vice-chairperson in this VSS as they were duly elected by their GB.

The introduction of VSS in a programme like CFM is very significant since it has direct bearing on not only its institutional sustenance, but also on that of its members in economic terms. If the institution is formed to regenerate and protect the degraded forest, it would take a longer time to reach sustainability level. In such case, these institutions need extended external aid and the sponsors have to be patient enough to wait until such forests reach a sustainable level. As Fabricius (2004) foresees, it requires decades, rather than years, before the institutions can sustain.

Among the 30 study VSS, barring few exceptions; most of them are already a decade or older (Table 3.2). The exceptional villages, fairly new to the programme of CFM, are Fakeerpet (OTV, Adilabad), Narayanpur Sakrinayak Thanda (OTV, Adilabad), Bhaktavatsala Colony (OTV, Chittoor) and Pamulavaka (MCV, Visakhapatnam). Technically, Fakeerpet (OTV, Adilabad) is the only village that is new to this concept, while other three villages have a connection with the VSS in one or the other interesting way. The VSS members of Narayanpur Sakrinayak Thanda (OTV, Adilabad) were a part of another neighbouring VSS village (Isapur Mathura). The VSS members of Bhaktavatsala Colony (OTV, Chittoor) belonging to the *Yanadi* tribe decided to move from the hamlet altogether for better livelihood prospects. After their complete migration, another set of tribals belonging to same *Yanadi* clan were handed the responsibility of the VSS forest protected by the previous 'community'. Only the chairperson of the earlier VSS now lives with his son in this new hamlet; he is included as a 'GB' member in the newly constituted VSS. In case of Pamulavaka (MCV, Visakhapatnam), the forest entrusted to the members of this village under a different scheme (NABARD) was completely handed over to the other VSS. Now the members have a different patch of forest for protection. This VSS is now sponsored by APCFM.

Significance of APCFM is that its members have a privilege of naming their VSS as they wish. It was interesting to note that only five VSS out of sample 30 had their VSS names different from their village names. All these five VSS belonged to Visakhapatnam District, and the VSS names were attributed to their religious deities, showing a strong bond with the forest, for these goddesses were equated with the 'forest mother'. However, when the members in the remaining VSS were enquired, as to why they did not name their VSS different from their village name, all of them said that they did not know about such option and the FD also did not care to inform them about it.

Social Composition and Human Capital of VSS Members

The caste composition of the 'community' is very important because social dynamics hold an immense influence and significance over the outcome of any communal activity. According to sample, 15 of the 30 VSS belonged to OTV, while the remaining 15 belonged to MCV. When the sample is more specifically observed, it presents further interesting dynamic characteristics.

Though tribal communities in the sample VSS have their own indigenous culture, tradition and gods; yet, most of them also worship the Hindu God Hanuman, and their method of worship is similar to that of the Hindus. All the respondents in non-tribal villages practice Hinduism, except for Ratnampeta SC colony, where the HHs carry dual religious identity of Hinduism and Christianity. Caste hierarchies were also prevalent among tribal communities. The PTGs are considered more backward than their other well-known brethrens. The different tribal sub-groups that specifically came across in the study are *Adivasi, Bagatha, Gond, Goudu, Kondh (PTG), Kolam (PTG), Konda Dora, Kummari, Koya, Lambada/Sugali, Malis, Manne Dora, Naik Pod, Nooka/Reddy Dora, Porja, Valmiki (ST) and Yanadi.*

As far as MCV members are concerned, it is BC dominance all the way in 10 of the 15 MCV having OC, BC, SC and ST population. Technically, in Peddapalli (MCV, Visakhapatnam), the *Kapus* (OC) not only dominate numerically, but also have a sway over others in all aspects of village and VSS affairs. According to the respective VSS members of Galetivaripalle (MCV, Chittoor) and Motlapalle (MCV, Chittoor), the *Reddys* not only have a hold on all the natural resources in their respective villages, but also in the administration of VSS, though their number is negligible. Kalampalle (MCV, Chittoor) has a reasonable number of *Raju* HHs in the village but only a couple of HHs are in the VSS; and though their interference in VSS or other matters is minimal as assessed by it chairperson, yet their dominant presence has the village in their grip. The same can be said about Netha Kuppam (MCV, Chittoor) where the *Kapus* are dominant with their numbers in the village; however, they have no members in the VSS; a few *Kamma* HHs have membership in the VSS. The non-tribal castes that were found in the sample villages are as follows: *Aare/Maratha, Besta/Gundla, Boya, Chakali (Rajaka), Ediga-Balija, Jalari, Kamma, Kammara/ Kammari, Kapu/Munnuru Kapu/Turupu Kapu, Kuruba, Kshatriya/*

Rajus, Madiga, Mala, Mali, Mangali, Muslim/Multani, Sali, Rajput/Thakur, Reddy, Relli, Vada/Wada-Balija, Valmiki, Velama/Koppala Velama, Wodlolu, Manne and Mannevaru (SC).

Age is an important factor in any arena of human activity. Especially in activities involving physical labour, it becomes even more necessary to be fit enough to carry the job. Farming in agriculture and/or carrying out silvicultural activities are no less strenuous jobs, for one has to toil hard in the fields to accomplish their tasks. A lot of walking is also required, particularly in the protection of forests.

All the 360 respondents interviewed are by default members of FPCs, while most of them also double up working in their own farms or in others as wage labourers – both require top physical state. Moreover, those involved in ploughing the hilly lands (*podu*) have to be extraordinarily fit, for it is most demanding on one's body to cultivate on the hills. It cannot be discounted that the physical fitness is at its peak in youth, and the prime age is usually between 18 and 45 years.

In the sample VSS, it is observed, that the respondents in the category of 18 to 45 are overwhelmingly high at 77.8 per cent, followed by 20.3 per cent in the category of 46 to 59, and also seven VSS members in an age range of 60 and above (Table 3.3). It is significant to note that six of them are from the district of Chittoor. This is because this district is comparatively more urban than the other two districts – where many of the members are found to be arm-chair members in executive. Otherwise, the popular trend is uniform across all districts and also in their respective stratums of villages in OTV and MCV, respectively.

Education has always been looked upon as a precious asset for a person, even dwarfing the materialistic wealth one might possess. A person with good education, or at least minimal of it, is expected to do better in society. Given the rural background of the respondents in the study, minimum literacy level would be a positive sign, since the VSS members, especially those in the executive positions of chairperson or vice-chairperson, have to handle many of VSS responsibilities that include keeping important books, viz., records of proceedings in the meetings, cheque books, joint account book, minute book, MC resolution

Table 3.3

Distribution of Respondents According to their Age

Age	*Adilabad*			*Chittoor*			*Visakhapatnam*			*Overall*		
	OTV	*MCV*	*T*	*OTV*	*MCV*	*T*	*OTV*	*MCV*	*T*	*OTV*	*MCV*	*GT*
18–45	57	41	**98**	24	45	**69**	64	49	**113**	145	135	**280**
	(79.2)	(68.3)	**(74.2)**	(66.7)	(75.0)	**(71.9)**	(88.9)	(81.7)	**(85.6)**	(80.6)	(75.0)	**(77.8)**
46–59	15	18	**33**	8	13	**21**	8	11	**19**	31	42	**73**
	(20.8)	(30.0)	**(25.0)**	(22.2)	(21.7)	**(21.9)**	(11.1)	(18.3)	**(14.4)**	(17.2)	(23.3)	**(20.3)**
60–99	0	1	**1**	4	2	**6**	0	0	**0**	4	3	**7**
	(0.0)	(1.7)	**(0.8)**	(11.1)	(3.3)	**(6.2)**	(0.0)	(0.0)	**(0.0)**	(2.2)	(1.7)	**(1.9)**
Total	72	60	**132**	36	60	**96**	72	60	**132**	180	180	**360**
	(100)	(100)	**(100)**	(100)	(100)	**(100)**	(100)	(100)	**(100)**	(100)	(100)	**(100)**

Key: OTV = Only Tribal VSS; MCV = Mixed-Caste VSS; T = Total; GT = Grand Total.

Source: Field Survey (Household).

Note: Figures in parentheses are the percentages of the respective counts.

Table 3.4

Distribution of Respondents According to their Literacy Level

Education	*Adilabad*			*Chittoor*			*Visakhapatnam*			*Overall*		
	OTV	*MCV*	*T*	*OTV*	*MCV*	*T*	*OTV*	*MCV*	*T*	*OTV*	*MCV*	*GT*
Illiterate	59	48	**107**	24	39	**63**	68	37	**105**	151	124	**275**
	(81.9)	(80.0)	**(81.1)**	(66.7)	(65.0)	**(65.6)**	(94.4)	(61.7)	**(79.5)**	(83.9)	(68.9)	**(76.4)**
< VII	10	5	**15**	5	10	**15**	4	11	**15**	19	26	**45**
	(13.9)	(8.3)	**(11.4)**	(13.9)	(16.7)	**(15.6)**	(5.6)	(18.3)	**(11.4)**	(10.6)	(14.4)	**(12.5)**
> VII	0	2	**2**	3	2	**5**	0	3	**3**	3	7	**10**
	(0.0)	(3.3)	**(1.5)**	(8.3)	(3.3)	**(5.2)**	(0.0)	(5.0)	**(2.3)**	(1.7)	(3.9)	**(2.8)**
X	1	2	**3**	3	6	**9**	0	6	**6**	4	14	**18**
	(1.4)	(3.3)	**(2.3)**	(8.3)	(10.0)	**(9.4)**	(0.0)	(10.0)	**(4.5)**	(2.2)	(7.8)	**(5.0)**
Inter	2	3	**5**	0	3	**3**	0	3	**3**	2	9	**11**
	(2.8)	(5.0)	**(3.8)**	(0.0)	(5.0)	**(3.1)**	(0.0)	(5.0)	**(2.3)**	(1.1)	(5.0)	**(3.1)**
Graduation	0	0	**0**	1	0	**1**	0	0	**0**	1	0	**1**
	(0.0)	(0.0)	**(0.0)**	(2.8)	(0.0)	**(1.0)**	(0.0)	(0.0)	**(0.0)**	(0.6)	(0.0)	**(0.3)**
Total	72	60	**132**	36	60	**96**	72	60	**132**	180	180	**360**
	(100)	(100)	**(100)**	(100)	(100)	**(100)**	(100)	(100)	**(100)**	(100)	(100)	**(100)**

Key: OTV = Only Tribal VSS; MCV = Mixed-Caste VSS; T = Total; GT = Grand Total.

Source: Field Survey (Household).

Note: Figures in parentheses are the percentages of the respective counts.

book, annual plan, master plan and documents of estimation for works. Being knowledgeable enough to read CFM GOs, micro-plans and annual plans would be an added advantage; they could find themselves in control of the VSS activities, rather than being helpless in the hands of the FD officials, only to be exploited, especially in financial matters.

The study throws a poor picture of the sample VSS members because the majority of the respondents (76.4%) are illiterate. The pattern is more or less same across both OTV and MCV; it is more acute – at 94.4 per cent – in the tribal villages of Visakhapatnam. District-wise, Chittoor is comparatively better for its less number of illiterates (65.5%). There are 12.5 per cent and 2.8 per cent respondents, respectively, who have studied up to VII and beyond upto IX. Those who have passed X are 5 per cent, while half of this percentage are through to Intermediate level. A lone individual from Gopalkrishnapuram (OTV in Chittoor) is a graduate – a silverlining among the 360 samples (Table 3.4).

Economic Status of VSS Members

Since the study is conducted in rural settings, and in the interiors of remote forests, expecting the standard of housing to be very good would be a high-ask. Yet, the findings are encouraging because only about 23.1 per cent of the sample respondents dwell in the cosy walls of huts, while the majority of the respondents, i.e., 41.4 per cent, reside in *pucca* houses, followed by 34.4 per cent living in semi-*pucca* houses (Table 3.5). The benefited respondents thank the 'houses-for-all' programmes initiated by the government for having reached even the remotest of the villages, especially those in the Scheduled Areas of Visakhapatnam. According to the scheme, even the poorest of the poor are eligible for a certain amount of money to build their houses. In the sample villages, the respondents benefiting from the 'housing schemes' acknowledged to have received a sum between ₹ 25,000 to ₹ 32,000 per HH. In some cases, entire houses have been built by a government agency and handed over to the occupants.

Bhaktavatsala colony (OTV, Chittoor) is one village where most of the respondents live only in huts. This is because the

Table 3.5

Distribution of Respondents According to the Type of their House

House Type	*Adilabad*			*Chittoor*			*Visakhapatnam*			*Overall*		
	OTV	*MCV*	*T*	*OTV*	*MCV*	*T*	*OTV*	*MCV*	*T*	*OTV*	*MCV*	*GT*
Hut	8	3	**11**	16	8	**24**	20	28	**48**	44	39	**83**
	(11.1)	(5.0)	**(8.3)**	(44.4)	(13.3)	**(25.0)**	(27.8)	(46.7)	**(36.4)**	(24.4)	(21.7)	**(23.1)**
Semi-pucca	22	23	**45**	2	3	**5**	50	24	**74**	74	50	**124**
	(30.6)	(38.3)	**(34.1)**	(5.6)	(5.0)	**(5.2)**	(69.4)	(40.0)	**(56.1)**	(41.1)	(27.8)	**(34.4)**
Pucca	42	34	**76**	18	47	**65**	1	7	**8**	61	88	**149**
	(58.3)	(56.7)	**(57.6)**	(50.0)	(78.3)	**(67.7)**	(1.4)	(11.7)	**(6.1)**	(33.9)	(48.9)	**(41.4)**
Others	0	0	**0**	0	2	**2**	1	1	**2**	1	3	**4**
	(0.0)	(0.0)	**(0.0)**	(0.0)	(3.3)	**(2.1)**	(1.4)	(1.7)	**(1.5)**	(0.6)	(1.7)	**(1.1)**
Total	72	60	**132**	36	60	**96**	72	60	**132**	180	180	**360**
	(100)	(100)	**(100)**	(100)	(100)	**(100)**	(100)	(100)	**(100)**	(100)	(100)	**(100)**

Key: OTV = Only Tribal VSS; MCV = Mixed-Caste VSS; T = Total; GT = Grand Total.

Source: Field Survey (Household).

Note: Figures in parentheses are the percentages of the respective counts.

village was very recently rehabilitated away from their old hamlet. They got the *pattas* after a long struggle for the lands where they have constructed their huts, and are expecting further monetary help from the government to turn their huts at least into semi-*pucca* houses. However, it is observed that, in general, those living in huts are the new families who have separated from their parents after marriage. Four respondents who are in the category of 'others' are either living temporarily with their relatives, or are singles who live in public places such as VSS community halls or temple premises.

Box 3.4

Rehabilitated Villages

Etapalli (MCV, Adilabad) was set up in the RFs by the then District Collector, when their village was hit by a cyclone in the early 1980s. The Etapalli villagers, along with their neighbouring villagers (Mathem), were allowed to settle on the highland, where they had taken refuge during that dreadful cyclone. They retained the name Etapalli for their newly rehabilitated village. Yet, they practise cultivation in their old lands. Gopalkrishnapuram in Chittoor is a rehabilitated village carved out for the poor tribes (Yanadis) in 1970s from the lands of the rich landlords, whose land was in excess and attracted the Land Ceiling Act. It was also one of the villages adopted then by the governor of the state. Similarly, the Yanadis were relocated in a new habitation by creating a colony on the outskirts of Bhaktavatsala village.

Source: Account of respondents in the field.

The finding reveals the fact that the majority (21.7%) of the farmers in the sample VSS are medium farmers (5–9.99 acres), followed by semi-medium (2.5–4.99 acres), marginal (0.1–1 acre) and small farmers (1.01–2.49 acres) with 14.7 per cent, 14.7 per cent and 12.5 per cent, respectively, in almost equal proportion. There are only 5 per cent of large farmers and it is observed that none of the respondents in Chittoor qualified in this category. It is seen that the majority (31.4%) of the total respondents have no land at all. Most of the landless VSS members are seen to be from Chittoor (42.7%), followed by 36.4

Box 3.5

Displacement Looming

Bleak future awaits three sample villages, because these poor villagers face the displacement threat. Also in jeopardy are the forest patches protected by them. These villages are one from each of three districts. If Dantanpalli (OTV, Adilabad) is under the threat of being taken over for mining, Borgam (OTV, Visakhapatnam) would be usurped for a power plant. In case of Gopalkrishnapuram (OTV, Chittoor) the submersion of this village under dam appears imminent.

Source: Account of respondents in the field.

per cent and 18.2 per cent in the respective districts of Visakhapatnam and Adilabad (Table 3.6).

Very interestingly, the respondents of those villages which are infamous for *podu* and encroachments are not too deprived of land compared to those where there is no history of either *podu* or encroachments. As far as *podu* is concerned, Visakhapatnam is well known, and Adilabad is the district, which has seen serious influx of '*lambadas*' into the district from Maharashtra State in 1970s and 1980s leading to mass encroachments as accounted by some of the VSS members in the study (Umri (Bojjuguda), OTV, Adilabad). The rehabilitated villagers of Bhaktavatsala Colony, OTV, Chittoor, are presenting their plea to the administration, to provide them with some land apiece. It appears as if there are more landless in MCV in Visakhapatnam – the figures are misleading because the economic status associated with the landless does not fit here, as one of the villages is a fishing village (Pudimadaka, MCV, Visakhapatnam), whose inhabitants depend entirely on fishing; they do not have lands for cultivation nor do they aspire to own any. Yet, the landless is seen to be more in MCV is because of poor SC members in its stratum.

Landholding titles are very important for the farmers. Permanent landholders enjoy security and confidence, while those with temporary titles are devoid of such luxury. People having temporary land titles are vulnerable to uncertainty ranging from not being able to sell the land in need, to the inability to obtain proper loans from banks.

Table 3.6

Distribution of Respondents According to their Landholdings

Farmer Type	*Adilabad*			*Chittoor*			*Visakhapatnam*			*Overall*		
	OTV	*MCV*	*T*	*OTV*	*MCV*	*T*	*OTV*	*MCV*	*T*	*OTV*	*MCV*	*GT*
Landless	12	12	**24**	19	22	**41**	12	36	**48**	43	70	**113**
	(16.7)	(20.0)	**(18.2)**	(52.8)	(36.7)	**(42.7)**	(16.7)	(60.0)	**(36.4)**	(23.9)	(38.9)	**(31.4)**
Marginal	8	5	**13**	8	14	**22**	8	10	**18**	24	29	**53**
	(11.1)	(8.3)	**(9.8)**	(22.2)	(23.3)	**(22.9)**	(11.1)	(16.7)	**(13.6)**	(13.3)	(16.1)	**(14.7)**
Small	2	9	**11**	2	13	**15**	12	7	**19**	16	29	**45**
	(2.8)	(15.0)	**(8.3)**	(5.6)	(21.7)	**(15.6)**	(16.7)	(11.7)	**(14.4)**	(8.9)	(16.1)	**(12.5)**
Semi-medium	12	12	**24**	6	7	**13**	11	5	**16**	29	24	**53**
	(16.7)	(20.0)	**(18.2)**	(16.7)	(11.7)	**(13.5)**	(15.3)	(8.3)	**(12.1)**	(16.1)	(13.3)	**(14.7)**
Medium	30	19	**49**	1	4	**5**	22	2	**24**	53	25	**78**
	(41.7)	(31.7)	**(37.1)**	(2.8)	(6.7)	**(5.2)**	(30.6)	(3.3)	**(18.2)**	(29.4)	(13.9)	**(21.7)**
Large	8	3	**11**	0	0	**0**	7	0	**7**	15	3	**18**
	(11.1)	(5.0)	**(8.3)**	(0.0)	(0.0)	**(0.0)**	(9.7)	(0.0)	**(5.3)**	(8.3)	(1.7)	**(5.0)**
Total	72	60	**132**	36	60	**96**	72	60	**132**	180	180	**360**
	(100)	(100)	**(100)**	(100)	(100)	**(100)**	(100)	(100)	**(100)**	(100)	(100)	**(100)**

Key: OTV = Only Tribal VSS; MCV = Mixed-Caste VSS; T = Total; GT = Grand Total; Landless = 0 Land; Marginal = 0.1–1 Acre; Small = 1.01–2.49 Acres; Semi-Medium = 2.5–4.99 Acres; Medium = 5.0–9.99 Acres; Large = 10 Acres and Above.

Source: Field Survey (Household).

Note: Figures in parentheses are the percentages of the respective counts.

Table 3.7

Distribution of Respondents According to their Landholding Titles

Land Title	*Adilabad*			*Chittoor*			*Visakhapatnam*			*Overall*		
	OTV	*MCV*	*T*	*OTV*	*MCV*	*T*	*OTV*	*MCV*	*T*	*OTV*	*MCV*	*GT*
Permanent	40	38	**78**	6	18	**24**	31	16	**47**	77	72	**149**
	(66.7)	(79.2)	**(72.2)**	(35.3)	(47.4)	**(43.6)**	(51.7)	(66.7)	**(56.0)**	(56.2)	(65.5)	**(60.3)**
Temporary	4	4	**8**	5	11	**16**	10	2	**12**	19	17	**36**
	(6.7)	(8.3)	**(7.4)**	(29.4)	(28.9)	**(29.1)**	(16.7)	(8.3)	**(14.3)**	(13.9)	(15.5)	**(14.6)**
None	16	6	**32**	6	9	**15**	19	6	**25**	41	21	**62**
	(28.7)	(12.5)	**(29.6)**	(35.3)	(23.7)	**(27.3)**	(31.7)	(25.0)	**(29.8)**	(29.9)	(19.1)	**(25.1)**
Total	60	48	**108**	17	38	**55**	60	24	**84**	137	125	**247**
	(100)	(100)	**(100)**	(100)	(100)	**(100)**	(100)	(100)	**(100)**	(100)	(100)	**(100)**

Key: OTV = Only Tribal VSS; MCV = Mixed-Caste VSS; T = Total; GT = Grand Total.

Source: Field Survey (Household).

Note: Figures in parentheses are the percentages of the respective counts.

However, it is encouraging to see 60.3 per cent of the total number of 247 respondents (only those holding lands out of total 360 HH samples) possessing permanent land titles. There were also 14.6 per cent of respondents who have temporary titles for their lands, while 25.1 per cent of the farmers do not have any land titles at all (Table 3.7). Usually, such 'officially landless' farmers either practice *podu* cultivation on hill tops, or encroach into forest lands. Most of such 'encroachers' belong to Adilabad and Chittoor districts, whereas those in Visakhapatnam are known as *podu* cultivators.

The findings show that a majority of the respondents (64.4%) in the sample are equally distributed among groups earning less than ₹ 10,000 a year and those earning between ₹ 10,001 to ₹ 20,000. Those earning under ₹ 10,000 annually are 65.3 per cent in the tribal villages of Visakhapatnam (Table 3.8). In contrast, none belonged to this slab in Adilabad tribal villages. This is mainly because the tribals in Adilabad have more options of earning and are better exposed to the outer world, where they work as labourers in construction sectors. Since the tribals in Visakhapatnam reside in remote villages, it has to be a complete migration for months together, if they have to go out for earning livelihoods or to earn meaningful wages in the towns.

A total of 24.2 per cent of the VSS members earn better, with an annual income between ₹ 20,001 to ₹ 50,000. About 11.4 per cent earn more than ₹ 50,001 or more in a year. Not surprisingly, none from the tribal villages in Visakhapatnam qualified in this category; it is disturbing to learn from the children in Madem Colony (OTV, Visakhapatnam) that their parents bring them out of schools to help them earn money to support family income. Children are rarely seen to study beyond VIII standard in this village. Ironically, this village also has a secondary school to cater. All of the interviewed VSS members (with a couple of exceptions) in the sample hold white ration cards,[4] not surprising, given their income status.

Source of livelihood is a vital activity that distinguishes the standard of living between the people. In the background of the rural setting, the resources through which one makes a living

Table 3.8

Distribution of Respondents According to their Total Annual Income

Income	*Adilabad*			*Chittoor*			*Visakhapatnam*			*Overall*		
	OTV	*MCV*	*T*	*OTV*	*MCV*	*T*	*OTV*	*MCV*	*T*	*OTV*	*MCV*	*GT*
Less than 10,000	0	2	**2**	13	12	**25**	47	42	**89**	60	56	**116**
	(0.0)	(3.3)	**(1.5)**	(36.1)	(20.0)	**(26.0)**	(65.3)	(70.0)	**(67.4)**	(33.3)	(31.1)	**(32.2)**
10,001 to 20,000	19	15	**34**	19	23	**42**	25	15	**40**	63	53	**116**
	(26.4)	(25.0)	**(25.8)**	(52.8)	(38.3)	**(43.8)**	(34.7)	(25.0)	**(30.3)**	(35.0)	(29.4)	**(32.2)**
20,001 to 50,000	32	28	**60**	3	22	**25**	0	2	**2**	35	52	**87**
	(44.4)	(46.7)	**(45.5)**	(8.3)	(36.7)	**(26.0)**	(0.0)	(3.3)	**(1.5)**	(19.4)	(28.9)	**(24.2)**
50,001 and above	21	15	**36**	1	3	**4**	0	1	**1**	22	19	**41**
	(29.2)	(25.0)	**(27.3)**	(2.8)	(5.0)	**(4.2)**	(0.0)	(1.7)	**(0.8)**	(12.2)	(10.6)	**(11.4)**
Total	72	60	**132**	36	60	**96**	72	60	**132**	180	180	**360**
	(100)	(100)	**(100)**	(100)	(100)	**(100)**	(100)	(100)	**(100)**	(100)	(100)	**(100)**

Key: OTV = Only Tribal VSS; MCV = Mixed-Caste VSS; T = Total; GT = Grand Total.

Source: Field Survey (Household).

Note: Figures in parentheses are the percentages of the respective counts.

are also limited, unlike in urban areas where one has numerous options to choose from. This is why people here have to depend on multiple options to earn.

The study reflects this precision because the respondents indeed indulge in more than one source for their living. Almost half of the income is drawn from traditional sources such as agriculture (28.4%) and agricultural wage-labour (19.7%). This pattern is consistent in all the districts. Income from non-agricultural wage labour is almost negligible (3.9%) because logistically, the sample villages, especially those in tribal areas in Visakhapatnam, are too far from places that fetch them any viable non-agricultural wage labour. However, the few who acknowledged to having gone out to earn go to nearby mandal or towns and stay there for weeks or months during lean periods. Many of the respondents in OTV work in one another's fields on mutual understanding. The 'other' sources of livelihoods (4.7%) are animal husbandry, which includes rearing milk-yielding animals besides goats, tailoring and petty business such as grocery shops (Table 3.9). Some of the respondents also carry out occupation-based traditions like washing clothes and fishing (Pudimadaka, MCV, Visakhapatnam). Another set of respondents are also found to maintain nurseries, or engaging in social service; there are a few political leaders too. A couple of them were housewives as well. One respondent claimed that a major part of his income came from serving as an informer to the FD, ever since he was a young boy.

About 12.7 per cent (more or less in the same range of percentage in all the three districts) of the respondents also earn their income by selling forest produce that includes fuelwood, bamboo works and bee keeping. The respondents in a couple of villages get some share of income annually out of *adda* leaves, *beedi* leaves and tamarind auctioning. Ratnampeta SC Colony (MCV, Chittoor) is one among other places where the respondents sell firewood for an income of about ₹ 30 per head load – that is the maximum they can collect from the forest in one day. During monsoon, they cannot carry out this work, hence, in the lean season they get to eat only once. A majority of the respondents (30.6%) has a share in the earning from wage works under

Table 3.9

Distribution of the Respondents According to the Source of their Livelihoods

	Source	*Adilabad*			*Chittoor*			*Visakhapatnam*			*Overall*		
		OTV	*MCV*	*T*	*OTV*	*MCV*	*T*	*OTV*	*MCV*	*T*	*OTV*	*MCV*	*GT*
Non-Forestry	Agri	60	48	**108**	14	41	**55**	60	24	**84**	134	113	**247**
		(33.9)	(27.0)	**(30.4)**	(17.5)	(29.3)	**(25.0)**	(33.1)	(21.2)	**(28.6)**	(30.6)	(26.2)	**(28.4)**
	AL	19	40	**59**	26	30	**56**	33	23	**56**	78	93	**171**
		(10.7)	(22.5)	**(16.6)**	(32.5)	(21.4)	**(25.5)**	(18.2)	(20.4)	**(19.0)**	(17.8)	(21.6)	**(19.7)**
	NAWL	1	11	**12**	5	12	**17**	1	4	**5**	7	27	**34**
		(0.6)	(6.2)	**(3.4)**	(6.3)	(8.6)	**(7.7)**	(0.6)	(3.5)	**(1.7)**	(1.6)	(6.3)	**(3.9)**
	Other	3	9	**12**	3	11	**14**	0	15	**15**	6	35	**41**
		(1.7)	(5.1)	**(3.4)**	(3.8)	(7.9)	**(6.4)**	(0.0)	(13.3)	**(5.1)**	(1.4)	(8.1)	**(4.7)**
Forestry	WW	64	47	**111**	19	40	**59**	61	35	**96**	144	122	**266**
		(36.1)	(26.4)	**(31.3)**	(23.8)	(28.6)	**(26.8)**	(33.7)	(31.0)	**(32.7)**	(32.9)	(28.3)	**(30.6)**
	SFP	30	23	**53**	13	6	**19**	26	12	**38**	69	41	**110**
		(16.9)	(12.9)	**(14.9)**	(16.3)	(4.3)	**(8.6)**	(14.4)	(10.6)	**(12.9)**	(15.8)	(9.5)	**(12.7)**
	Total	177	178	**355**	80	140	**220**	181	113	**294**	438	431	**869**
		(100)	(100)	**(100)**	(100)	(100)	**(100)**	(100)	(100)	**(100)**	(100)	(100)	**(100)**

Key: OTV = Only Tribal VSS; MCV = Mixed-Caste VSS; T = Total; GT = Grand Total; Agri = Agriculture; AL = Agricultural Labour; NAWL = Non-Agricultural Wage Labour; WW = CFM Wage Works; SFP = Sale of Forest Produce.

Source: Field Survey (Household).

Note: Figures in parentheses are the percentages of the respective counts.

Table 3.10

Distribution of the Respondents According to their Income (in ₹) from VSS Wage Works (per annum)

Income Slab	*Adilabad*			*Chittoor*			*Visakhapatnam*			*Overall*		
	OTV	*MCV*	***T***	*OTV*	*MCV*	***T***	*OTV*	*MCV*	***T***	*OTV*	*MCV*	***GT***
0	7	13	**20**	14	22	**36**	13	23	**36**	34	58	**92**
	(9.7)	(21.7)	**(15.2)**	(38.9)	(36.7)	**(37.5)**	(18.1)	(38.3)	**(27.3)**	(18.9)	(32.2)	**(25.6)**
1 to 1,000	0	0	**0**	3	9	**12**	35	22	**57**	38	31	**69**
	(0.0)	(0.0)	**(0.0)**	(8.3)	(15.0)	**(12.5)**	(48.6)	(36.7)	**(43.2)**	(21.1)	(17.2)	**(19.2)**
1,001 to 2,500	32	25	**57**	13	22	**35**	23	15	**38**	68	62	**130**
	(44.4)	(41.7)	**(43.2)**	(36.1)	(36.7)	**(36.5)**	(31.9)	(25.0)	**(28.8)**	(37.80	(34.4)	**(36.1)**
2,501 to 5,000	33	22	**55**	6	7	**13**	1	0	**1**	40	29	**69**
	(45.8)	(36.7)	**(41.7)**	(16.7)	(11.7)	**(13.5)**	(1.4)	(0.0)	**(0.8)**	(22.2)	(16.1)	**(19.2)**
Total	72	60	**132**	36	60	**96**	72	60	**132**	180	180	**360**
	(100)	(100)	**(100)**	(100)	(100)	**(100)**	(100)	(100)	**(100)**	(100)	(100)	**(100)**

Key: OTV = Only Tribal VSS; MCV = Mixed-Caste VSS; T = Total; GT = Grand Total.

Source: Field Survey (Household).

Note: Figures in parentheses are the percentages of the respective counts.

CFM; and very few who have leased-in lands are included in agricultural labour.

The break-up of the income from VSS wage works is important since the support through this incentive has direct impact on the protection of forest; this is expected to serve the economic needs of the VSS members until their forest reaches sustainable stage, while they are protecting their forests.

Estimating the share of income earned from wage works helps to understand as to how far the CFM programme was able to influence the lives of the VSS members. It is seen that 36.1 per cent of the total respondents in the sample of 360 VSS members earn an amount of ₹ 1,001 to ₹ 2,500 per year through VSS wage works, whereas, 19.2 per cent of them earn between ₹ 1 to ₹ 1,000 per year on an average. The same percentage of respondents earned a better amount of ₹ 2,501 to ₹ 5,000 from VSS works. The VSS members from OTV in Adilabad appear to be more fortunate than their other district counterparts, because the maximum number of earners (41.7%) are seen from this category (Table 3.10).

Further, it is seen that 25.6 per cent of the total respondents across all the three districts do not earn any income from the VSS wage works because of various reasons. If some feel that the wages are less, others feel that the payment is not made on time; in some instances, the respective VSS does not get any work for months or even years. Some voluntarily refuse to work, either because they think it is below their prestige to work with labourers or that forest work is hard and only tribals can do it. Many of these disgruntled members acknowledged that they got reasonable amount of money and work during the initial period of VSS formation, a phase which did not last long.

In the past, dependence of poor rural communities, especially tribals, on forests was near total for food, shelter and other needs. With the passage of time, the scenario started changing. Today, the dependency is reduced due to settled agriculture that fulfils the food needs and financial needs by working as labourer in other's fields or as casual labour.

Table 3.11

Distribution of the Respondents According to their Income from Forest Produce Sale (per annum)

Income Slab	*Adilabad*			*Chittoor*			*Visakhapatnam*			*Overall*		
	OTV	*MCV*	***T***	*OTV*	*MCV*	***T***	*OTV*	*MCV*	***T***	*OTV*	*MCV*	***GT***
0	36	45	**81**	23	54	**77**	46	48	**94**	105	147	**252**
	(50.0)	(75.0)	**(61.4)**	(63.9)	(90.0)	**(80.2)**	(63.9)	(80.0)	**(71.2)**	(58.3)	(81.7)	**(70.0)**
1 to 1,000	10	0	**10**	6	6	**12**	17	2	**19**	33	8	**41**
	(13.9)	(0.0)	**(7.6)**	(16.7)	(10.0)	**(12.5)**	(23.6)	(3.3)	**(14.4)**	(18.3)	(4.4)	**(11.4)**
1,001 to 5,000	26	15	**41**	7	0	**7**	9	10	**19**	42	25	**67**
	(36.1)	(25.0)	**(31.1)**	(19.4)	(0.0)	**(7.3)**	(12.5)	(16.7)	**(14.4)**	(23.3)	(13.9)	**(18.6)**
Total	72	60	**132**	36	60	**96**	72	60	**132**	180	180	**360**
	(100)	(100)	**(100)**	(100)	(100)	**(100)**	(100)	(100)	**(100)**	(100)	(100)	**(100)**

Key: OTV = Only Tribal VSS; MCV = Mixed-Caste VSS; T = Total; GT = Grand Total.

Source: Field Survey (Household).

Note: Figures in parentheses are the percentages of the respective counts.

When VSS members from the sample villages were asked about their source of income, their response suggested that 18.6 per cent of the total 360 respondents earned between ₹ 1,001 and ₹ 5,000 from the sale of forest produce. In the respective districts, Adilabad had a share of 31.1 per cent, while Chittoor had a paltry 7.3 per cent, and Visakhapatnam 14.4 per cent. Adilabad accounted for more income share because the timber species is comparatively better here, and moreover, thinning in teak and bamboo forest is permitted for Adilabad VSS members. Besides, coppiced branches of teak have enough market to fetch them a good income. Though, Chittoor also has timber species in its VSS forest, it is not as rich as in Adilabad. Visakhapatnam forest does not have timber like Adilabad forest, but it has good NTFP (*usiri, adda* leaves, tamarind). However, collection and sale of these items does not fetch them more than meagre sustainable income. The group of respondents in the income range of ₹ 1 to ₹ 1,000 per annum is 7.6 per cent in Adilabad, 12.5 per cent in Chittoor and 14.4 per cent in Visakhapatnam. Yet, the total per cent of income earners from the sale of forest produce among all respondents put together is only 30.0 per cent (Table 3.11).

In the overall assessment, only Lalghad (MCV, Adilabad) and Gopalkrishnapuram (OTV, Chittoor) are the two villages that stand out for doing well in earning better from forest produce sale, not only due to enhanced forest condition after VSS, but also because of equitable distributional practices (from tradition) among their VSS members. When income from forest produce sale and VSS wage works is compared (Tables 3.10 and 3.11), the majority of VSS respondents were found to be earning more from VSS wage works than forest produce sale, showing a decline on forest dependency for livelihoods among the supposedly forest-dependent communities.

The issues presented above sets the study in context to help in understanding the administrative area chosen. At the same time, information on natural and physical profile of the study VSS villages throws light on the facts of functioning of the members in VSS activities. The scientific method used for choosing the districts from their respective regions and also the selection of 30 villages for the study is expected to cover the intended objective to generalise the outcome of the research for CFM in the state of AP. Coming to the characteristics, there appears a marked difference between the MCV and OTV villages. Be it in the matters of infrastructure, and other vital indicators like the distance between VSS forest and the villages where community dwells. In regard to stakeholder, i.e., 'community', the description of their backdrop in terms of the caste, age, education level and their livelihood aspects helps in understanding the behaviour of the forest-depending people in CFM.

Notes

1. Tribal VSS are comprised of only tribal communities including PTGs.
2. Mixed-caste VSS are comprised of more than two castes, including tribals. Ratnampeta SC Colony in Chittoor is an exception in this stratum for having exclusively SC members in its VSS.
3. Works like digging contour trenches, digging fire lines in the forest, planting saplings, building check dams, pruning and other forest regeneration activities.
4. The families below poverty line are given white ration cards. In Andhra Pradesh, 173.76 lakh families are identified as BPL families. With effect from July 2008, families earning below ₹ 60,000 per annum in rural areas and ₹ 75,000 in urban areas qualify for this category.

4

Community Participation and Decision-Making in CFM

Introduction of JFM by AP government in 1990s following the national guidelines was conceived as a democratic step towards enhancing the relationship between traditional forest user communities and the FD, which is a legal custodian of the rich forest resources in India since its establishment during British rule. In 2003, JFM was modified into CFM to strengthen community's status in the management of forests by bringing in favourable amendments in its institutional set-up of governance.

In the absence of constitutional status to the policy of CFM, which is only a GO, there is always uncertainty and fear hovering among the communities about their future with the forest, where they have invested their labour for years in its regeneration and protection. These fears are compounded further with the incidences of the FD overshadowing the community with its coercive authority. In anticipation of such irregularities, the theorists like Rich et al. (1995) cautioned that the government agency should remain active only while creating the institution and not after its formation. With the interference of government bodies in the day-to-day affairs, freedom of decision-making is bound to be affected. In the absence of such important freedom, Singleton (1998), Blair (2000) and Larson (2002) envisaged no positive outcome in the decentralised environmental governance. Equally important is the freedom within the 'community' to participate in every aspect of the institutional affair.

In pursuit of understanding such dynamics in the APCFM, this chapter focuses on the participation in the decision-making process and the capabilities of 'communities' in the institutional structure of CFM, and also investigates the influence of FD in the governance of these institutions.

Constitution of VSS

Constitution of the CFM institutions and their executive body (MC) in a transparent and democratic manner is a first step towards devolving the rights for the management of forests to the community. Less of FD and more of community is what an ideal foundation would be for the success of such community-oriented programme.

When the all-important question about formation of VSS was put to the members in the sample villages, the majority of members in 22 (73.3%) VSS (including all eight VSS in Chittoor) said that it was initiated by the FD. Members in only eight (26.7%) VSS acknowledged that they initiated on their own. Some of the members in the villages that have applied on their own to form VSS have interesting tales to narrate. Fakeerpet (OTV, Adilabad) got VSS after applying repeatedly for four years. Their claim was ignored because this village has a history of encounters between the Naxalites and police. So, there was a fear factor and mistrust between the villagers and the FD. Finally, they were allotted VSS, with the hope of curbing smuggling activities in the adjoining forest with the help of these villagers.

The elders of Chamanpalli (MCV, Adilabad) decided to apply for VSS as they were frustrated when their forest was entrusted to their neighbouring villagers under VSS. The implication was that the entire village that was bringing fuelwood from the forest since their ancestry, was now found to be barred from entering it. The motivation to win back their rights to use their forest did not deter them even from spending about ₹ 1 lakh for lobbying. The villagers of Peddapalli (MCV, Visakhapatnam) learnt about VSS and its benefits through news reports; they were also prompted to apply after seeing the allocation of VSS to their neighbouring villages. However, it was only after several rounds to the FD that they were allocated VSS. This was because the FD initially refused to entertain them on the ground that their village did not have enough forest-dependent communities, and the majority in the village belonged to *Kapu*, a forward caste (OC). Pudimadaka (MCV, Visakhapatnam) members also applied for the VSS after learning about the programme from the newspapers. But they had to wait for six months before they finally succeeded. It was an ex-Member of Legislative Assembly (MLA) in Pamulavaka (MCV, Visakhapatnam) who asked the villagers, especially the landless SC, to form VSS and avail wage-labour benefits.

As for the remaining villagers who initiated to form VSS on their own, they applied to the FD after finding the neighbouring villagers benefiting out of it. They hoped that they too could reap similar benefits by protecting their forest.

Participation of Community in the VSS Affairs of Decision-Making

Constitution of GB

The decision-making process for the VSS members begins precisely from their choice to be its member. It all begins when a forest officer of not below the rank of Forest Range Officer (FRO) calls for a meeting comprising all the adult members residing in the village/hamlet/cluster of hamlets situated within 5 km of their forest boundary. After that, they are explained the rights and responsibilities of the members of the VSS as per GO 13 (2002). When the members in the sample were enquired regarding such exercise, the majority of them acknowledged that such meetings were indeed called for by the then FRO of their respective villages and the rights and responsibilities of the members of the VSS were also explained. At the same time, they also confessed that they did not attend the formal meeting because they were either not available in the village or were too busy with their personal work; because the chairperson-in-waiting did not bother to call the GB and managed with only his few yes men, or the cluster of hamlets were so big (Veernamala Thanda, OTV, Chittoor) that the villagers just did not realise when all this happened. This is why many of the members learnt about their membership in the VSS through others, days after the so-called meeting was held for the constitution of VSS. However, according to official records, the constitution procedure was perfect with all the formalities, including the names of the VSS members, along with their signatures/thumb impressions on the Memorandum of Understanding (MoU).

The VSS is entitled to form only when a minimum of 50 per cent households (HHs) agree in writing for its constitution. The procedure is followed up by sending the proposal to the DFO for his consent (GO 13, 2002). Many HHs of the dominant community do not depend on the forests in the MCV villages, and hence they are presumed not to join the VSS. Therefore, the FD classified the poor, especially the SCs or STs separately, created a colony out of such HHs and allotted VSS to them. In other instances, a big village like Patha Bellampalli (MCV, Adilabad) was given two VSS when another community was also willing to be a part of CFM. However, in some villages, the FD did not bother to create a colony as in Netha Kuppam (MCV, Chittoor); although this village has numerically more non-OC population, while a majority of the VSS members is SC. It appears that 50 per cent of village HHs' consent is not respected because the proportion of VSS HHs to that of village HHs is much lower than 50 per cent.

Nevertheless, after the DFO's approval, the FRO enrols the villagers as members of VSS after meeting further conditions, such as two members from each gender for every HH (in Scheduled Areas, the tribal membership has to be always more than that of non-tribals). In consistence with GO 13 (2002), all the VSS in the sample are found to have given equal representation to both the genders, though in Pudimadaka (MCV, Visakhapatnam), only the names of male members were found in VSS GB records. However, equal numbers of women members have representation in the MC, and they take part along with their male counterparts in all activities of the VSS.

According to GO 13 (2002), SC and ST HHs are entitled to be automatic members of the VSS. Except in Sankaram (MCV, Visakhapatnam), Etapalli (MCV, Adilabad) and Lalghad (MCV, Adilabad), all the other 12 villages of the MCV have the presence of SCs. As it is already clear, OTV villages are all ST and discriminative exclusion is not expected at a large level; but an instance of 10 HHs belonging to *Konda Doras* in Madem Colony (MCV, Visakhapatnam) not being invited for membership has surfaced as an exception because the remaining majority belonging to *Kondhs* (PTG) did not desire their membership in the VSS with them. *Kondhs* (PTG) are said to have not protested against this prejudice to maintain harmony in the village. A serious allegation of discrimination against SCs is reported in Pamulavaka (MCV, Visakhapatnam). The reigning chairperson is accused of not inviting the 100 SC HHs while reconstituting the VSS under CFM. He is alleged to be playing party politics and ignoring a majority of the SC HHs, who incidentally happen to be the supporters of a rival political party. However, the chairperson denied all the allegations against him (for details see Chapter 6). Contrastingly, SC HHs in Kongaravaripalle BC colony (MCV, Chittoor) have voluntarily refused to be VSS members because they felt that the wages are not feasible, and also feared that they would be dominated by other VSS members belonging to *Valmiki* and *Kamma* communities.

When the members of their respective VSS in the sample were enquired to sum up the entire VSS constitution procedure, majority of them agreed that during the initiation of VSS, none of them would have opposed the formation because nobody knew what this programme would be like. Many saw it as another poverty alleviation programme to improve their lives. But there were a few who had apprehensions if their village got VSS. Navegaon (MCV, Adilabad) villagers thought that it was a ploy by the FD to deny some landless HHs from cultivating patches of forest land. The villagers of Veernamala Thanda (MCV, Chittoor) were still confused whether the programme was aimed at bettering their well-being or it was a pretence to refute goats' entrance into forest for grazing, because a majority of the

Box 4.1

VSS Membership for Sale!

Two villages, Peddapalli (MCV, Visakhapatnam) and Sankaram (MCV, Visakhapatnam) stand out from rest of the villages because VSS members here had to pay money for their membership. If ₹ 50,000 each was allegedly charged in Peddapalli (MCV, Visakhapatnam), ₹ 40 was collected from each member in Sankaram (MCV, Visakhapatnam). In Peddapalli (MCV, Visakhapatnam), huge money was collected towards 'community fund' because the members were given individual plots in VSS forest. All the members grow cashew in the plots carved out from the VSS forest. There is also a competition among the non-VSS members belonging to the wealthy sections to lure the SC members to sell their membership for a suitable price. The Sankaram (MCV, Visakhapatnam) VSS members claim that their chairperson collected ₹ 40 from each member, instilling fear of not inviting them for forest wage works if they did not pay him the bribe.

Source: Field survey.

HHs owned goats and made a living through them. Similarly, Ratnampeta SC colony (MCV, Visakhapatnam) members knew that it was a well-planned programme to get cheap labour to work in the forest, and also to stop their income-earning profession of fuelwood selling. The Madem colony (OTV, Visakhapatnam) and Goppulapalem (OTV, Visakhapatnam) members still rue over their lost *podu* land under VSS. All these disgruntled villages expressing their ire were those where VSS was initiated by the FD and not demanded by villagers.

Constitution of MC

After constituting the VSS GB, the Forest Section Officer (FSO) convenes a meeting to supervise the election of the MC of 15 members; among them, eight members have to be women, and it is mandatory for one woman to be in an executive position of chairperson or vice-chairperson, or both. In the Scheduled Areas, all the MC members have to belong to either SC or ST, while in the non-Scheduled Areas, their membership is determined by the proportion of their HHs. The tenure of an elected MC is three years (GO 13, 2002).

When the members in the sample VSS were asked about the procedure to hold VSS GB meeting to elect their MC, all of the members in 24 VSS out of 30 sample acknowledged that meetings were indeed held to elect the MC members, including the chairperson and vice-chairperson. But only 13 (43.3% acknowledged as fair) of them thought that the elections in their VSS were fair and democratic, and that they actually participated actively in the elections. Most of such VSS were from OTV across all the three districts. The remaining 11 (36.7% acknowledged as partially fair) were neither happy nor unhappy because they felt meetings were held for formality sake and they had no voice in the process because of the local elite and FD's dominating presence. And yet, they were not against any executive member (chairperson and vice-chairperson) because if they had no reason to support, they also had no issue against them either. Another important reason was that, during the initial phase of VSS, especially during JFM, the members were unaware that holding positions in VSS is a matter of importance, as many VSS members perceive it now. Hence, many did not mind to have anybody as their chairperson, vice-chairperson or MC members. In Veernamala Thanda (OTV, Chittoor) people still do not know who among them is a MC member. Moreover, holding MC membership was not taken seriously by any of the VSS members because, they felt MC members practically do not carry much weight in the VSS set-up. There were two exceptions in M. Kongaravaripalle BC Colony (MCV, Chittoor) and Peddapalli (MCV, Visakhapatnam), where MC membership is respected by its VSS.

Members in six (20%) VSS were completely disappointed with their MC members including chairpersons and vice-chairpersons. A majority of the VSS members of Galetivaripalle (MCV, Chittoor) and Motlapalle (MCV, Chittoor) felt that the local elites used their clout to manage all the process in their own backyard without calling any meetings to form VSS. In the former VSS village, non-OC members felt that they paid for the favours taken from the OC by remaining silent during the formation of VSS. In the latter VSS village, an almost certain SC candidate's name for chairpersonship was conspicuously changed at the last minute at the behest of an OC member who himself later became its chairperson. Some other members (Bhaktavatsala Colony, OTV, Chittoor; and Netha Kuppam, MCV, Chittoor) felt that the FD and the chairperson were in collusion and did not allow any democratic procedure to take place; they simply nominated whosoever they wanted in the MC, sometimes even the members themselves were not aware of their membership. In one instance (Ramachandrapuram, OTV, Visakhapatnam), two of the VSS members were removed from their VSS altogether when they protested against the chairperson for his authoritarian attitude. In another village (Pamulavaka, MCV, Visakhapatnam), the members were so upset not only with MC election, but with the entire VSS formation, that they lodged compliant with the DFO and the police.

However, two VSS stand apart from the majority of the sample VSS for being different (rather normal), because their constitution was executed in letter and spirit of the GO 13 (2002). Those VSS are Gopalkrishnapuram (OTV, Chittoor) and Peddapalli (MCV, Visakhapatnam). The VSS members of Peddapalli (MCV, Visakhapatnam) and the then officers stuck to the procedure; they elected their MC members including the chairperson and vice-chairperson unanimously without any formal elections. In Gopalkrishnapuram (OTV, Chittoor), the MC election for the second phase under CFM took place in a very professional manner. For the chairperson's post, the contestants literally challenged each other in the hardest manner though democratically, and were elected through secret voting. The chairperson, giving an account of the election, said that even police were present to avoid any untoward happening.

Even after a decade, only 10 villages, viz., Kortheguda (OTV, Adilabad), Chamanpalli (MCV, Adilabad), Lalghad (MCV, Adilabad), Gopalkrishnapuram (OTV, Chittoor), Veernamala Thanda (OTV, Chittoor), Netha Kuppam (MCV, Chittoor), Goppulapalem (OTV, Visakhapatnam), Tarlaguda (OTV, Visakhapatnam), Pamulavaka (MCV, Visakhapatnam) and Peddapalli (MCV, Visakhapatnam) experienced changes in their MC set-up, including the chairperson and vice-chairperson. Otherwise, the same sets of members are still continuing since JFM in MC and executive positions (chairperson and vice-chairperson) in the rest of the VSS. Many of the VSS members in the sample did not know that executive members have to be elected after every three years. Only the chairpersons of Pamulavaka (MCV, Visakhapatnam) and Goppulapalem (OTV, Visakhapatnam) knew about such clause. As far as proportional representation of the STs in the MC is concerned, VSS records in the sample VSS suggest them to be in tune with the clauses in GO 13 (2002). With regard to SC representation in MC, they were also represented in their proportion, with an exception of Peddapalli (MCV, Visakhapatnam), where all the MC members are OCs belonging to *Kapu*.

Micro-Plan: The Constitution of VSS

Micro-plan is a document prepared as per CFM guidelines by the members of MC and GB, including the weaker sections, viz., SCs, STs, BCs and women, through participatory and equitable process. It contains plans for the development of village, forest, maintenance of bio-diversity and, soil and moisture conservation. It also provides for livelihood support to the forest-dependent communities and management of forest in a sustainable way. Issues like harvesting details, regeneration plan and prescription for grazing in consistency with overall working plan, are mentioned in the micro-plan. In addition, priority over species selection is bestowed to the members subject to forest laws. The micro-plan is reviewed every year for updating. All the estimates going into the micro-plan are prepared by the responsible FD officer and reviewed by the MC, which seeks the advice of the advisory council if needed. Changes to the micro-plan are made by the MC with the approval of the GB. In case the advisory council does not agree to any of the provisions, the issue is again placed before the GB and their advice is incorporated if agreed by a majority of the members. However, the final approval is given by the DFO after ascertaining that the provisions have not contravened with the national or state legislations. In case of such inconsistencies, the micro-plan is sent back to the MC for incorporating the necessary changes and after obtaining approval of the GB, for resubmission. At the close of the financial year, a complete report showing the activities planned in the micro-plan, the works undertaken, and the amount spent is placed before the GB to seek its approval for deviations, if any (GO 13, 2002). This arrangement sounds like what Vincent Ostrom (1990) had recommended about delegating options for the users to frame rules at multiple levels.

The above description makes clear the importance of a micro-plan in the functioning of VSS. However, the information gathered from members in the sample VSS is not too encouraging because the awareness level of the respondents about it was found to be very low. As high as 85 per cent of the total respondents were unaware of the existence of anything called micro-plan (Table 4.1).

They were not even aware that it looks like a book and contains information about their village and VSS. The ignorance level was almost uniform across OTV and MCV villages and also districts. When the respondents were not aware what micro-plan is, there was no question of them knowing their role in preparing this document, especially in matters related to species selection, grazing, harvesting benefits, regeneration plan and also about the provisions to change their micro-plan. This was confirmed from them when these details were asked and explained to them very specifically. Even many of the vice-chairpersons never heard about this book, leave alone the MC members. But a few members recalled that they were told by someone or the other about some book that contains details about the VSS. However, even they never imagined that it contains such vital information and it should be with them to view anytime they wanted. It is not surprising to mention that except in seven villages, viz., Bommena (OTV, Adilabad), Dantanpalli (OTV, Adilabad), Patha Bellampalli (MCV, Adilabad), Navegaon (MCV, Adilabad), Gopalkrishnapuram (OTV, Chittoor), Kalampalle (MCV, Chittoor) and

Table 4.1

Are You Aware of Micro-Plan?

Response	*Adilabad*			*Chittoor*			*Visakhapatnam*			*Overall*		
	OTV	*MCV*	**T**	*OTV*	*MCV*	**T**	*OTV*	*MCV*	**T**	*OTV*	*MCV*	***GT***
Yes	5	7	**12**	8	11	**19**	7	16	**23**	20	34	**54**
	(6.9)	(11.7)	**(9.1)**	(22.2)	(18.3)	**(19.8)**	(9.7)	(26.7)	**(17.4)**	(11.1)	(18.9)	**(15.0)**
No	67	53	**120**	28	49	**77**	65	44	**109**	160	146	**306**
	(93.1)	(88.3)	**(90.9)**	(77.8)	(81.7)	**(80.2)**	(90.3)	(73.3)	**(82.6)**	(88.9)	(81.1)	**(85.0)**
Total	72	60	**132**	36	60	**96**	72	60	**132**	180	180	**360**
	(100)	(100)	**(100)**	(100)	(100)	**(100)**	(100)	(100)	**(100)**	(100)	(100)	**(100)**

Key: OTV = Only Tribal VSS; MCV = Mixed-Caste VSS; T = Total; GT = Grand Total.

Source: Field Survey (Household).

Note: Figures in parentheses are the percentages of the respective counts.

Sankaram (MCV, Visakhapatnam), this document was not readily available with the VSS. Those chairperson or MC members, who were aware about some book like this, understand that it was either with the FD or Community Extension Worker (CEW[1]). Although Kortheguda (OTV, Adilabad) and Chamanpalli (MCV, Adilabad) members had the books, they could not furnish them because the chairperson of the former village was not available and in the latter village, the chairperson who had taken over the reins just some days before, was yet to take over the documents from the relinquished former chairperson. Peddapalli (MCV, Visakhapatnam) members deliberately did not show their micro-plan probably fearing the allegation against them for tampering with the membership would be revealed. Coming to the 15 per cent respondents who were mostly those in positions of chairperson, vice-chairperson or MC members, they were aware about micro-plan but were not sure they knew what the document actually contains; moreover many of them were illiterate to read it on their own. Most of them only knew about the existence of such a book superficially and remember that it was mentioned in the training sessions. In a couple of VSS, those in executive positions (chairperson and vice-chairperson) heard about it only while helping either the FD staff or NGOs when they were conducting Participatory Rural Appraisal (PRA) (not necessarily with the participation of all the VSS members) to prepare the document.

Annual plans are prepared by the MC at the beginning of every financial year to review and update micro-plan. When the members of their respective VSS were enquired about this, it was found that members in 25 (83.3%) VSS in the sample of 30 had no idea about such procedure. The annual plan was prepared only in 5 (16.7%) VSS. It is only in these villages, that the VSS members discuss issues beyond VSS wage works and payment, mainly because the chairpersons are active or the entire MC is well aware about following such procedures. These villages are Chamanpalli (MCV, Adilabad), Gopalkrishnapuram (OTV, Chittoor), Motlapalle (MCV, Chittoor), Peddapalli (MCV, Visakhapatnam) and Pudimadaka (MCV, Visakhapatnam).

Selection of species for plantation in the VSS forest has to be decided by the VSS members subject to the forest laws in vogue. But in none of the VSS across the three districts or in the OTV or MCV community in the sample of the study, the members were given the freedom to select the species of their choice for plantation. In fact, some of the members in MCV wanted to plant cashew in their VSS, but they were desisted by the FD officials citing that it does not go with the 'forest law in vogue'. For the same reason, OTV members were discouraged in many places from planting coffee in their VSS.

There is a mention in the 'micro-plan' about grazing measures; the VSS members can adopt to protect their forest from not only other of their member's cattle but also from outsiders. The members of their respective VSS in the sample, barring Navegaon (MCV, Adilabad) have acknowledged of having continuous trouble with regard to grazing from within the VSS or their village members, because, the VSS members and other non-VSS members of this village have scant regard for the VSS rules. The FSO and the VSS chairperson were slapped with an 'atrocity case'[2] when they tried to prevent some of the members from taking their goats into the forest. The FSO and chairperson have now given up the fight against such offenders after bailing themselves out with great difficulty from the 'atrocity charges'. Now, it is free for all in this forest. In Veernamala Thanda (OTV, Chittoor) the VSS members openly disagree with the grazing measures targeted against goats under CFM, because they see it a policy against certain communities and their livelihoods. There were also instances of serious conflicts between the VSS members and other villagers over grazing (for details, see Chapter 6).

Meetings: A Dimension of Participation

Theoretically, there are two dimensions of participation, direct and indirect. If forest protection is taken as an example, the stakeholders in direct participation involve themselves in forest protection meetings, labour contribution and forest management through monitoring and patrolling. Whereas, in indirect participation, the individuals simply follow forest protection rules, motivate others including their own families, and see that equity, justice and transparency in forest management are ensured (Ostrom, 1990; Sarin, 1996; Silwal, 1986; Singh, Ballabh and Palakudiyil, 1996). Direct or indirect participation may make the community custodians of natural resources, but they will be sustainable only when empowered not only to participate, but also to take action in their 'own backyard' (Cuthill, 2002), to make the NRM more effective and meaningful.

The basic element towards meeting this criterion is through the meetings between the 'community' members involved in the management of forests. It is this forum where the execution of their plans is given shape and reviewed. In such background, understanding the level of participation and decision-making process among the VSS members in the APCFM becomes more significant. A look at the GO 13 (2002), gives a hope of respite, but it is ground reality that matters, especially when the downtrodden and disadvantaged are the supposed beneficiaries of the programme. The GB meetings are to be held at least once in every six months to discuss the implementation of the micro-plan/annual plan and to review all related transactions.

When the question of conducting meetings in their VSS was put to the respondents, members in only seven (23.3%) VSS have acknowledged, that they conduct meetings to discuss the VSS issues. There is no specific pattern among the villages with regard to meetings, as far as OTV and MCV villages are concerned. But, the OTV and MCV villages in the Visakhapatnam appear to be least interested in attending the GB meetings. One of the chairpersons alleged that 'the people are too lazy to meet'. The members in other 23 (76.7%) VSS have stopped meeting after showing interest during the initial years (1 to 2) of formation of VSS. The lack of interest among them ranged from reasons of the chairperson's one-man show, to domination by the FD, ignorance of the GB by the MC, and above all, inconsistency in allocation or payment of wage works. All such demotivating factors led to dwindling numbers to the extent that not even one-tenth of the quorum was met (officially specified quorum is two-thirds, including 50% women).

Moreover, it is now understood by the members that the meetings are nothing but discussion about the wage works, release of funds, and payment. Hence, they think it is wastage of time to meet, more so, when they get to learn about works through the chairperson who spreads the word, or sometimes through personal visits by the MC members at their doorsteps. Many also think they can earn wages elsewhere utilising the valuable time instead of wasting it there, although in a year, they are required to meet for only two days. Even where the meetings are held in accordance with GO 13 (2002), the procedural seven-day notice prior to convening the meeting is not followed. Because GB meeting is conducted in convenience to majority of the members, so that nobody has any grievance as far as the timings set for the meetings are concerned. In most of the villages, meetings are held in the evenings when all the VSS members are expected to be available, after returning from their work. In some villages, they meet in the mornings, at 7 am and finish by 10 am. Sometimes, these VSS fall short of quorum (at least 50% of the members), yet they carry forward the task of meeting.

Under special circumstances, GB meetings can be convened by the FSO, provided one-third of the VSS members request for such meeting. This clause was utilised by the VSS members of Chamanpalli (MCV, Adilabad) when they suspected their chairperson's involvement in stealthily selling VSS forest timber. In the meeting he admitted his offence, upon which, he was slapped with a penalty of ₹ 30,000 and dismissed from the post. Bommena's (OTV, Adilabad) former chairperson was also removed in the same fashion when the VSS members found out his corrupt practices.

MC meetings are to be held once every month with a minimum quorum of two-thirds. The presence of 50 per cent of women members is mandatory. The meetings could be convened either on the predecided date by the members or through an advance notice of three days. These meetings are convened by the chairperson of the respective VSS.

Responses from the sample villages suggest that members in only 10 (31.3%) VSS carry out MC meetings regularly. Most of these VSS are the same ones that hold GB meetings as per norms.

The MC members of Peddapalli (MCV, Visakhapatnam) have even the fixed date for the meetings – they meet on 8th of every month in *'Raithu Sangh Bhavanam'* because they do not have a VSS community hall. In M. Kongaravaripalle BC colony (MCV, Chittoor), the MC meeting used to be held on the 16th of every month until their forest division was shifted from Tirupathi to Chittoor. They had to stop (since one year) the meetings because no FD official visited them since then. Kalampalle (MCV, Chittoor) hold meetings every month (GB and MC combined), in the evening, between 5 pm and 8 pm. The chairperson informs the VSS members by visiting their houses three to four days in advance. District-wise, Chittoor appears to be marginally better as far as conduction of MC meetings is concerned.

The FSO has the right to convene MC meetings similar to GB in the absence, or in the case of the chairperson not doing his duty for any reason. This was not required in any of the sample VSS. However, in one instance (Peddapalli, MCV, Visakhapatnam), the FSO was informally informed about a meeting wherein their agenda was to remove their chairperson. There were no reports of MC assigning duties and responsibilities by constituting sub-committees to ensure the implementation of VSS micro-plan or annual plan in the sample VSS.

Disadvantaged Sections, Women and the Dynamics of Power Struggle

The aim of any developmental project is to empower the poor and marginalised to take decisions favourable to them (World Bank, 1994). APCFM is also looked upon as a developmental project covering about 7 lakh people from the SC and ST sections, besides a substantial segment of BCs (APFD, 2005). With such hype, it is a challenge for the government to see that it works on the ground with equal zeal.

The BC, SC and ST sections are not only socially disadvantaged, but also economically poor; and their working alongside 'local elites' or OC in the Indian setting of caste system presents a more testing situation. This has to be taken into consideration while implementing projects like CFM. McCay (2003) also observed that dynamic communities present different levels of sharing, dependence, or care for the resources. However, Baland and Platteau (2000) find no harm in heterogeneity when the collective user interests remain in tact, despite their economic inequalities. Similarly, Bardhan and Dayton-Johnson (2003) explain the possibility of coexistence of social or cultural heterogeneity with pronounced economic heterogeneity. To support their view, they illustrate an example of 'unequal agrarian societies' occasionally exhibiting 'adherence to a hierarchical ideology' that helps in the enforcement of cooperative agreements.

Before going into details of the attitude of the local elites (OC and dominant BC) towards the disadvantaged sections (SC, ST and Poor BC), there is a need to deduct 16 VSS from the sample of 30 for analysis, as these are the VSS which are homogeneous, composed of only ST/PTG or SC groups. Among them 15 villages are from OTV by default as per the methodology adopted for the study, the remaining one is from MCV, where only SCs are exclusive members in its VSS (Ratnampeta SC Colony, Chittoor). Moreover, the respondents from all these 16 VSS acknowledged that they do not have any 'serious discriminations' in their institutions on sub-caste or class grounds.

As far as the remaining 14 VSS are concerned, the members of their respective VSS excluding the local elites (OC members and dominating BC VSS members in their respective VSS) revealed a mixed picture of these privileged sections; if majority of the members in eight (53.3%) VSS found 'local elites' neutral in their attitude towards disadvantaged sections, in the other six (40%) VSS, all of the disadvantaged members have acknowledged of being literally discouraged in every aspect of their existence as VSS members. A startling reality was that none of the local elite members in these 14 VSS encouraged disadvantaged sections by giving them freedom to be on their own in the affairs of VSS. Even in the eight VSS where disadvantaged sections found the local elite's attitude to be neutral, except two VSS in Adilabad (Lalghad and Patha Bellampalli), members in the remaining five could feel the uneasiness and negative vibes especially from the OCs.

The local elites appeared to be complying only because the GO 13 (2002) had made statutory provisions for the participation of the disadvantaged sections. A good example is that of Kallampalle (MCV, Chittoor), whose chairperson is Rocka Rockalla Gynaiha, 62, belonging to SC. He observed that OCs in his VSS started behaving aggressively when he was unanimously elected as *Sarpanch* from his village, because they started pestering him soon after, to resign either from VSS chairpersonship or his *Sarpanch* post citing 'one man one post' policy. According to him there is no provision as such to not hold these two posts together and feels they are doing it being unable to digest a '*dalit's* rise'. With such examples, Chittoor stands apart from other districts in behaving poorly with the disadvantaged sections, with as high as 80 per cent (4 out of 5 MCV villages).

Following are the illustrations on various discriminations the disadvantaged sections suffer in the sample VSS. The experiences are narrated by all of disadvantaged section members in their respective VSS in a separate FGD.

Peddapalli (MCV, Visakhapatnam) is composed of OCs (*Kapu*), SCs and BCs. *Kapus* are also overwhelming in numbers in this VSS. SCs are nearly 10 per cent of the total composition, yet, they are not given any representation in the MC, even when the GO 13 (2002) is clear about proportional representation to them in the MC. In Pamulavaka (MCV, Visakhapatnam), about 100 SC HHs were denied membership following the reconstitution of VSS under CFM, even when they were the members in the previous VSS under JFM; this was in complete violation of the GO 13 (2002), which mentions clearly that the SC or ST HHs can have automatic membership in the VSS subject to their wish. The matter was referred at DFO and Deputy Commissioner level, but they were not entertained. The irony in this imbroglio was that this village is a segment of the AP assembly constituency from where Ayyana Patrudu was elected as an MLA and who latter went on to become the Minister of the FD during the Telugu Desam[3] regime. However, even those few SC members are discriminated and branded as 'lazy and troublesome' by the chairperson who belongs to a dominant BC

(*Koppala Velama*) community. This chairperson is not only alleged of hiring non-VSS workers for wage works in the VSS forest, but also using machines to get work done in the forest, without passing resolution in the MC or obtaining approval from the GB for using machineries as per GO 13 (2002).

The *Reddys* in Galetivaripalle (MCV, Chittoor) and Motlapalle (MCV, Chittoor) are accused by the non-OC VSS members that they do not go to work in the forests because they think it lowers their prestige. They are also alleged of trying to remain in the positions of influence in the VSS by sticking to chairperson's post when the majority of the VSS members are non-OC. Similarly, the *Rajus* in Kallampalle (MCV, Chittoor) are also alleged of giving a miss to the VSS works for the same reason, even though a woman member from their community is a vice-chairperson.

A serious allegation against the landholding OC community chairpersons in the villages of their dominance (Galetivaripalle and Motlapalle, MCV, Chittoor) is that they manage the FD officials to delay the plantation in the VSS forest during monsoon because they fear that the labourers will go to work in the forests for better wages than what is given by them, which in turn would hamper their agricultural prospects. As a result, plantation in the forests is always carried out after the monsoons only to see the saplings dying prematurely. As a result of poor survival rate, forest regeneration is said to be taking a back seat in such VSS.

Women in VSS

Since women are active contributors to their households from the forest produce, and they tend to work towards environmental sustenance and equilibrium (Omvedt, 2005), APCFM provided an apt platform for them by reserving half of the membership in all capacities possible, right from GB to executive positions in its institutional set-up. The role envisaged for women was expected to yield results in the form of their active participation in the institutional affairs of APCFM. The moot question is how well are they co-opted into the decision-making process, in a rural society known for prejudices against women?

In the sample VSS, it is observed that women belonging to forward/dominant communities in Galetivaripalle (MCV, Chittoor), Motlapalle (MCV, Chittoor), Pamulavaka (MCV, Visakhapatnam) and Peddapalli (MCV, Visakhapatnam) do not participate at all in the affairs of VSS. Whereas, women belonging to BCs, SCs and STs play a decisive role in forestry aspects by contributing their worth to the VSS and also their HH economy by not only working in the VSS wage works, but also bringing NTFP both for household consumption and for selling. The contribution of women in OTV villages is especially decisive.

When the women members of their respective VSS in the sample were enquired about their status in the decision-making process of VSS and also the attitude of the VSS male members towards them, it was found that majority of the women in 13 (43.3%) VSS found themselves encouraged by men. Men in OTV villages across the three districts were more supportive (53.3%) towards their women folk. Overwhelming encouragement from men was received by the women in Visakhapatnam OTV, with 83.3 per cent, i.e., five out of seven VSS. However, there were also nine VSS (30%) where, the attitude of the men was neutral; most of them belonged to Adilabad.

The overall picture from the sample VSS is that of mixed attitude of the men; the women in the study VSS were not so sure whether their reservation in the VSS GB and MC was justified or not, because they are hardly exposed. This lack of exposure is because of two reasons: first, the VSS meetings are not conducted in the majority of the VSS, and second, their family members usurp their rights leaving them to be mere dummies and take decisions on their behalf. A good example is the former chairperson, belonging to Netha Kuppam (MCV, Chittoor), whose brother was everything as far as VSS affairs was concerned, even the FD dealt with him when his sister was the official chairperson; she was used only for withdrawing funds from bank. Surprisingly, she was content with her subdued role and had no complaints or regrets whatsoever. Many other women did not feel different from her line of thinking.

Box 4.2

All-Women MC is Only a Gimmick

Galetivaripalle and M. Kongaravaripalle BC Colony are the two sample villages representing MCV, Chittoor District, where the VSS MC members are all women. There are 213 such VSS under APCFM (APFD, 2005). In spite of that, M. Kongaravaripalle BC Colony VSS had to nominate one male member from GB to look after the VSS paper work and also to deal with the FD, since women found it hard to cope with the FD. It only shows how difficult the circumstances are for women to function freely. However, in Galetivaripalle, the VSS members who belong mostly to BCs are unhappy that their chairperson, a male member belonging to OC (Reddy) has deliberately chosen women members in the MC only to gain total control over the VSS; because, in this way, he can have a free hand in the functioning of the VSS, as women in this village have less awareness and cannot voice against an OC chairperson out of their shyness and village tradition. From the women's perspective, it could be understood that they are only used to satisfy vested ends of men in the garb of emancipating them.

Source: Field survey.

From the sample VSS, it is quite revealing that a majority of the women members are not aware about their rights; this is consistent with other studies (Sarin et al., 1998). Besides institutional functions, they are also not aware about some of their rights. They do not know that CEWs are drawn from the VSS members to oversee the VSS-related book-keeping works, and also that 50 per cent of them have to be women (one CEW is appointed over five VSS). Wages are still discriminative against them except in five villages, viz., Narayanpur Sakrinayak Thanda (OTV, Adilabad), Chamanpalli (MCV, Adilabad), Patha Bellampalli (MCV, Adilabad), Gopalkrishnapuram (OTV, Chittoor) and Kallampalle (MCV, Chittoor). Male chauvinism was at its ugliest when the VSS members in Navegaon (MCV, Adilabad) defended discriminative wages against women by saying that if they are paid equal wages according to VSS GO 13 (2002), women will raise their hood and demand same sort of equal wages in the other village wage works, which according to them was undesirable. In Borgam (OTV, Visakhapatnam),

Box 4.3

Reservations for Women in VSS is a Bane, not a Boon

Many women executive members (chairperson and vice-chairperson) are rather irked for making one of them signatories to draw money, which in fact, is a trouble – going to bank all the way only to hand over drawn money to the FD officials or to their chairperson or vice-chairperson. Narrating her anguish, the vice-chairperson of Bhaktavatsala Colony (OTV, Chittoor) said that she suspects her signatures are being forged by their chairperson or FD officials to withdraw money from the joint account, so she is in constant fear that she would be held responsible for the offence committed by others in her name. She has made up her mind to resign from her position and wants to be left alone, away from VSS affairs for good. Like her, a majority of the women feel that they are made VSS members only to fill in the quotas as per statutory requirement, and there is no complimentary atmosphere for them to prosper. Hence, the MC and executive membership are nothing but fraud according to them.

Source: Field survey.

women are literally asked not to attend VSS and *Panchayat* meetings. The *Kammas* and *Valmikis* in M. Kongaravaripalle BC colony (MCV, Chittoor) also behave similarly with the 'other' BC and SC women members when it comes to VSS business. The FD officials are also to blame because they insist on interacting only with men, even in VSS headed by women.

In all the 30 VSS, there is a presence of women Self-Help Groups (SHGs); yet they are still under the hegemony of men. There is no clear distinction between the plight of women belonging to any caste, tribe/non-tribe or OC; all are at the mercy of their menfolk. The only consolation was that some tribal women, especially those belonging to *Sugali/Lambada or Valmiki*, show signs of valour to speak up vociferously for their cause.

Freedom of free participation in the decision-making process starts right from the initiation of the institution of the CFM. In the sample VSS, it appears that this freedom was chocked since the beginning itself. Most of the VSS were imposed by the FD on the community, apparently to meet their targets in their respective divisions. Moreover, many VSS members admitted that if they were given a free choice, they would not have agreed to become VSS members at all. This opinion was almost uniform across tribal and mixed caste VSS. Furthermore, even after the formation of VSS GB, the members did not enjoy the freedom to participate and elect MC members of their choice, mostly because such exercise simply did not take place in most of the villages across the three districts. The FD and would-be chairpersons got their proxies into MC and subsequently, themselves, to the executive posts (chairperson and vice-chairperson).

Important area where 'community' participation is seen as decisive in the CFM was while preparing the 'micro-plan'. This is the main document on which the future activities of VSS are determined, which, in turn, is determinant to the successful sustenance of their institution, forest and livelihoods. Ironically, many of the VSS members in the sample, including most of the chairpersons and vice-chairpersons were also not aware of the 'micro-plan', its preparation and importance. This implies that no efforts were made to prepare this important document with the participation of the VSS members.

Another dimension of participation is through regular meetings between the VSS members at GB and MC levels to discuss the course of their VSS activities and implementation of the plans to keep the democratic practice alive. The study shows the participation, or rather the lack of it, on part of the communities in a very poor light, and does not augur well with the institutional tenets of CFM. This activity became extinct after the initial enthusiasm (one or two years of VSS formation) in a majority of the sample VSS, cutting across tribal and mixed-caste VSS, though a couple of Adilabad VSS are still carrying forward the formalities. Otherwise, the meetings have come to be looked upon as only discussions about wages and wage payments, and not issues like forest regeneration or protection.

The attitude of local elites towards the disadvantaged is not too encouraging, especially among Chittoor VSS. Similarly, the condition of women in the sample VSS is not any good or improved. Irrespective of their castes, they are still looked down upon as inferiors in most of the VSS. They are discriminated on wages as well. However, the silverlining in this case is the tribal VSS in Visakhapatnam, where women are enjoying equal status with their male counterparts, thanks to their tradition. As for overall comparison between the study districts is concerned, no remarkable consistency is found to establish the differences on aspects of participation and decision-making in the institutional set-up of CFM, though; clear variations are observed between the OTV and MCV at not only district level but also within their respective districts.

Notes

1. One CEW is appointed over five VSS villages to oversee the VSS-related bookkeeping works.
2. The Scheduled Castes and Tribes (Prevention of Atrocities) Act, 1989 was enacted by the Government of India in order to prevent atrocities against the SCs and STs. The purpose of the Act was to prevent atrocities and help in social inclusion of Dalits into the society.
3. One of the leading political parties in the state.

5

Transparency and Accountability in CFM

All talk about effective decision-making in decentralised environmental governance proves to be meaningful only when downward accountability to resource users is guaranteed (Crook and Manor, 1998; Agrawal and Ribot, 1999; de Oliveira, 2002; Ribot, 2002). This is possible only when mediums such as structures and institutions are assured of democratic practices, integrated with accountability of public officials for their actions, and further complemented by adequate and accessible information systems (Kaufmann et al., 2008). APFD claims to possess everything that is required by any community institution in order to maintain transparency and accountability in its implementing document (GO 13, 2002). This chapter presents the assessment of the field investigation to find gaps, if any, between the claims of APFD on paper, and the actual implementation.

Transparency in the Management of VSS

Transparency is mainly synonymous with finances; therefore, when transparency in the management of VSS is talked about, the issue directly leads towards entitlement to the funds in the

VSS, as mentioned in the micro-plan for undertaking various activities for the following five years. Every year, annual plans are prepared in order to decide on taking up proposed works. So, it becomes necessary for the members to know how much money they are going to receive for the current financial year. All this information is disseminated in the GB and MC meetings, including the necessary changes or deviations, which can be made if the majority of the members in the GB agree.

The funds for VSS are accessed through a 'joint account'[1] operated by its chairperson and vice-chairperson. The deposits received into the account have to be reported by them to the MC and a resolution passed to its effect to record in the minute book. Withdrawal of funds from the VSS account also has to be reported to the MC, either on the day of withdrawal or the next, to keep its members informed of the developments. A copy of the resolution passed to withdraw money against the work done is sent to the FSO by the Forest Beat Officer (FBO)/assistant FBO, to keep the FD informed of the work done and the funds withdrawn. A muster roll register is maintained on a permanent basis with the names of the persons engaged in various works. The register needs to show the total amount payable or the amount already paid to each member who worked in the VSS. The FSO or FBO/assistant FBO signs this register. It is the responsibility of the FSO to cross check the details of the funds withdrawn, including the cheque numbers and the amount disbursed (GO 13, 2002).

When the members in the sample VSS were asked about the financial procedure and allocation of all funds to their VSS (Table 5.1), the opinion expressed by them was not too encouraging; 75 per cent of them were found to be unaware of the financial matters, in particular, the members in OTV from Visakhapatnam had absolutely no knowledge about such funds or the financial procedures. Though, a majority of them knew that VSS is allotted funds particularly for wage works, they were not sure about how much their VSS receives. In the OTV across the three districts, even the chairperson and vice-chairperson are found to be kept in the dark about financial details by their respective FSO and FBOs. About 25 per cent of

Table 5.1

Are You Aware of all The Financial Allocations to Your VSS?

Response	*Adilabad*			*Chittoor*			*Visakhapatnam*			*Overall*		
	OTV	*MCV*	***T***	*OTV*	*MCV*	***T***	*OTV*	*MCV*	***T***	*OTV*	*MCV*	***GT***
Yes	21	22	**43**	8	17	**25**	0	22	**22**	29	61	**90**
	(29.7)	(36.7)	**(32.6)**	(22.2)	(28.3)	**(26.0)**	(0.0)	(30.7)	**(16.7)**	(16.1)	(33.9)	**(25.0)**
No	51	38	**89**	28	43	**71**	72	38	**110**	151	119	**270**
	(70.8)	(63.3)	**(67.4)**	(77.8)	(71.7)	**(74.0)**	(100.0)	(63.3)	**(83.3)**	(83.9)	(66.1)	**(75.0)**
Total	72	60	**132**	36	60	**96**	72	60	**132**	180	180	**360**
	(100)	(100)	**(100)**	(100)	(100)	**(100)**	(100)	(100)	**(100)**	(100)	(100)	**(100)**

Key: OTV = Only Tribal VSS; MCV = Mixed-Caste VSS; T = Total; GT = Grand Total.

Source: Field Survey (Household).

Note: Figures in parentheses are the percentages of the respective counts.

the total respondents who were aware of the financial allocations to their VSS were mostly those in the position of chairperson, vice-chairperson and MC members.

GO 13 (2002) mentions about provisionally displaying the details of year-wise funds released, the list of the works carried out annually and the expenditure incurred in a prominent public place in the village in order to encourage transparency in the working of the VSS. This duty was to be carried out by the chairperson/MC and the FD. But a probe with the members of their respective VSS in the sample shows that only two (6.7%) VSS do this every year. They are Dantanpalli (OTV, Adilabad) and Peddapalli (MCV, Visakhapatnam); and six (20.2%) VSS had such details painted at a public place at the end of first year of initiation of VSS. However, 22 (73.3%) VSS, a majority in the total of 30 have never bothered to display the VSS details publicly. Interestingly, even the display of such information in some VSS villages had no impact as nobody ever spared a thought to understand what it was about. Besides illiteracy, lack of courage to speak up against the dominant chairpersons was among the reasons why important information remained under wraps. The VSS members of Narayanpur Sakrinayak Thanda (OTV, Adilabad) recalled that the FD had collected ₹ 2,500 from them to get the information written on the school building, but even after a year this has not been done.

Working of the Elected Representatives and their Accountability

Common resource management is a group-oriented entity, and leadership is an important ingredient that has a potential to influence such programmes either way. In the midst of such expectations, it would be interesting to learn how the leaders (here, chairpersons) in the study VSS fared.

According to GO 13 (2002), the VSS chairperson is required to fulfil many duties that determine the success of CFM. Such duties include operating the government account (a joint account with the vice-chairperson and an FD official) for receiving government funds and to disburse it judiciously to every member in line with the implemented project plans.

The performance of the chairpersons in the sample appears not so good as revealed by the members of their respective VSS. A majority of the members in only six VSS (20%) thought that their chairperson was doing a good job as he/she is required to do according to the rules and regulations of the CFM. Whereas, a majority of the members in seven (23.3%) VSS felt that their chairpersons were not honest in executing their financial obligations as the disburser of the VSS funds. Most of such VSS were from MCV villages and the members of these respective VSS had concrete evidences against the integrity of their chairpersons. Many of these respondents acknowledged that these chairpersons were hard to dislodge because, while some belonged to influential castes, others developed a clout with the FD. A majority of the members in 17 (56.7%) VSS felt that the question of judging does not arise at all in their VSS, either because there is simply no role played by the chairperson, or they are not allowed to play their role by the FD. Officers of the rank of FSO or below manage everything by keeping not only the chairperson and vice-chairperson, but all members from the MC and

Box 5.1

Villages in High Profile Assembly Constituencies

'Veernamala Thanda' is a tribal hamlet in Chittoor, which falls under the Assembly Constituency of the former Chief Minister Chandra Babu Naidu, who is considered as a strong supporter of J/CFM. It is widely believed that his active involvement resulted in the formation of a huge number of VSS in AP. Moreover, he is also known as an anti-goat campaigner for his anti-goat statement in the Assembly (Ravinder, 2003). It is important to mention this because Chittoor, and this particular hamlet in his constituency, have a menacing goat problem. Similarly, Pamulavaka in Visakhapatnam is another village that has Ayyanna Patrudu representing their legislative assembly constituency. He was also a Forest Minister during the reign of N. Chandra Babu Naidu. Strangely, both these VSS are nowhere near the ideals of CFM in performance, nor are their chairpersons able to emulate the leadership traits of their respective MLAs who are well known for their acumen skills.

Source: Field survey.

GB in the dark about all transactions. They simply dictate terms to the VSS members, caring little for the chairperson or community, for whose sake the programme exists. The chairpersons of such VSS are only used for withdrawing money from the joint account. Incidentally, 11 such VSS (73.3%) belonged to OTV, including all six of this category from Visakhapatnam.

Wage Works

VSS wage works in the CFM have been the motivating factor for many of the VSS members to involve themselves in this programme of forest regeneration and protection (Reddy et al., 2004). This is because the VSS members get to work in the forest regeneration activities that include digging trenches, planting trees, digging fire lanes, weeding and pruning branches of trees. Therefore, it is vital on the part of the chairperson to see that every member gets work and the due payment is made in accordance with the rules, regulations and their basic expectations.

The investigation in the field (Table 5.2) from the sample VSS found the chairpersons to be on the positive side with as many as 73 per cent of the respondents acknowledging their chairperson's honesty in considering them for wage works. Some VSS members (Lalghad, MCV, Adilabad and Gopalkrishnapuram, OTV, Chittoor) were very happy for the comparatively high wages they consistently got in the VSS.

There were, however, about 16.7 per cent of the VSS members, who complained that they were ignored and not considered for the works in the VSS. When the reasons behind the denial of works to the rightful members of the VSS were further probed, the respondents cited many startling reasons. Patha Bellampalli (MCV, Adilabad) VSS members alleged that their chairperson's husband (de facto) and vice-chairperson hire members of *Manner* community to earn commissions (because this community works for much less wages by VSS estimation or general standards). The same allegation was levelled against the Bhaktavatsala colony (OTV, Chittoor) chairperson by his VSS members. While M. Kongaravaripalle BC colony (MCV, Chittoor) chairperson was unpopular for inviting

Table 5.2

Does your Chairperson Consider You for Wage Works when Micro-Plan is Executed in Your VSS?

Response	*Adilabad*			*Chittoor*			*Visakhapatnam*			*Overall*		
	OTV	*MCV*	*T*	*OTV*	*MCV*	*T*	*OTV*	*MCV*	*T*	*OTV*	*MCV*	*GT*
Yes	71	40	**111**	17	40	**57**	60	36	**96**	148	116	**264**
	(98.6)	(66.7)	**(84.1)**	(47.2)	(66.7)	**(59.4)**	(83.3)	(60.0)	**(72.7)**	(82.2)	(64.4)	**(73.3)**
No	0	13	**13**	17	9	**26**	8	13	**21**	25	35	**60**
	(0.0)	(21.7)	**(9.8)**	(47.2)	(15.0)	**(27.1)**	(11.1)	(21.7)	**(15.9)**	(13.9)	(19.4)	**(16.7)**
Refused voluntarily	1	7	**8**	2	11	**13**	4	11	**15**	7	29	**36**
	(1.4)	(11.7)	**(6.1)**	(5.6)	(18.3)	**(13.5)**	(5.6)	(18.3)	**(11.4)**	(3.9)	(16.1)	**(10.0)**
Total	72	60	**132**	36	60	**96**	72	60	**132**	180	180	**360**
	(100)	(100)	**(100)**	(100)	(100)	**(100)**	(100)	(100)	**(100)**	(100)	(100)	**(100)**

Key: OTV = Only Tribal VSS; MCV = Mixed-Caste VSS; T = Total; GT = Grand Total.

Source: Field Survey (Household).

Note: Figures in parentheses are the percentages of the respective counts.

only MC members for works, Sankaram (MCV, Visakhapatnam) chairperson was accused of favouritism. In Galetivaripalle (MCV, Chittoor), it was found that the reins of VSS was in the hands of a stooge appointed by its non-resident chairperson. It is he who decides who should work and who should not, and forces the VSS members to quit when they demand proper wages.

As per GO 13 (2002), the MC is allowed to employ skilled workers or use hired machinery when the VSS members are faced with difficult jobs like uprooting shrubs, removing rocks and clearing forests of unwanted weeds. However, such decision needs proper sanction from the GB, and should be implemented only after the chairperson discusses the issue with MC, recording the details in the minute book. Yet, the chairpersons of Navegaon (MCV, Adilabad) and Pamulavaka (MCV, Visakhapatnam) are accused of using hired machinery without completing the above-mentioned formalities. When enquired about this, the chairperson of Navegaon (MCV, Adilabad) defended his action by explaining that he was compelled on one hand by the FD which pressurises him to finish the given task on time, and on the other hand by the VSS members who do not want to work; they want money without contributing seriously to the task, because they treat the VSS as a charity organisation.

The chairperson of Pamulavaka (MCV, Visakhapatnam) was found to be deliberately denying the rights of the SC members and other poor sections of people, not only due to political rivalry but also because he has a very low opinion about SCs and, in particular, their way of working. His reasoning was that the SC HHs send only old men to work under VSS. According to him, the SC members migrate to the town and hence it is difficult to find them on time for work in the VSS. The VSS members of Veernamala Thanda (OTV, Chittoor) held the FD responsible for not giving their VSS big works; they are diverted to contract labour. Further, the small works offered to them do not attract their interest because there is not sufficient work to employ a cluster of 12 villages like theirs even for a week.

With regard to VSS members who have voluntarily refused to work, it was found that around 10 per cent of the respondents decided so, because they had their own lands to work on – especially the large landholding members; others were busy with their regular professions such as tailoring, dry cleaning or grocery shop keeping. Others simply refused because they believed that it is against their prestige to work along with the labourers who work for them in their fields. Such members belonged to forward communities like *Reddys*, *Rajus* and *Kapus*, who have a sizeable land of their own. In a unique case at Ratnampeta SC colony (MCV, Visakhapatnam), the members refused to work in VSS because the wages were not sufficient. Moreover, they are daily wage earners, who need wages by the end of the day to run their houses; they were not sure when they would be paid for their work done in the VSS.

Most of the chairpersons and vice-chairpersons draw wages only for supervising because they think that it is a thankless job and so they deserve to be paid for it. Such elected

Box 5.2

Chairperson Forced to Hire Contractor to Complete VSS Works

The Ratnampeta SC colony (MCV, Chittoor) chairperson Singanapalli Gangaraju is an unhappy man. He must be one of the exceptional few VSS chairpersons in AP, who would be pleased to relinquish their positions. His tale of woe is that his VSS members are not willing to work in the forest, the reasons being: (1) they are underpaid in comparison to the wages outside; (2) the wages are not paid on any fixed date; and (3) the work is hard in the forests, to put it in their own words, "forest work is difficult; only tribals can do it". On the other hand, he claims that the FD pressurises them to complete the work in the stipulated time, which is no less than a torture. Left with no choice, he delegates forest work to a labour contractor. His anguish ends only after the work is finished to the satisfaction of the FSO; until then, he remains tense fearing that the officer may hold back the sanction of money. On asking why the FD does not derecognise their VSS, the chairperson replies that doing so would end the FSO's side-income in the form of cuts received on VSS funds.

Source: Account of respondent in the field.

executives (chairperson and vice-chairperson) belonged to MCV only. In OTV, however, they too work alongside their other VSS members on an equal platform. This distinct behaviour shows that the objectives and the socio-economic positions of the chairperson and vice-chairpersons in the OTV are similar to the rest of their VSS members, while those in the MCV are diverse across all three districts in more or less same proportion.

Assessing the Performance of MCs

It appears that, as many as 45.6 per cent of the total respondents in the sample VSS are not sure whether they are happy with their MC or not. This state of dilemma is more among the VSS members of OTV with 63.9 per cent. The figure is 90.3 per cent for those belonging to OTV in Visakhapatnam. The reason is that their MC members including chairperson and vice-chairperson are only puppets controlled by the FD, and so they cannot morally blame their MC; the same is the reason for the Adilabad OTV, where 52.8 per cent feel uncertain about assessing their MCs. However, there were 23.6 per cent of the total respondents who were bold enough to voice that they were unhappy with their MC for being incompetent and corrupt in connivance with the FD.

The frustration galore of some respondents is due to the fact that their chairpersons either belong to the local elite class or have started behaving indifferently to the problems of the poor VSS members by being elusive to them. The MC members in these VSS are merely there to make the numbers. Nevertheless, there were also 30.8 per cent of the respondents, who are happy with the performance of their elected executive heads and MC members (Table 5.3).

Power Relations between FD and User Community

CFM responsibilities are actually extended duties for the forest officials in addition to their routine work. Yet the obligations on part of the FD are very imperative because the GO 13 (2002) envisages a facilitator's role for them. In the study, the members

Table 5.3

Are you Happy with the Performance of Your MC?

Response	*Adilabad*			*Chittoor*			*Visakhapatnam*			*Overall*		
	OTV	*MCV*	*T*	*OTV*	*MCV*	*T*	*OTV*	*MCV*	*T*	*OTV*	*MCV*	*GT*
Yes	28	20	**48**	13	15	**28**	1	34	**35**	42	69	**111**
	(38.9)	(33.3)	**(36.4)**	(36.1)	(25.0)	**(29.2)**	(1.4)	(56.7)	**(26.5)**	(23.3)	(38.3)	**(30.8)**
No	6	26	**32**	11	24	**35**	6	12	**18**	23	62	**85**
	(8.3)	(43.3)	**(24.2)**	(30.6)	(40.0)	**(36.5)**	(8.3)	(20.0)	**(13.6)**	(12.8)	(34.4)	**(23.6)**
Can't say	38	14	**52**	12	21	**33**	65	14	**79**	115	49	**164**
	(52.8)	(23.3)	**(39.4)**	(33.3)	(35.0)	**(34.4)**	(90.3)	(23.3)	**(59.8)**	(63.9)	(27.2)	**(45.6)**
Total	72	60	**132**	36	60	**96**	72	60	**132**	180	180	**360**
	(100)	(100)	**(100)**	(100)	(100)	**(100)**	(100)	(100)	**(100)**	(100)	(100)	**(100)**

Key: OTV = Only Tribal VSS; MCV = Mixed-Caste VSS; T = Total; GT = Grand Total.

Source: Field Survey (Household).

Note: Figures in parentheses are the percentages of the respective counts.

of their respective VSS expressed their opinion on the issue, which are presented as under.

The FD has to share 50 per cent of the value of the produce above ₹ 100 with the VSS within the prescribed time, as a reward for apprehending the forest offenders. When asked about such situation and the FD's role, all the members of four VSS admitted that they received their share of 50 per cent. These villages were Narayanpur Sakrinayak Thanda (OTV, Adilabad), Lalghad (MCV, Adilabad), Kallampalle (MCV, Chittoor) and Pamulavaka (MCV, Visakhapatnam). They received ₹ 7,000, ₹ 1,500, ₹ 500 and ₹ 500, respectively, so far. Such promptness in payment encourages the VSS members to protect their VSS forest and the adjacent RF more efficiently. The majority of the members in most VSS admit that they do not encounter such offences in their villages anymore; though they claim to have caught many of such offenders and handed them over to the FD even before CFM (during JFM there was no such norm). The villagers of Chamanpalli (MCV, Adilabad) and Pudimadaka (MCV, Visakhapatnam) had caught truck loads of timber worth ₹ 1 lakh a decade before, but they were saddened to learn that the FD released the culprits through underhand dealings.

The story of Fakeerpet (OTV, Adilabad) is unique because this village was given VSS only to take their assistance in apprehending the smugglers, whose activity is rampant here. All the members of this VSS are now unhappy because they did not get any share on apprehending smugglers along with 12 cartloads of teak; instead, the FD field officers released the smugglers without booking any case. Now they do not bother to apprehend smugglers even when they witness 50 cartloads of teak being smuggled every night through their village route. Since they are not apprehending the smugglers, the FRO and FSO have asked the chairperson not to visit their office seeking VSS works. Since then, their VSS is not getting any wage works. The VSS members claim that smuggling takes place with tactical support from some of the FD officers (FRO and FSO) who have an unholy nexus with the smugglers. In some instances, fingers are pointed at FSO and chairperson nexus as well, One VSS member of Kortheguda (OTV, Adilabad) accuses the former chairperson of holding 10 cart loads of teak that were caught before 2002 (before CFM), in his custody. In another case, the former chairperson of Chamanpalli (MCV, Adilabad) wonders why the FD has not removed the logs of teak (valuing more than ₹ 1 lakh) that is still remaining in his house. His VSS patrolling members had confiscated this catch when it was being smuggled in a truck way back in 2002.

The next important duty that establishes trust between the community and the FD is with preparation of estimates before undertaking any VSS wage works. Most of the members in only seven (23.3%) VSS have expressed their happiness with the FD on this count, while members in the majority, i.e., 23 (76.7%) VSS are frustrated because the FD officials do not prepare transparent estimates. As per procedure, the estimates are prepared

Box 5.3

Villagers Shocked by Researcher's Visit

Fakeerpet (Adilabad) is a village situated in the interiors of the Adilabad forests. According to the members of this village, it became infamous for the naxalite movement, for it was in the vicinity of this village, back in 1993, firing was exchanged between the police and Naxalites. Since then, this village has been under scanner of Naxalites and police alike. While the police suspect villagers of being sympathisers of Naxalites, the outlawed outfit suspects the villagers of being informers to the police. In such volatile situation, the people have been suffering silently, devoid of basic amenities that villages normally receive under various State and Central Government schemes, because no government officials dared to visit this village, fearing for their own lives. They just meet the available member from Fakeerpet in another village, a junction where many people congregate to buy basic needs or look for a wage work. The villager's observed that the officials, including those from the FD, have not spent more than 10 minutes at a stretch in Fakeerpet, even when they were required for directing VSS works to its members. Instead, they communicated with them in another village, where they felt they were safe. This is why the researcher was questioned hundreds of times by the villagers, why he visited their village and stayed for so long.

Source: Field experience.

by the FSO/FBO for the works to be undertaken, and then the copies of the forest schedule rates are handed over to the VSS MC to facilitate the review of the cost of works. Only upon revision of the rates, the works are undertaken (GO 13, 2002). Due to non-implementation of this procedure, the members feel cheated each time. They become more aggravated when they find that higher wages are being paid to their neighbouring VSS members for the same kind of work and on the same type of soil as in their forest.

Providing Non-Timber Forest Produce (NTFP) permit sanctions, signed by the DFO and handed over by the FSO to the VSS members is another pro-poor initiative to reduce the hardships of the VSS members when they venture into forest to collect the NTFP items. When the VSS members in all the sample villages were enquired about this, it was found that an overwhelming number of them were not aware of their entitlement to get such cards; surprisingly, even a majority of the FD officers of the rank of FSO or below were not aware about this. However, the people have no complaint for not possessing these permit cards because they do not face any hardship without them; there is no access restriction to the RF after the advent of the VSS.

The FD officials, especially those below the rank of FRO are expected to visit forests more often after the advent of VSS for wage works assessment. The resultant interaction with the community was expected to build a healthy rapport and relationship between the VSS members and the FD, and also to erase the longstanding suspicion between these two stakeholders. When the members of their respective VSS were asked about this, the majority of the members in the 13 (43.3%) VSS acknowledged that they now experienced a comparatively better behaviour from the FD, due to frequent visits by the FD officials of various ranks such as FSO, FBO, ABO or guard. However, most of the members in 17 (56.7%) VSS were unhappy because of the unimproved behaviour of the FD officials. The respondents in these VSS mentioned how the FSOs preferred to talk only with the chairperson and not with other VSS members, displaying their continued arrogant style of functioning. The VSS members of Umri Bojjuguda (OTV, Adilabad) and M. Kongaravaripalle BC colony (MCV, Chittoor) were also unhappy, because no FD officer visited them for the past six months in the former, and for the past one year in the latter village.

On asking about the higher official's inspection visits to their VSS to take stock of the situation, the poor members in the sample recounted as to how, they are 'pressed' in advance to speak good about ground level FD staff. The VSS members were also threatened with consequences if they speak the truth against the local officials. Left with no choice, the hapless members would impress the visiting officers by sending the message that everything is going well according to the rules in their VSS. Such incidents are more common in OTV villages across all the study districts. On enquiring what they meant by consequences, the VSS members informed that they would be denied access into the forest to collect everyday needs, debarred from VSS wage works and would be subjected to abuses and misconduct.

Role of FD in Financial Matters under CFM

Under JFM, the power to withdraw money from the VSS account rested jointly with an FD official and the president (now chairperson). In CFM, the FD official is replaced by the vice-chairperson, thus giving more autonomy to 'community' (see Table 2.1 in Chapter 2).

Elucidating the actual situation in regard to financial autonomy and the transparency they are expected to enjoy under CFM in their VSS. A majority of the members in only three (10%) VSS of the total sample of 30 acknowledged of experiencing an improvement.

A majority of the members in 19 (63.3%) VSS found the condition worsening, while most of the members in eight (26.7%) VSS were not sure whether the situation has changed or not, because they have not experienced a comparative situation; they were never in a position of assertion either during the JFM or CFM phase. All the OTV members in Visakhapatnam found it to be worsened because the harassment faced by the chairperson and vice-chairperson at the hands of FD has increased manifold after they were made signatories to withdraw money.

Actually, the provision in the GO 13 (2002) was an earnest effort to make money withdrawal a foolproof exercise, and to weed out the possibility of any exploitation by the FD. The provision stated that the chairperson and vice-chairperson would operate the account and withdraw money, that too, only after passing a resolution in the MC. They are also required to enter the cheque details and the purpose of withdrawal in the minute book either on the day of withdrawal or the next. But on ground, the picture is different.

In majority of the VSS, the estimates are not prepared as prescribed. The FD officials just order the members to work. Upon completion of the task and its so-called inspection, the chairperson and the vice-chairperson are summoned to the FD's office from where they are taken to the bank to withdraw only such amount of money as dictated by the officials. In many instances, they write all the particulars on the cheques, and just take the thumb impressions from the respective elected executive heads. After the withdrawal, the money is snatched from the chairperson and both of them are taken back to the FD premises to settle the cut (which varies from one village to another depending upon the vulnerability of the community). Many of the VSS members give an account of how, from lower rank officials to the FRO in the FD office, each takes their share from the withdrawn amount. The majority of the VSS members feel what they get is merely a left-over amount. The story is similar even in the well-aware villages, the only difference being the magnitude of the treatment. If the chairpersons and vice-chairpersons in the OTV are literally taken captives during entire process of withdrawing money from the bank, the MCV elected executive heads manage the FD by settling with some percentage. From the sample 30 VSS, only three VSS chairpersons could say that they were not exploited, and that they have not allowed the FD to exploit them; instead, they claimed to deal with them on equal footing. These VSS are Kortheguda (OTV, Adilabad), Gopalkrishnapuram (OTV, Chittoor) and Pudimadaka

(MCV, Visakhapatnam). The reason was their unity and the bold nature of the respective communities to question injustice.

Besides taking commissions from the VSS funds, the FD staff at the ground level are also accused by some VSS members of taking money for petrol expenses for visiting their village during VSS works and photocopying the VSS-related documents. They are also alleged of collecting high charges for transporting saplings from nurseries to the VSS village or forest. In case of M. Kongaravaripalle (MCV, Chittoor), VSS members were shocked on learning about their FSO retiring from the service only to disappear with their VSS wage works money. The members of this VSS were yet to get their money when they were interviewed. Perhaps such disgraceful track record of the FD may have incited the former MLA of Narsipatnam constituency in Visakhapatnam and resident of Pamulavaka (MCV, Visakhapatnam) during the interview, to place the FD only next to the Police Department among all the departments in the state who are involved in corrupt practices.

Community's Verdict on FD

After interview with the members in each of the sample VSS, many of them used to have a puzzled look on their faces, as they realised how ignorant they were about their rights in the VSS. In majority of the VSS, especially in the OTV, the MC members, including the chairperson and vice-chairperson too were unaware of many of their own rights. So, a question was asked to them to find out, who they would hold responsible for their ignorance.

The response revealed by them (Table 5.4) puts FD in poor light because 56.1 per cent of the total respondents held them responsible for their sorry state; they expected the FD to train the VSS members and make them self-reliant; or at least leave them without interfering in their day-to-day affairs, which would have helped them become aware on their own. Instead, they are seen as wilfully concealing all the important information from the VSS members, may be with an intention to exploit their innocence to meet their vested ends. More forthright views were expressed against the FD by the OTV members, because 72.8 per cent held a poor image of the FD. Further, 25.6

Table 5.4

Who do you Hold Responsible for Your Ignorance of VSS Affairs Including Financial Allocations?

Response	*Adilabad*			*Chittoor*			*Visakhapatnam*			*Overall*		
	OTV	*MCV*	*T*	*OTV*	*MCV*	*T*	*OTV*	*MCV*	*T*	*OTV*	*MCV*	*GT*
Chp	13	29	**42**	15	43	**58**	14	17	**31**	42	89	**131**
	(17.3)	(29.9)	**(24.4)**	(28.8)	(34.4)	**(32.8)**	(16.3)	(22.1)	**(19.0)**	(19.7)	(29.8)	**(25.6)**
V-Chp	0	8	**8**	2	22	**24**	0	0	**0**	2	30	**32**
	(0.0)	(8.2)	**(4.7)**	(3.8)	(17.6)	**(13.6)**	(0.0)	(0.0)	**(0.0)**	(0.9)	(10.0)	**(6.3)**
MC	0	0	**0**	1	7	**8**	0	0	**0**	1	7	**8**
	(0.0)	(0.0)	**(0.0)**	(1.9)	(5.6)	**(4.5)**	(0.0)	(0.0)	**(0.0)**	(0.5)	(2.3)	**(1.6)**
FD	59	44	**103**	24	48	**72**	72	40	**112**	155	132	**287**
	(78.7)	(4.1)	**(59.9)**	(46.2)	(38.4)	**(40.7)**	(83.7)	(51.9)	**(68.7)**	(72.8)	(44.1)	**(56.1)**
NA	3	16	**19**	10	5	**15**	0	20	**20**	13	41	**54**
	(4.0)	(16.5)	**(11.0)**	(19.2)	(4.0)	**(8.5)**	(0.0)	(26.0)	**(12.3)**	(6.1)	(13.7)	**(10.5)**
Total	75	97	**172**	52	125	**177**	86	77	**163**	213	299	**512**
	(100)	(100)	**(100)**	(100)	(100)	**(100)**	(100)	(100)	**(100)**	(100)	(100)	**(100)**

Key: OTV = Only Tribal VSS; MCV = Mixed-Caste VSS; T = Total; GT = Grand Total; Chp = Chairperson; V-Chp = Vice-Chairperson; MC = Managing Committee; FD = Forest Department; NA = Not Applicable.

Source: Field Survey (Household).

Note: Figures in parentheses are the percentages of the respective counts.

per cent of the respondents also accused the chairperson of concealing information from them in collusion with the FD. The accused chairpersons belonged mostly to the MCV category and more so, where they did not belong to a caste of majority of the VSS members. This trend is more prominent in Chittoor (34.4%). A small minority, i.e., 6.3 per cent and 1.6 per cent, of the respondents also had grievances against the vice-chairperson and MC members, respectively. However, none in Visakhapatnam held them responsible. In Adilabad also, none of the VSS members held their MC members or their vice-chairperson responsible for their ignorance.

On a positive note, a section of respondents (10.5%) felt that this query does not apply to their VSS. On asking about the reason, they replied that whatever information any member in their VSS (whether he/she is a GB, MC or the chairperson and his/her deputy) gets to know about VSS on any issue is immediately disseminated to all the other members. They also do not suspect that the FD may have concealed anything from them either. When they were asked whether the reason for their positive opinion is because their chairperson properly maintains records such as: (1) records of proceedings in the meetings; (2) cheque book; (3) joint account; (4) minutes book; (5) MC resolution book; (6) estimates for works; and (7) muster roll register. All the respondents were unanimous in not crediting the transparency in their VSS in such record maintenance; according to them the credit goes to their community's healthy tradition of practising 'participatory democracy' and in conducting VSS business transparently even without the book-keeping exercise.

Given the poor reputation developed by the FD among the VSS villagers, the respondents were asked whether the government should go a step further from community to 'only community' by withdrawing the FD from the forest jurisdiction.

The response from the members in the sample VSS (Table 5.5), was quite interesting because only 18.9 per cent were categorical in getting rid of the FD. They thought that the FD staff are not only corrupt but also arrogant in their conduct in executing VSS tasks and also in general. About 44.4 per cent of

Table 5.5

Given the History, Do You Think the FD Should Completely be Withdrawn from Your Area?

Response	*Adilabad*			*Chittoor*			*Visakhapatnam*			*Overall*		
	OTV	*MCV*	***T***	*OTV*	*MCV*	***T***	*OTV*	*MCV*	***T***	*OTV*	*MCV*	***GT***
Yes	7	3	**10**	6	12	**18**	32	8	**40**	45	23	**68**
	(9.7)	(50.0)	**(7.6)**	(16.7)	(20.0)	**(18.8)**	(44.4)	(13.3)	**(30.3)**	(25.0)	(12.8)	**(18.9)**
No	60	35	**95**	9	25	**34**	39	32	**71**	108	92	**200**
	(83.3)	(58.3)	**(72.0)**	(25.0)	(41.7)	**(35.4)**	(54.2)	(53.3)	**(53.8)**	(60.0)	(51.1)	**(55.6)**
Don't know	5	22	**27**	21	23	**44**	1	20	**21**	27	65	**92**
	(6.9)	(36.7)	**(20.5)**	(58.3)	(38.3)	**(45.8)**	(1.4)	(33.3)	**(15.9)**	(15.0)	(36.1)	**(25.6)**
Total	72	60	**132**	36	60	**96**	72	60	**132**	180	180	**360**
	(100)	(100)	**(100)**	(100)	(100)	**(100)**	(100)	(100)	**(100)**	(100)	(100)	**(100)**

Key: OTV = Only Tribal VSS; MCV = Mixed-Caste VSS; T = Total; GT = Grand Total.

Source: Field Survey (Household).

Note: Figures in parentheses are the percentages of the respective counts.

the Visakhapatnam villagers in OTV strongly held this view; they felt that it would be a good riddance for having suffered atrocities at their hands since the establishment of their department. However, only 7.6 per cent of the members in Adilabad thought in a similar fashion; about 25.6 per cent were non-committal, because they were not sure if it would be good for them and the forest. However, a majority, with 56.6 per cent gave a clear no, most of whom were from Adilabad. These people felt that in spite of all the atrocities experienced at the hands of the FD, it would not be wise to wish away with an entire department; according to them, in the absence of an authority like the FD, it would be anarchy all over, and whatever remains of the forest they see today would vanish. They also wanted the FD because they are professionals trained for protecting forests. On the other hand, the community who have to look after their farms cannot concentrate on what is happening in the forest all the time even if they are VSS members.

Importantly, these respondents found fault not with the FD but with a few of its low-ranking officials. They remember many officials who were good to them and understood their sensitivities. They were all praise for the officials of DFO rank, because they were compassionate with them. Nevertheless, all the respondents expected better behaviour and humane treatment from the ground level staff added by the qualities of sincerity, accountability and honesty, especially while discharging their duties as facilitators under the aegis of CFM.

FD on its Role in CFM

To get a balanced analysis on the role the FD in the affairs of CFM, opinions from the FD staff were also recorded, to hear their side of the story, especially on the issues that were held against them by the 'communities'. In all, 30 forest officials ranging from the rank of guard to DFO were interviewed individually and their views elicited.

The FD officials found themselves in a very uncomfortable position. They were agitated either while defending themselves or their department, when questioned on the corruption charges levelled against them. None of the interviewed officials admitted to have taken money or commission from the VSS members; they even rubbished petty allegations of collecting money towards petrol expenses[2] or for photocopying the VSS-related documents. They also refused to admit the serious charges of keeping the chairperson and their deputies captives while withdrawing money from the VSS bank account. They categorically dismissed all the charges of collecting cash or kind for allowing grazing in the forest. When enquired further on their nexus with the smugglers, most of them turned furious and tried to excuse themselves from talking further.

S. Mannaiah, leader of Association of field level forest officials declares that the CFM programme is a failure. He feels that the survival rate of the plants is diminishing as the FD officials do not inspect the sites where communities undertake plantation work. Many officers across all the three districts unanimously held the view that micro-plans are not practical. They blame not only their own department but also the NGOs for not preparing 'micro-plans' by adopting the PRA method. They accuse them of indulging in malpractices like copying the contents of one VSS micro-plan to another. Charging the NGOs of dishonesty, they also accuse them of delegating and outsourcing the VSS work to other NGOs having no experience in VSS activities.

Talking on encroachments, the majority of the officers are irked by the people's behaviour when they try to fool the FD to

Box 5.4

Why a Good VSS Goes Defunct?

A good example is Kortheguda, where its own chairperson slashed 25 acres of VSS forest to plant 'kanuga', declaring it as his individual plot as he was fed up with FD's indifferent attitude. He is now emulated by his other VSS members who are also taking separate plots for themselves by clearing teak forest. Such level of demotivation is the result of the FD refusing to act tough with the 'thieves' and 'smugglers' who have been denuding their VSS forest at every opportunity. According to these villagers, a 'Range Officer' is quoted on record for advising the VSS members to 'not take forest protection seriously thinking VSS forest would remain with them forever'.

Source: Account of respondents in the field.

claim the land in the VSS forest by showing forged *pattas*. They claim that chairpersons who are not happy with the lower level officials try to take revenge by threatening to complain against them to the DFOs, on the pretext of excesses committed by them. The officials also complain that some of the chairpersons are so arrogant that they demand food and other treats when they are called to the office in relation to VSS work; they otherwise threaten to complain of ill-treatment to their higher-ups in the FD. According to officials of the ranks FSO and below, the chairpersons get audience with DFO anytime they wish, while it is very difficult for them to get an appointment with the DFO. On the issue of VSS wage payments, some of the officials held a curious view that only such persons should be made chairperson, who would be able to pay the wage works from his/her pocket until the payment is transferred to the VSS account upon inspection of the works.

On drawing their attention to the fact that VSS members find DFO level officers to be honest, one of them quoted a proverb in Telugu, which meant: "the hills, when seen from far look smooth, it is only after closing-in, one sees its roughs". What he meant to say was that, these officers visit the VSS occasionally and speak good things to them, which impresses the communities. On the other hand, most of the lower officials visit them on a regular basis and take tough measures against communities on violation of forest rules, so they become undesired faces.

The FD officers across all the three districts are unanimous in their view on the shortage of manpower in proportion to the huge forest jurisdiction. Therefore, they see an urgent need to recruit ground level staff to ward off this problem. They also stress upon equipping the officers at least of the rank of FRO with the modern and sophisticated firearms to match with the ever-improving smugglers' armoury. The officers of Adilabad and Chittoor explained how they work under serious threats to their lives from the mafias involved in smuggling teak and red sanders. Adilabad officers hold the Multani[3] community responsible for rampant smuggling because of their daredevilry. On asking about continuous dent made by the smugglers, the

Box 5.5

Forester's Woes

An officer of FSO rank in a MCV in Adilabad who was nearing retirement blames Naxalism for forest degradation. He elaborates that this trend started in 1976, reached its peak in 1982, and still continues. For him, allotting natural forest (composed of indigenous tree species; non-exotic) to VSS makes little sense. He also faults the policy of allowing existing forest to be cut, only to plant new saplings. He likens this practice to what economists call 'Keynesian Theory' of digging mud and filling it up to generate employment. He claims of appraising the ground realities to their higher ups, only to learn their department's helplessness against the state's committed policy towards involving people in the protection of forests. His poor opinion on community is due to people's lack of concern for forest and indifference towards it. Shifting to other issues, he cites examples of how some of the tribals, with their increasing population are always on an encroaching mission; how some caste groups barge through the fences into forests for grazing their cattle in spite of requesting them not to; and how people try to encroach forest lands armed with 'bogus pattas'. He claims that in some areas like his, the FD officials live in acute terror, fearing attacks on them by Naxalites, even at home. He claims to have survived an attack on his life when the extremists burnt his jeep to ashes. He is also disillusioned with the 'atrocity act', which has become a tool to get back at the FD officers; he too was one such victim. Throwing a final salvo, he does not see any future for the CFM programme, more so, when the funds stop.

Source: Field interview.

officials blame it on the laxity of the Indian criminal law, and interference from political leaders such as MLA, Zilla Parishad Territorial Constituency (ZPTC) and *Sarpanchas* in their affairs. They pointed out various loopholes in the law through which the forest offenders are released on bail within hours of being arrested with tactical support from some of the politicians. Hence, Prabhakar (DFO, Adilabad) demands stringency in the law; echoing the voice of his subordinates, he suggests treating forest crime as a non-bailable offence. Highlighting the misuse of the 'atrocity act', the forest officials describe how poor people belonging to SCs and STs, even those who are VSS members are deliberately used by the smugglers to not only cut the tress but as fronts to threaten the officials of slapping the 'atrocity case' against them on being apprehended. The FD officials also point to those selected pockets of forest areas, where VSS members belonging to these communities also threaten the officials of filing such suits if they are questioned for anti-forestry acts. According to the interviewed officials, such pressure and blackmail tactics are affecting forest protection, so the FD officials are demoralised to work to their full potential under constant fear of being framed under atrocity cases.

Summing up, transparency and accountability depend not only on the kind of structure any institution provides, but also on the attitude of the stakeholders involved in it. The institution discussed here is VSS and the stakeholders are the FD and community. From the findings analysed in the above discussion based on 30 sample VSS, it can be concluded that there is an acute dearth of awareness among the community to avail the benefits envisaged for them. While some are found to be exploited for their shortcomings by their own members, heading the executive positions (chairperson or vice-chairperson), the majority are seen to be at the mercy of the FD in spite of its reduced role under CFM. The chairperson, being a representative of the VSS members, is entrusted with preserving transparency by bestowing him with the responsibility of maintaining important documents that has everything to do with VSS activities, especially financial aspects. But such records were rarely seen to be available with the VSS to enable the community to give a thought to the members to find out what is happening in their institution. The working of the MC appears to be least tested because in most of the VSS, it is either the chairperson or the FD who dominate the VSS affairs. However, barring a couple of VSS chairpersons, imposing leadership was not witnessed in the study from the sample VSS.

In spite of the FD's reduced role in the financial matters under CFM, severe irregularities are seen on the ground, especially among the OTV due to their ignorance and the FD's dominance. The majority of the VSS members found the FD, followed by chairpersons responsible for keeping them in the dark about VSS activities which serve their interests. This belief was stronger among the OTV than the MCV. Even while holding the FD responsible for many of the shortcomings in the CFM, the VSS members did not want its complete withdrawal; they want an authority to control the people and the forest and to keep mafias and smugglers at bay.

Then again, the FD staff have their own reasons for not living up to the expectations; these include not only poor working conditions and salaries, but also outside interference in their job. From the districts' point of view, not much difference was found in the analysis on the issues discussed in the study. However, there were marked differences between the OTV and MCV, which have been appropriately mentioned.

Notes

1. Compounding fees, project funds, other resources received from government and internally-generated funds are the sources of funds going directly into the VSS account for their exclusive use.
2. According to the FD officials, only under FDA, they are given ₹ 500 per month for petrol allowance but not under APCFM.
3. According to the locals, they are a community, believed to have settled in Adilabad during Mughal Emperor, Aurangazeb's time when he brought them as soldiers from the present-day Multan in Pakistan (Source: Field Survey). They are dominant in the villages of Keshavpatnam, Gundela, Sirikonda, Gundi, Chikli and Dedva and Bazar Hatnoor of Adilabad District.

6

Determinants to Sustenance of CFM

Providing for an institutional mechanism to manage 'forests', in itself, does not mean that the objectives of an institution like CFM would be achieved as desired. Ensuring devolution of powers and transparent process in the institutions are mere steps towards basic process of democratisation. There are many different factors outside the purview of governance principles, that also determine the course of community-based institutions. This chapter assesses the causes of such decisive issues which have the potential to influence the CFM programme.

Assurances of Securities and Incentives: Impact on VSS Performance

Rangachari and Mukherji (2000) stress that better protection of forests is always a possibility, when the community is secure about their tenure rights and assured access to the resources and related benefits. The CFM has provisions for the community to avail most of these (GO 13, 2002). In fact, these very inducements have been the driving force for many communities to form VSS. However, it would not be possible for

Table 6.1

What Benefits were Envisaged by You to Join VSS?

Benefits	*Adilabad*			*Chittoor*			*Visakhapatnam*			*Overall*		
	OTV	*MCV*	***T***	*OTV*	*MCV*	***T***	*OTV*	*MCV*	***T***	*OTV*	*MCV*	***GT***
Better protection of forest resources	48	24	**72**	12	24	**36**	8	36	**44**	68	84	**152**
	(19.0)	(22.2)	**(20.0)**	(12.8)	(17.9)	**(15.8)**	(4.4)	(24.8)	**(13.4)**	(12.9)	(21.7)	**(16.6)**
Secure livelihoods from forest	60	12	**72**	12	12	**24**	59	12	**71**	131	36	**167**
	(23.8)	(11.1)	**(20.0)**	(12.8)	(9.0)	**(10.5)**	(32.2)	(8.3)	**(21.6)**	(24.8)	(9.3)	**(18.2)**
Sense of ownership	60	24	**84**	12	24	**36**	48	36	**84**	120	84	**204**
	(23.8)	(22.2)	**(23.3)**	(12.8)	(17.9)	**(15.8)**	(26.2)	(24.8)	**(25.6)**	(22.7)	(21.7)	**(22.3)**
Wage-employment	72	31	**103**	36	47	**83**	57	33	**90**	165	111	**276**
	(28.6)	(28.7)	**(28.6)**	(38.3)	(35.1)	**(36.4)**	(31.1)	(22.8)	**(27.4)**	(31.2)	(28.7)	**(30.1)**
Other	12	12	**24**	16	20	**36**	0	21	**21**	28	53	**81**
	(4.8)	(11.1)	**(6.7)**	(17.0)	(14.9)	**(15.8)**	(0.0)	(14.5)	**(6.4)**	(5.3)	(13.7)	**(8.8)**
None	0	5	**5**	6	7	**13**	11	7	**18**	17	19	**36**
	(0.0)	(4.6)	**(1.4)**	(6.4)	(5.2)	**(5.7)**	(6.0)	(4.8)	**(5.5)**	(3.2)	(4.9)	**(3.9)**
Total	252	108	**360**	94	134	**228**	183	145	**328**	529	387	**916**
	(100)	(100)	**(100)**	(100)	(100)	**(100)**	(100)	(100)	**(100)**	(100)	(100)	**(100)**

Key: OTV = Only Tribal VSS; MCV = Mixed-Caste VSS; T = Total; GT = Grand Total.

Source: Field Survey (Household).

Note: Figures in parentheses are the percentages of the respective counts.

'community' to avail all such benefits at the time of forming VSS. For example, it takes a few years for a degraded forest to regenerate before it yields any benefits. Hence, there were also incentives in the form of 'entry point programme' through which the community was kept interested in the management, by sanctioning some funds for the common benefit of the village.

As discussed above, APFD offered benefits related to both forest and non-forest works through 'entry point programmes' for the community. When asked about peoples' own reasons to join VSS, interesting facts came to the fore; benefits through forest sustenance appeared to be less important for them than the non-forestry-related benefits like wage works.

Forest-related Primary Benefits

In the order of preference expressed by the members in the sample VSS, wage-employment, with 30.1 per cent, was found to be the popular motivation, followed by sense of ownership and secure livelihoods from forests, with 23.3 per cent and 18.2 per cent, respectively. The reason why sense of ownership attracted fewer respondents to VSS membership was that the respondents confessed that they did not trust the FD and its promises. Around 16.6 per cent of the total respondents joined VSS in pursuit of better protection. Only 4.4 per cent members from OTV in Visakhapatnam gave a serious thought to this aspect because in the scheduled areas, they do not see much threat to the forests from smugglers, compared to its magnitude in the forests in the non-scheduled areas (Table 6.1).

There is a significant variance among the OTV and MCV over secure livelihoods. Only 9.3 per cent in the MCV thought they could get secure livelihoods by forming VSS, while it was 24.8 per cent in the OTV. This indicates the difference between the qualities of the forests OTV and MCV are protecting. All the MCV are near urban settings and have degraded forests. About 8.8 per cent of the total respondents had other benefits on their minds; benefits such as getting a share in the apprehending fees, which would amount to a substantial sum in the smuggling-ridden VSS villages like Fakeerpet (OTV, Adilabad); Adilabad region is known for its high-priced teak. Another attraction was harvesting benefits, where timber protection on degraded forestland is possible. For some, it was an extra source of income. VSS membership was also seen as boosting social prestige, especially if one is in the executive position of chairperson. Such members belonged mostly to the OCs and BCs of relatively wealthy background. There were also 3.6 per cent of the total respondents, who were apprehensive that by becoming VSS members they would lose their freedom to practise *podu* or cultivation of the patch of forestland they were either eyeing on, or were already cultivating. Interestingly, the members from Ramachandrapuram (OTV, Visakhapatnam) were fearful when the FD made them VSS members because they thought the FD was shifting its job onto them; they feared attacks from thieves and wild animals if they ventured into the forest for its protection.

According to GO 13 (2002), VSS is entitled for forest produce such as all non-timber forest produce (NTFP), all intermediate yield obtained from silvicultural operations in natural forests, and all timber and bamboo (including yield from bamboo plantations) harvested from the forest managed by them, except in case of plantations.[1] The members of the respective VSS in the sample were enquired to find out the availability of such benefits to them.

Firewood is an important basic need of many residing in the rural areas. This is because rural India still depends on the traditional mode of energy for cooking. In the sample of 30 VSS, only Patha Bellampalli (MCV, Adilabad) is special as most of their VSS HHs use cooking gas cylinders. In the remaining VSS, every HH depends on firewood for cooking. The majority of the members in their respective VSS have free access into their VSS and RF, from where they bring the required firewood. A few VSS have enough firewood in their own agricultural farms; they need not go into either VSS forests or RF. The VSS members of Ratnampeta SC colony (MCV, Visakhapatnam) complain about harassment by the FD. However, this action by the FD is more to do with the members' persistent indulgence in selling head loads of wood from the forests even after years of being VSS members. Besides, what irks the FD to behave in such harsh manner is that the members of this VSS refuse to work in the forests. Therefore, they mark the members not attending the

VSS works and catch hold of those bringing firewood for whatever purpose. Some members from Bhaktavatsala Colony (OTV, Chittoor) have similar complaints of harassment and the FD's actions were for the same reasons. Here, the FD snatches their axes only to return them after the offenders make several rounds to the FD's office, which is quite far from their houses. Navegaon (MCV, Adilabad) is an exception because its members shell out ₹ 100 to 200 annually to the FD staff for collecting firewood. However, they do not get any receipt for the payment made.

Fodder for livestock is an important issue for those having cattle. Even those HHs in the rural areas which are not in the business of animal husbandry have one or more sheep or goats. Agriculturists invariably possess cows or oxen; among the 30 study VSS, none of the VSS members having livestock face problems to graze their animals. They have *porambok* (common) lands and open pastures, besides unrestricted access into VSS and RF to satisfy the needs of their livestock. Only in Chamanpalli (MCV, Adilabad), the VSS members have serious restrictions, and anyone found with their cattle either from their own VSS or neighbouring villages have to pay a penalty to the tune of ₹ 100 to ₹ 500 each time. They buy fodder from the markets for their cattle. Similarly, Patha Bellampalli (MCV, Adilabad) HHs, buy fodder from Luxettipet, a nearby village. However, there is a variance in the fodder's need in different VSS villages. While it is minimal in one village (Bhaktavatsala Colony, OTV, Chittoor), it is quite high in others like Veernamala Thanda (OTV, Chittoor), depending on the number of cattle owned by the respective VSS villagers.

NTFP are an important source of income for the forest-dependent communities. More the prospects of items in the forest, more self-reliant the VSS is expected to become in future. The enhancement of this is what is promoted through VSS. In the degraded forests, these species are planted, and where they are already available, care is taken to protect them: *biduru, jeedipappu, chinta pandu, ashwagandha, cheepiri pullalu, chikudukai, lakka, phanasa pandu, jafra, jama, kalabandha, kanuga, mamidi, marri pandu, neredu pandu, seethaphal, tumma, usiri, vepa, vippa puvvu and alla neredu, adda leaves, tunuka leaves, that-mokkalu, vyapa, karaka kaya, chenega and indigenous* grass (used for roof tops in the respective regions) are some of the prominently found species in the study VSS forests, besides a range of other medicinal plants and timber, viz., teak, silver oak and eucalyptus. Most of the VSS members in the sample VSS collect these NTFPs for their own HH consumption. Very few sell them in the markets. M. Kongaravaripalle BC Colony (MCV, Chittoor) is an exception because non-MC VSS members do not collect anything from their VSS.

The chairperson of Gopalkrishnapuram (OTV, Chittoor) claimed that each VSS member earns anywhere between ₹ 3,000 to ₹ 4,000 per annum from NTFP sale. In the same way, Lalghad (MCV, Adilabad) and Navegaon (MCV, Adilabad) members claim to earn a good amount of money from *beedi* collection. In fact, Lalghad (MCV, Adilabad) has earned a specific amount of ₹ 80,000 in *beedi* auctioning. In Kortheguda (OTV, Adilabad), the VSS members were yet to receive 50 per cent of the money in their VSS account from *beedi* auctioning; however, the members who were involved in collection of *beedi* leaves got 50 per cent of money individually. According to the VSS members of Galetivaripalle (MCV, Chittoor), they too would have been happier but for their chairperson's questionable role in tamarind auction. Peddapalli (MCV, Visakhapatnam) and Umri Bojjuguda (OTV, Adilabad) VSS members also earn good revenue respectively from '*chutta*' (cigar) rolling and *beedi* collection. With an exception of some VSS like Gudamaliput (OTV, Visakhapatnam), Pamulavaka (MCV, Visakhapatnam) and Ratnampeta SC Colony (MCV, Visakhapatnam), access into VSS or RF is relatively free, although none of them have the 'permit cards' signed by the DFO of the respective VSS.

Regarding marketing for the produce collected from forests, most VSS villages have no major problems. Only the members of Lalghad (MCV, Adilabad) expressed the fear of selling forest produce to private traders. They also expressed that the private traders also fear to buy the items directly from the villagers. Hence, the produce is always sold through official auctioning. However, in the remaining sample villages including those in scheduled areas, where GCC has monopoly on a number of items, the tribals manage to sell their items to whomever they want, depending on the prices.

Intermediate and final harvests have been one of the attractions for the VSS members in certain villages having timber as the major species in their forests. Every VSS forest in the sample has timber along with other NTFP, either planted or protected. But none of them are enjoying these benefits, either because their forest has not yet reached the stage of harvest, or they have not been permitted to harvest it by the FD. Patha Bellampalli (MCV, Adilabad), Goppulapalem (OTV, Visakhapatnam), Peddapalli (MCV, Visakhapatnam) and Pudimadaka (MCV, Visakhapatnam) have timber ready for harvesting. The members of these VSS are growing impatient because of delaying tactics adopted by the FD to permit them to crop, in spite of repeated pleas. This attitude of the FD has not gone well with the morale of the VSS members. Many of the agitated VSS members have claimed to have broken their links with the VSS following the FD's attitude. Goppulapalem (OTV, Visakhapatnam) villagers were asked ₹ 10,000 to cut their eucalyptus from the first batch of plantation, when the worth of the plantation itself was only ₹ 20,000. Hence, the VSS members of Peddapalli (MCV, Visakhapatnam) and Pudimadaka (MCV, Visakhapatnam) have decided to harvest the first batch of eucalyptus soon, without the FD's permission. Their forest has ₹ 10 lakh worth of eucalyptus (as estimated by its VSS members). The VSS members of Patha Bellampalli (MCV, Adilabad) and Goppulapalem (OTV, Visakhapatnam) may not be bold enough to declare open defiance, but they (as confessed by some of the members) have already started cutting the yield (eucalyptus) stealthily in proportion to their share.

Entry Point Programme Benefits

Entry point programme benefits include construction of community halls and other village utility buildings such as bus shelters, temples, concrete bridges over small streams, or any other construction through which villagers can benefit. The choice mostly rests with the GB of the VSS. Then again, the FD comes up with many other options that may serve the respective

VSS members either individually or at the village level. Such options can be income-enhancing enterprises such as providing a public address system, utensils for cooking at functions, tents (*shamianas*), music bands, vermicompost, incense-stick-making machines, leaf-stitching machines and honey-making boxes. When the members of their respective VSS were enquired about the entry point programme benefits availed by them, members in 16 (53.3%) VSS acknowledged to having benefited from such programme in one or the other form. If some VSS villages benefited through utility buildings, others benefited from the schemes at the individual level described above. However, between the three districts, VSS in Visakhapatnam appears to have had comparatively lesser benefits, with members from only 4 of its VSS acknowledging it, while the number of VSS having benefited from entry point programme in Adilabad and Chittoor were comparatively more in proportion.

Sanction of certain benefits through entry point programmes does not necessarily amount to its usefulness to all of the VSS members. It could either be useful to the entire VSS including its villagers, or to only a few VSS members or individuals. In other occasions, it may not be useful to anyone after a period of time. Hence, an attempt has been made in the following to qualitatively measure the depth of entry point programme's usefulness.

In some VSS, community halls are used for purposes other than VSS meetings. The Etapalli (MCV, Adilabad) community hall is rented to a grocery shop. Lalghad (MCV, Adilabad) hall is being used to keep musical instruments. Navegaon (MCV, Adilabad) hall has been taken over by an old man, who is living there since a few years. Incidentally, it was on his land that the community hall was constructed; he was, of course, compensated with another land in the VSS. In the same way, the ruined community hall in Gudamaliput (OTV, Visakhapatnam) is being used for sheltering cattle. The Sankaram (MCV, Visakhapatnam) community hall is half constructed; the members of this VSS are awaiting the construction of its roof. Madem colony (OTV, Visakhapatnam) hall is now deserted, because the tins used for the roof were so thin that some flew away when strong winds blew sometime after its construction.

The then FSO who supervised its building, had even tried to siphon away ₹ 4,000 from the wages of the VSS members who had rendered their services to construct the hall. However, he was forced to yield under the villager's pressure. Whereas in Kortheguda (OTV, Adilabad), the former chairperson is accused of selling the roof tins from the community hall. The community halls that were found to be in the best of condition among the entire study VSS are Bommena (OTV, Adilabad) and M. Kongaravaripalle BC colony (MCV, Chittoor). In spite of this, the community hall in the former village is not usable, because it echoes; the community hall in the latter village appears to be the only one serving its purpose to the optimum.

A small bridge constructed over a small stream in Peddapalli (MCV, Visakhapatnam) is proving to be useful to its villagers. Navegaon (MCV, Adilabad) and Kallampalle (MCV, Chittoor) utilised VSS money to build small bus shelters in their villages.

The women members of Dantanpalli (OTV, Adilabad) VSS are happy though vermicompost proved to be a failure in their village, because the 'bamboo slicing machine' used in making 'incense sticks' is providing an extra income to them. In Etapalli (MCV, Adilabad), honey-keeping boxes were provided to each HH, but they had to be taken back by the FD when they found lack of interest among its VSS members. Lalghad (MCV, Adilabad) members expressed their happiness for being given bullock carts for only ₹ 2,500 in addition to fertilisers for their farms at a very subsidised price. In Motlapalle (MCV, Chittoor), the VSS members got bore-wells sunk in their village for common use. The SC HHs received smokeless stoves, while the BCs preferred gas connections through the VSS entry point programme. Interestingly, the VSS HHs in Galetivaripalle (MCV, Chittoor) voluntarily refused gas connections fearing that "the daughters-in-law and mothers-in-law in the families will use it to kill each other to settle their legendary fights". Narayanpur Sakrinayak Thanda (OTV, Adilabad) got money to start 'tent-house businesses',[2] while Umri Bojjuguda (OTV, Adilabad) are yet to get the same as promised by the FD, even though it has exhausted its quota of money earmarked for building a community hall that collapsed. According to the members of this

VSS, the FD official who supervised its construction is said to have compromised on the quality of construction material.

In the opinion of an overwhelming majority of the respondents across all VSS in the sample, constructions like community halls and other measures undertaken to improve the livelihoods of the VSS members are mismanaged by the forest officials in the field, to benefit themselves more than the community.

Conflicts: Blockade to CFM Objective

All institutions tend to face situations of conflict in one form or another; sometimes within the institution, and sometimes due to external forces. Such hostilities cannot be simply wished away. They need to be addressed to quell further damages to the commons, as well as the integrity of the institution itself. As a consequence to such scenario, Gupta (1990) recommends rule-framing mechanism for 'conflict resolution' in resource management institutions, which according to Ostrom (1990), has to be a low-cost method, in order to achieve long-run objectives (Rangachari and Mukherji, 2000).

Among the 30 sample VSS there was no institution that had not encountered any sort of conflict at one point of time or the other. However, the frequency varied from one VSS to another. Majority of the members in their respective VSS identified the major causes of conflicts as theft, smuggling, grazing, conduct of VSS members and hostilities from the non-VSS HHs in the same village.

Theft tops the cause of conflict with 20 (35.7%) VSS. The offenders were invariably the neighbouring villagers. According to the majority of the VSS members in the sample VSS, it happens because the neighbouring village HHs suddenly find themselves barred from entering into a forest from where they have been collecting firewood for domestic consumption. In some cases, it was to eke out their livelihoods by selling firewood, while artisans like ironsmiths and washermen collected firewood to sustain their traditional occupations. In the opinion of the VSS members, most of the offending neighbours were finally convinced not to enter their forests, though it took sometime for them to see reason. Now, they are said to be

Box 6.1

VSS Members Victimised for Stern Protection

Many villages refused to form VSS in its initial phase buckling under Naxalites dictates to stay away from this government programme, which they saw as a ploy to corner their activities; they feared that, their hideouts would be visible when VSS members begin 'singling' work in the forests. In such hostile atmosphere, only Kortheguda (OTV, Adilabad) along with another village (Munjampalli) among many of their neighbouring villages agreed to form VSS, in 1995, to protect their demarcated forest. All the HHs in this village belonged to one big family of Rajgonds or Koyas as they are known here.

Theirs was an ideal VSS that had formed a special 15–member patrolling team, two of which took turns to patrol their forests during the night. Within days, they started catching people, often from their neighbouring village, Katepalli, stealing teak from their forest. Following their stern stand on protection, enmity between Kortheguda members and other villagers indulging in the illegal activity of stealing timber from their forest intensified. As Nandram, the then chairperson of Kortheguda VSS claims, a plan was hatched by the Katepalli villagers, who belong to *Arya* and *Golla* communities, to implicate him in a case alleging him to be a sympathiser of Naxalites, only to get back at him for not allowing them to have their way. As a result, he was picked by the police along with 25 other people, including government school teachers on charges of supporting Naxalites; he was jailed in 1996. To this day, he is fighting his case. He relinquished his post of chairperson in 2006 after becoming PDS dealer.

The Kortheguda VSS members are now disillusioned not only for what happened to Nandram in the Naxalite case, but also for the way the FD is turning a blind eye to the ongoing rampant denudation of forest and indiscriminate encroachments. For example, when their neighbouring villagers (Kukuda) were cutting the forest with machines and backhoes, the Kortheguda members tried to resist them; and on realising that they were outnumbered, informed the FD. The then FRO, who instead of taking any action against the offenders questioned VSS members, saying "why do you bother? After all, the forest is not yours. Even in the VSS forest, you are only a labour and not its owner".

Source: Account of respondents in the field.

using other, alternatives to fulfil their firewood needs. Some adamant villages were also awarded with VSS to pacify them. However, people who exploit the forest for smuggling keep clashing with the VSS members quite often. Kortheguda (OTV, Adilabad) and Chamanpalli (MCV, Adilabad) are two VSS that experienced serious conflicts (see Boxes 6.1 and 6.2 for details). In Sankaram (MCV, Visakhapatnam), some of the VSS members narrated how they were beaten up by their neighbouring villagers when they were passing through their village in revenge to their opposition to let them steal wood from their forest. However, now, the chairperson of this VSS is himself alleged by his members to have compromised with the offenders for allowing them to steal wood from their forest for a sum of ₹ 100 to ₹ 200 per cart (incidentally, their forest has only one route that passes through their village).

Enquiring on the absence of conflicts arising within the VSS over theft, many of the VSS members in the sample appeared to be going easy on their VSS members and also non-VSS members of their village when they bring timber from the forest (VSS and RF) for constructing houses or for preparing agricultural implements just to avoid disturbing the harmony in the village. Only Pudimadaka (MCV, Visakhapatnam) was exceptionally strict with its members during the initial stage of VSS formation, when a case against their villagers including their VSS members on charges of theft was booked. Throwing light on the FD's insensitive attitude, the Pudimadaka (MCV, Visakhapatnam) chairperson recalled an incident whereby the FD officials uprooted half-cut poles in their VSS forest only to remove the traces of evidence of theft and save themselves from their higher officials' enquiry.

Conflicts arising out of smuggling have been reported by 5 (8.9%) VSS – four from Adilabad district and the remaining one from Chittoor. Smuggling is a more serious offence compared to theft as for this study is concerned. While smugglers are professionals who execute the offence with meticulous planning, thefts are committed by the poor only to sustain themselves. All the VSS suffering from smuggling are in the districts known for timber that fetches good remuneration both in open and black

Box 6.2

Politicians Interfering with VSS Affairs

Chamanpalli (MCV, Adilabad) villagers are committed VSS members, who take the task of protecting their forest seriously. Lakshman Chanda is their neighbouring village, whose HH members often trespass into Chamanpalli VSS to graze their cattle and steal timber. One day, the Chamanpalli VSS members along with their neighbouring VSS members (Sawanpalli), decided to confront them. As anticipated, when the offenders were returning from the forest with stolen wood on their cattle, the VSS members of these two villages stopped them; the offenders responded by attacking two of the VSS members with blows on their heads. In retaliation, the VSS members also counter attacked, which resulted in serious injuries to both the parties. The issue ended up in the Police Station, followed by First Information Report (FIR) being filed against the two sides. The Lakshman Chanda villagers defended themselves saying they were permitted to go into the forest by their MLA. When the VSS members contended that he had no business to interfere into VSS affairs, the Rural Development Officer (RDO), acting on behalf of the MLA tried to prevail upon the VSS members by asking them not to think the VSS forest was their property. When the VSS members protested against his irrational argument and questioned his authority to interfere in their affairs, he retreated. However, the MLA, when later confronted by the VSS members in his mandal headquarters, is said to have denied asking Lakshman Chanda villagers to enter the forest; he claimed to have only asked them to take their cattle to the river and not into the forest.

Source: Account of respondents in the field.

markets alike. None of the 30 study VSS villages belonged to Visakhapatnam district because of their remote typology, poor road connectivity, and absence of priced timber. Although Kallampalle (MCV, Chittoor) does not have timber of significance in its forest, the VSS members claim to suffer from smugglers' offensives because the offenders use a route that bypasses their village to smuggle red sanders from the forest situated on the other side of the hill and adjacent to their forest. They are threatened with dire consequences if they ever inform

Box 6.3

Adilabad Reeling under Multani Terror

Multanis are increasingly seen as a single community which has become a thorn in flesh for the entire district administration, including the FD and Police Department in Adilabad, for their indulgence in several crimes including wood smuggling. Many FROs, FSOs, VSS members and other victims like the truck owners consider these people – including their women folk – to be criminal minded; they are seen to have scant regard for people or law, to the extent that, even the Police do not dare to go into their village without proper protection – not even to summon an offender to the Police Station. Not long ago, some FD officers including FRO, FSO and guards were mercilessly beaten up by the Multanis in their village (Chikli, Ichoda). Their intolerant level is said to be such that they kill cattle which stray into their fields. They are also blamed for stealing government property like pipes or iron implements passing through their fields, although they posses 30 to 40 acres of land per HH (allegedly encroached from forest).

Strangely, they all have leanly built frames; their looks do not give away their background. Asgar (Gundala), who had leased land in Fakeerpet (OTV, Adilabad) is a sad man for the alleged criminal indulgence of his brethren Multanis. According to his assessment, 75 per cent of them are indeed criminals, while the remaining 25 per cent are good. The Fakeerpet (OTV, Adilabad) VSS members see Asgar in the latter category.

A local truck owner, who was found running from pillar to post in the Adilabad FD office to get his truck released, narrated how his truck, on its way to deliver cement, was hijacked by the Multanis; they asked for a lift and after travelling a distance of about 20 km, they beat up the driver and his helper and threw them out of the truck. He claims that such activities are increasing with each passing day. He blames some of the FD and Police officials for patronising the Multanis to such alarming levels. According to him, such officers enter into deals with big builders in Hyderabad and use these Multanis as foot soldiers for a paltry labour of either ₹ 200 or some commission from the big deals. He also suspects some of the officials to be informers of the Multanis, and holds 'long standing officials' in both of the departments of FD and Police responsible for corrupting these departments. He suggests that if consumption of wood is discouraged, the smuggling will stop on its own.

Source: Account of respondents in the field.

about this activity to the FD or police. There have been occasions when they were actually beaten up by the smugglers. The *Yanadis* belonging to Malchuri village who are hired as labour by the smugglers also behave aggressively with the VSS members of Kallampalle (MCV, Chittoor). The VSS members of Fakeerpet (OTV, Adilabad), Chamanpalli (MCV, Adilabad), Lalghad (MCV, Adilabad) and Navegaon (MCV, Adilabad) have similar complaints. But except for Lalghad (MCV, Adilabad), the members in other two VSS from Adilabad are not taking on the smugglers any more, thanks to the Forest and Police Departments' repeated failure to act honestly upon their information. However, Lalghad (MCV, Adilabad) tried to fight the smugglers only when they are patrolling in a group (15 batches of 10 members each); otherwise they, avoid themselves from, their attacks – the criminals use sickles to attack if found alone. These smugglers usually slip into Maharashtra to evade from being brought to book, as this VSS borders with that state.

Box 6.4

Smuggling Has Dropped in VSS Forest but Not in RF

Many of the VSS members refused to speak on smuggling that supposedly takes place in the RF. However, some of them dared to speak about it and explained how it happens. As already mentioned, in Fakeerpet (OTV, Adilabad) smuggling is rampant – every day, about 50 cartloads of teak is claimed to be smuggled through this village. People belonging to all communities (OC to SC and BC) in the neighbourhood of Kortheguda (OTV, Adilabad) use machineries like 'saw machines' and 'backhoes' to cut teak and smuggle in small vehicles like cars and jeeps to Hyderabad. The FD field staffs are accused of remaining silent in spite of being aware of this. Similarly, smugglers around Chamanpalli (MCV, Adilabad) forests are mostly Wadlolu and Lambadas from Dhimmadhurthi, Singapur, Sangyam and Woodepally villages. They go in 20 to 30 numbers with chilli powder and cell phones while smuggling, and it is dangerous to combat them. Lalghad (MCV, Adilabad) is located on the AP-Maharashtra border; hence the villagers have recommended a check-post on top of the hill in

Cont'd...

...Cont'd

the forest to keep a better watch on the smugglers slipping into the neighbouring state with teak laden on animals and cycles. The VSS members of Galetivaripalle (MCV, Chittoor) claim to witness smuggling from the RF on the other side of their village hills that has an easy road access, but they do not want to inform the FD because these VSS members are convinced that, the FD just stages the catching of the smugglers, only to release them later after making shady deals. Therefore, they want to avoid conflicts with the smugglers. Similarly, most of the Kallampalle (MCV, Chittoor) VSS members also remain silent when they see smugglers passing through their village with the loot, though a few members inform the FD. In fact, the chairperson himself claims to be an informant of the FD. He suggests that the FD should provide each VSS chairperson with a 'cell phone' so that they pass on the information as soon as they see anything suspicious in the forest. Pamulavaka (MCV, Visakhapatnam) and Peddapalli (MCV, Visakhapatnam) VSS members show concern for the ongoing smuggling in the RF bordering their VSS, because of the availability of an access route through the forests to roads. The chairperson of the former VSS believes that he can protect his VSS from possible smuggling by constructing a boundary wall around their VSS and expects the FD to sponsor the funding. It was only in Madem Colony (OTV, Visakhapatnam) where the VSS members have acknowledged that smuggling in the RF has come down after the initiation of VSS. Ironically, the poor locals used as labour to cut the timber and transport get only ₹ 200, an insignificant amount compared to the value of the actual loot.

Source: Account of respondents in the field.

Grazing is a problem that creates a conflicting situation in 10 (17.9%) VSS villages. This happens when cattle from neighbouring villages stray unintentionally or sometimes are herded deliberately into the VSS forests. However, the magnitude of the problem in Galetivaripalle (MCV, Chittoor) is very huge (thousands of goats from neighbouring villages are herded into their forest every day for grazing). Enough energy is wasted by the VSS members in containing this menace unleashed by their neighbours who herd thousands of their goats into the forest, destroying its vegetation in an unprecedented proportion. Thanks to this problem, the VSS members could not save even 10 per cent of the plantation over the years. The VSS members were a disillusioned lot after fighting unending and hopeless battles with the goat herders and not receiving any support from the FD, in spite of lodging complaints repeatedly. The story of Veernamala Thanda (OTV, Chittoor) is quite interesting because the majority of the VSS members own goats and all of them take their goats into the forest. The FD officials collect money for each animal grazed in the forest, but rarely give receipts for this payment. To make their forest more secure from grazing animals, the VSS members of Peddapalli (MCV, Visakhapatnam) proposed to construct a shed with water and fodder facility to shelter the cattle caught while straying into the forest for claiming penalty from their owners.

Box 6.5

A Dynamic and Courageous Leader

The way the issue of grazing[3] was dealt with in Gopalkrishnapuram (OTV, Chittoor) is very praiseworthy and encouraging. After failing to see anything coming out of the requests made to the villagers to hold back their goats from entering into the forest, Chengal Rayudu (chairperson) issued a notice to all the villagers belonging to all communities to sell off their goats in the interest of forest, before a deadline decided by him. On the day his ultimatum ended, he called a truck and packed all goats into it and sent them away for sale. He also took utmost care to see that the amount from the sale was properly distributed among the owners. It was a courageous decision on any count for someone belonging to a tribe of *Yanadi* to take on the possible ire of fellow villagers including the dominant OCs.

Source: Account of respondents in the field.

The most discouraging aspect for CFM among all conflicts is that of VSS members fighting among themselves. This kind of conduct within the VSS was experienced in 16 VSS (28.6%) villages. This happens almost uniformly across OTV and MCV in all three districts. There is, however, an encouraging trend from the sample Adilabad OTV villages where internal conflicts are not reported, very much in contrast to their counterparts in Visakhapatnam. The cause of the members fighting among themselves is basically over the non-payment of wages on time and also not paying of the expected wage rate by their respective chairpersons, which happens because the ground level FD officials cheat them of their rightful and anticipated share. Invariably, the quarrels flare up when members are in inebriated condition. Overall, the conflicts appear to be more among the MCV villagers (33.3%) compared to OTV villagers (23.1%), to some extent because of the dynamics in the composition of its members.

There were five VSS (8.9%) in the sample, where the members and non-members clash for one reason or the other. These VSS villages are Kortheguda (OTV, Adilabad), Netha Kuppam (MCV, Chittoor), Pamulavaka (MCV, Visakhapatnam), Peddapalli (MCV, Visakhapatnam) and Pudimadaka (MCV, Visakhapatnam). The non-VSS HHs in Kortheguda (OTV, Adilabad) and Pamulavaka (MCV, Visakhapatnam) allege that their chairperson and MC members deliberately keep them out of VSS membership. Personal rivalry is cited as the reason in the former VSS village, while party politics laced with caste discrimination is seen to be the reason in the latter. Whereas, Peddapalli (MCV, Visakhapatnam) and Pudimadaka (MCV, Visakhapatnam) VSS members allege the non-VSS members of being greedy, wanting to share the fruit – the forest benefits – nurtured by them. This problem keeps coming up now and then in the former village, while in the latter, the issue has reached the court; the battle is being fought for over a year now, hampering regular VSS activities because FD has kept this VSS under suspension since then. In Netha Kuppam (MCV, Chittoor), there is no direct conflict between the VSS and non-VSS members, though the VSS members share uneasy relations with the other members of the village. Most of the VSS members belong to SC and BC, while the non-VSS HHs belong to the dominant *Kapu* community.

Podu/Shifting Cultivation

The term *podu* is elucidated in different ways by different people. In general terms, *podu* is 'slash and burn' cultivation, a lengthy procedure implying clearance of the forest on hill slopes, burning the trees and growing crops in the ashes, and after a certain period, shifting the cultivation to a new hill slope to allow soil fertility and forest on old plots to regenerate. However, since the 20th century, because of increasing tribal population and reduced forest extent, *podu* rotations have been reduced to two or three years from ten years of fallow period.

According to WCFSD (1999), the communities indulging in shifting cultivation are the poorest of the poor, Besides, doing without inputs like bullocks, agricultural implements, and manure for *podu* cultivation, the other advantage of growing different kinds of cereals and vegetables in one single plot is an allurement for the poor tribals to resort to with such insecure and uncertain nature of output, both in terms of yield and legal consequences.

Given APFD's stand on *podu* – treating it as an encroachment (APFD, 1999), and the accusations against it for grabbing tribal's traditional lands using J/CFM as an excuse (Sarin, 2003), the respondents in the sample VSS were queried to understand their experience in this regard. Members in 11 of these VSS have acknowledged of having certain impact on some of their members, after the advent of J/CFM. The VSS villages having *podu*/encroachment problems were Umri Bojjuguda (OTV, Adilabad), Narayanpur Sakrinayak Thanda (OTV, Adilabad), Navegaon (MCV, Adilabad), Netha Kuppam (MCV, Chittoor), Borgam, Gudamaliput, Goppulapalem, Madem Colony, Ramachandrapuram and Tarlaguda, all in OTV of Visakhapatnam district, and Sankaram (MCV, Visakhapatnam).

In a total of 30 sample villages, only 11 VSS have a *podu*/encroachment problem in their villages. In a total of 132 VSS members in these 11 villages also, only 67.4 per cent of them were actually affected by the initiation of CFM for merging their land with VSS forest. The mode of acquisition differed in each case. While some claimed to have surrendered by their own free will, others complained of forceful evacuation. The most affected among all the districts, obviously belonged to villages in the Visakhapatnam district, especially those in OTV, with 83.3 per cent of the district's total respondents. As far as 32.6 per cent of the unaffected respondents are concerned, these HHs had several reasons: (1) they had no such lands of dispute; (2) their lands, though disputed are still with them; (3) they may have freshly acquired the land into VSS; (4) they reverted back to their lands even after the FD took away their land; or (5) they have encroached into fresh patches of land elsewhere outside VSS (Table 6.2). In Umri Bojjuguda (OTV, Adilabad) nine HHs have 2 to 3 acres of land each in the middle of the VSS forest. Curiously, the FD is said to have ignored this because the respondents were able to produce temporary *pattas*.

When the affected respondents were further questioned as to how exactly the loss of land impacted them, the fallouts were described as reduced income, food insecurity and having to work as labourers in other's fields. The worst affected were those suffering from food insecurity because they have very little alternative for their living; this was either because they do not get assured wage works from the VSS or they do not have anybody to work for. Those working in other's fields have no alternative lands in the form of permanent or temporary *pattas*. Contrarily, the least affected among them were those suffering from reduced income because they have alternative lands with either temporary or permanent *pattas*.

Describing the methods employed by the FD to recapture *podu* lands from the tribals, the members of such VSS revealed during FGD as to how the FD used convincing, compensation and coercive tactics selectively with the communities, based on their background. The officer dealing with the issue is also said to have made the difference. In case of more aggressive communities, the FD tried convincing methods or provided quicker compensations. Naïve communities such as the PTGs were rarely treated with respect, and their lands were simply seized and merged into the VSS forest. Likewise, the more compassionate the officer, better were the alternatives provided to the community.

There was a section of VSS members who were furious at not receiving the promised compensation. When the issue was raised with the FD officials who belonged to the jurisdiction of the aggrieved VSS members, they denied making any such promise of compensations; instead they maintained that the land belonged to the FD, and hence they need not pay any compensation to claim it back. Some officers even went to the

Table 6.2

Are you Affected by the Advent of CFM?

Response	*Adilabad*			*Chittoor*			*Visakhapatnam*			*Overall*		
	OTV	*MCV*	***T***	*OTV*	*MCV*	***T***	*OTV*	*MCV*	***T***	*OTV*	*MCV*	***GT***
Yes	14	5	**19**	0	6	**6**	60	4	**64**	74	15	**89**
	(58.3)	(41.7)	**(52.8)**	(0.0)	(50.0)	**(50.0)**	(83.3)	(33.3)	**(76.2)**	(77.1)	(41.7)	**(67.4)**
No	10	7	**17**	0	6	**6**	12	8	**20**	22	21	**43**
	(41.7)	(58.3)	**(47.2)**	(0.0)	(50.0)	**(50.0)**	(16.7)	(66.7)	**(23.8)**	(22.9)	(58.3)	**(32.6)**
Total	24	12	**36**	0	12	**12**	72	12	**84**	96	36	**132**
	(100)	(100)	**(100)**	(100)	(100)	**(100)**	(100)	(100)	**(100)**	(100)	(100)	**(100)**

Key: OTV = Only Tribal VSS; MCV = Mixed-Caste VSS; T = Total; GT = Grand Total.

Source: Field Survey (Household).

Note: Figures in parentheses are the percentages of the respective counts.

extent of demanding penalty from the offenders to send strong signals to desist others from such encroachments.

While assessing the impact of the *podu*/encroachment issue on the performance of CFM, it was observed that it had, and is still having, a negative bearing due to the rigid and indifferent approach adopted by the FD towards the tribals practising *podu* – ignoring their traditional rights and economic implications. Hence, many resorted to cultivation on their previous land (officially now under VSS), while some are seriously considering to go back to their old lands or want to occupy new patch of lands. Navegaon (MCV, Adilabad) is an example, where five HHs are practising agriculture on two patches of land (11 + 5 = 16 acres) on what is supposed to be VSS forest.

Coordination between CFM and Other Departments

The Revenue Department, TWD, Livestock Department, Department of Rural Development, ITDA, Defence Research and Development Organisation (DRDO), Drought Prone Areas Programme (DPAP), GCC, *Velugu*,[4] NGOs and SHGs are some of the government departments, cooperatives and organisations that have a direct or indirect influence on the outcome of the CFM programme. All these organisations work in the same jurisdiction as the CFM. Interdepartmental coordination becomes all the more vital when the roles of such departments are defined in the GO 13 (2002) on whose basis the CFM functions. The role of many of these departments is limited to advisory level, while certain other bodies, organisations, and cooperatives like the Panchayat, ITDA, GCC and NGOs have a far bigger role to play in the day-to-day working of CFM. In the following sections, only such organisations are discussed that have a defining influence on the outcome of the CFM. The analysis is based on the views expressed during FGD by the members of their respective VSS in the sample.

The Revenue Department plays a key role while dealing with land rights, especially on the sensitive issue of encroachment. If there is proper coordination, unnecessary and unpleasant situations could be avoided. As claimed by some of the FD officials, the Revenue Department is alleged of issuing *pattas* to the people without verifying their credentials on the lands that are deep in the RF (e.g., Umri Bojjuguda, OTV, Adilabad). According to them, this is not only creating bad vibes between the people and the FD but also is leading to mistrust between them. Next is ITDA, this is the only organisation about which the VSS members have positive opinion. All these members have benefited from the schemes carried out by the ITDA in one or the other way. In the Visakhapatnam tribal belt, many of the VSS members are grateful to them not only for helping them with the coffee, silver oak and pepper plantation, and also seeing through the stages of its growth, but also for their enhanced economic condition. According to the information gathered from the respondents, the ITDA has an active presence only in this district. GCC was looked upon to do a lot of good to the tribals in general, and VSS members in particular, but the VSS members appear to have lost faith in this cooperative. They are now seeing them as their exploiters, not any different from the *Sahukars* (see Box 6.6 for details).

Box 6.6

Mobile GCC and PDS

In the tribal areas, the GCC's role is very vital. But increasing resentment among the people over the behaviour of the staff that runs the cooperative is a matter of concern. The GCC staff are accused of behaving rudely with the illiterate and innocent tribals, besides cheating them in measurements when they bring forest produce for sale.

As a possible solution, the VSS members recommend that the GCC should operate on wheels, visiting each village to collect the items. The vehicle should bear the updated price list painted in bold on the body of the vehicle, in the local scripts. This is expected to give confidence to the tribals for being on home ground and to overcome their timid nature, which is exploited by the GCC staff when they go to their depots. Tribals want experiment on similar lines with PDS as well, since they suffer, an equally harsh treatment from its staff. They also expect this reform will save them a lot of travelling time.

Source: Suggestions of respondents in the field.

The role of panchayats, according to GO 13 (2002), commences right from marking the boundaries for the VSS forests when the FRO consults the Sarpanch of the particular village for the task. The Panchayat Sarpanch is also one of the members of the advisory council constituted by the FRO; in fact, he chairs its meetings. The other members in the advisory council include FSO, FBO, FABO, representatives of village ITDA, Village Agriculture Officer (VAO), locally involved NGO and the village school headmaster/mistress. The advisory council meets as often as required to facilitate inputs to the micro-plan and annual plans; evaluate, and coordinate the other activities of other departments at the VSS level. It also reviews the micro-plan and annual plans.

Despite the Panchayat Sarpanch's role explicated in the GO 13 (2002) in the preparation of all important VSS documents,

Box 6.7

Is Caste Panchayat Good?

Since India's independence, every effort has been made through the means of the constitution and government to root 'caste system' out of our ethos and to establish an egalitarian society. Every right thinking individual supports this. But the crucial role played by Chamanpalli (MCV, Adilabad) 'caste Panchayat' in reviewing their forest is commendable. The 'Caste Panchayat' in this village constitutes members from every caste residing in this village. These members are elderly citizens who have taken upon themselves to motivate their own caste members to work towards forest regeneration irrespective of their needs in the forest or the availability of funds. Everybody has to contribute their services even if wages are not enough and, even if they are not official members of their VSS; nobody can question the decision of the 'Caste Panchayat' as it is the supreme body in this village; the VSS is also dictated by this body. On failing to yield to the dictate, the erring member has to face social boycott and penalties. It is a mixture of fear and urge to improve their forest; these villagers believe that they were able to bring about a sea change in the cause of their forest regeneration. On a more positive note, none of the members, including those belonging to lower strata of society have complained about this 'Caste Panchayat', instead they acknowledge it as a 'just' and respected body.

Source: Field survey.

viz., micro-plan and annual plan, none of the members in the sample VSS have seen interaction between the panchayat and the VSS at any level. Though each VSS has one or two VSS members from the panchayat as members, sometimes even from ranks such as Sarpanch, they have never seen any interaction between the VSS and the panchayat. However, only in Ramachandrapuram VSS (OTV, Visakhapatnam), the Panchayat Sarpanch at least enquires about the developments of the VSS. Fakeerpet (OTV, Adilabad) was unique from the Panchayat perspective because it is a constituent of exclusively Girijan Panchayat (Nerangonda Panchayat), along with 14 other neighbouring villages.

NGOs

Many observers of NRM like Silva (1994) and Blair (1996) have cited the importance of NGOs in contributing to the environmental cause. Undoubtedly, the role of such organisations is central, particularly when the government is short of manpower and funds. Their role becomes all the more crucial when the community has reservations on the credibility of the official departments. In such circumstances, NGOs are expected to win their confidence in cruising towards brighter future. Banking on such positive wisdom, CFM also envisaged a positive role for the NGOs in its set-up through CFM GO 13 (2002). They were expected to prepare micro-plans, train VSS members on marketing and value addition of the forest produce, micro-credits, accounting procedures, awareness creation/capacity building and conflict resolution.

When the members of their respective VSS were asked to explain about the presence of NGOs, only Peddapalli (MCV, Visakhapatnam) members in the entire sample of 30 VSS acknowledged that they played an active role in their VSS by creating awareness among their members about the CFM programme. Whereas, members in nine VSS found NGOs limiting themselves to only preparation of micro-plan during the initiation of J/CFM, and that too only a few of them are said to have carried out PRA to prepare this all important document. Members in the 20 VSS (majority) admitted NGOs' presence to be almost negligible. Of these, 12 VSS happen to be in remote tribal areas, where the presence of NGOs is most required.

The nine NGOs that were involved even for a brief period with the sample VSS villages were MASS (Patha Bellampalli, MCV, Adilabad), RAIDS (Navegaon, MCV, Adilabad), I Rose (Gopalkrishnapuram, OTV, Visakhapatnam), Sri Sai Krishna Rural Education and Development Seva Samithi (SKREDSS) (Netha Kuppam, MCV, Chittoor), Girijan Jyothi (Gudamaliput, OTV, Visakhapatnam), Sri Rama Association (Pamulavaka, MCV, Visakhapatnam), Triveni Yojana (Ratnampeta SC colony, MCV, Visakhapatnam), Grama Abhivrudhi Samstha (Sankaram, MCV, Visakhapatnam) and Navasadan (Madem colony, OTV, Visakhapatnam).

Among the above-mentioned NGOs, Navajeevan is the only VSS that is active in Peddapalli (MCV, Visakhapatnam), though it began working with them only recently, i.e., 2005. Narrating their experience with the NGO, the members of this VSS explained how they were initially skeptical about the intentions of their NGO; they feared that they may ask for a share in the VSS benefits or may charge money for their services. However, their fears were short lived. The VSS members acknowledged that their NGO's presence definitely made a positive impact on them and helped them understand the CFM programme better, though many of these VSS members were not naïve themselves. A Girijan Jyothi (Gudamaliput, OTV, Visakhapatnam) official, who was very active for sometime in the beginning of VSS formation, is said to have distanced himself from the VSS, dissatisfied, following the FD's indifferent attitude towards him and his ideas on the implementation of the programme.

Sharing their bitter experience with an NGO, Madem colony (OTV, Visakhapatnam) VSS members recounted, how they got tired of paying ₹ 750 to their NGO (Navasadan) every time they get payment for their VSS wage works. On the other hand, it is difficult to judge the activities of Sri Rama Association (Pamulavaka, MCV, Visakhapatnam) as it is said to have ventured into CFM very recently.

In an interview with 30 NGO officials, from field staff to state level office bearers, who were working or had worked in the proximity of the study villages to understand the probable causes of certain situations in particular study VSS, revelations were interesting and intriguing.

Mamidi Satyam, Director of AKKA NGO (Jannaram, Adilabad) did not hesitate to declare VSS to be a failure. For this he holds responsible the forest and police departments' incompetence in checking rampant encroachments even in VSS forests by dominant and aggressive communities such as the *Kapu* and *Lambadas*. These departments are said to be turning a blind eye to what is happening around them in spite of people lodging FIR with the Police. He claims that such developments have disillusioned even committed VSS members. Another reason according to him is not granting permission to harvest the benefits. Giving account of the quality of forest elsewhere in Jannaram Division, he says that one can see only contours in the forest and no trees because the FD officials themselves are involved in cutting the forest in collusion with contractors for a commission. Talking about smuggling, he says that even a child knows that tonnes of teak from RF are cut and thrown into the river only to be received by their gang members on the other side in Karimnagar.

S. Vishwanth, Director, Sanghamitra Service Society (NGO), Chandragiri, Chittoor, was involved with 20 VSS (sponsored by both World Bank and Central Schemes) when he was associated with CORE (NGO). He is of the view that, the FD's volte-face in regard to sharing benefits is increasingly distancing the VSS members away from CFM. To gain the VSS members' confidence back into CFM, he recommends horticultural species for 'gap plantation' and wants the government to do something on the FD officials' (ground level) complaint of overwork and the burden of additional responsibilities under CFM. He is all for increased role for NGOs in the decision-making at the village level; at the same time he is also weary about NGO representatives turning corrupt when they are given powerful positions such as VSS chairpersonship.

Roop Sunder Rathod (SKREDSS) is a well-known personality in his mandal (Ramachandrapuram, Chittoor) for his social activities which include running education institutions. He was actively involved with seven VSS, for which he prepared micro-plans. But, the FD did not pay him the promised amount of ₹ 35,000. He too has come to the conclusion that CFM is a failure and blames the

FD for such a poor state, thanks to their careless attitude towards this programme. He recommends reducing the role of the FD by revamping the entire programme at the VSS level.

Similarly, many of the other NGOs were not too enthusiastic and claimed that they were no more interested in VSS because of non-cooperation from the FD and also because they felt the programme has lost its purpose and objective. On enquiring from them as to why NGOs do not like to visit remote VSS villages where their presence is more important, the majority of the ground level NGO staff questioned back, why government teachers dread to go to such remote villages/hamlets; when teachers are not being taken account, then why should NGO staff be, when this staff are comparatively in an insecure job.

Importance of Training

Under the CFM project, the FD claimed to have undertaken capacity building and awareness building programmes by giving training to the VSS members, especially the chairpersons, vice-chairpersons and MC members. Emphasis was laid on training in financial management and book-keeping activities to selected members of the VSS, to improve their skills in record maintenance, minute writing, forest management, orientation and demonstration. Training was also given on specified forest-based micro-enterprises so that VSS members can have synergy and sustainable dependence on forests. Use of Global Positioning System (GPS), map interpretation, silviculture nursery raising and grafting of high-yielding varieties were also some of the other areas on which the FD had set agendas to train the VSS members (GO 13, 2002).

When the members in the sample VSS were enquired whether they have attended any training programme and whether it proved beneficial to them and their VSS, only 19.4 per cent of the total 360 sample VSS members confirmed it. The majority of such members were chairpersons, vice-chairpersons or MC members. When the members who attended the meeting were asked about the utility of the training, half of the respondents acknowledged to have benefited, while the other half did not agree on benefiting in any way. The reason why the members had a mixed opinion about training was because half of them, like Ratnampeta SC colony (MCV, Visakhapatnam) VSS chairperson, felt that in the name of training, they had something of a tourism exposure; they were taken to the places of interest in Hyderabad such as the Golconda Fort, Birla Mandir and Tank Bund. However, some members such as Kalampalle (MCV, Chittoor) VSS chairperson were thankful to the training programme because they were able to completely understand the VSS concept. Women in Dantanpalli (MCV, Adilabad), Madem Colony (OTV, Visakhapatnam) and Pamulavaka (MCV, Visakhapatnam) were happy to have been trained in incense stick-making and leaf plate-making.

However, the study revealed that none of the members in the sample VSS received any high profile trainings like usage of GPS, map interpretation or micro-enterprising. Their training was claimed to be limited to basics on plantation techniques, in addition to book-keeping and account maintaining. Many of the members confessed that they did not pass on to their GB about what they learnt in training either because their GB was not interested, the chairperson cared little to consider this needful, or in some cases also because of his incompetence to impart what he learnt in the training. In view of this, Peddapalli (MCV, Visakhapatnam) VSS members wanted the VSS GB to decide who should go for training, instead of sending only chairperson and vice-chairperson by virtue of their positions.

All the training expenses are borne by the FD; yet it is ironical to find that VSS funds are being misused in the name of training by some members. The Galetivaripalle (MCV, Chittoor) vice-chairperson accused her chairperson for asking her to sign on a cheque to draw ₹ 8,000 towards travelling and lodging expenses to one of their MC members and an NGO representative to attend the training programme in Hyderabad. On other hand, most of the VSS members across both OTV and MCV in all the three districts accused the FD for not compensating them in anyway for forgoing their daily wages during training at mandal level. In contrast, those going beyond mandal levels to towns and cities for training have acknowledged of receiving good hospitality from the FD.

External Funding for CFM

In APCFM, the funds are also required to provide wage works to the VSS members to keep their motivation alive until the forest regenerates to provide benefits to its members. In such backdrop and amid the increasing reports of wage works emerging as the backbone to sustain the CFM programme (Reddy et al., 2004), when members in the sample VSS were asked whether they agreed with the notion that the CFM lasts only as long as it provides wage works, 33.3 per cent of the total respondents were sure that VSS will lose its meaning in the absence of monetary motivation. Already some VSS members like Netha Kuppam (MCV, Chittoor) have weaned away from CFM. In such VSS, forests have not reached any sustainable level, and they do not see it reaching any beneficial stage because of poor management by the FD and the chairperson, due to rampant corruption on all matters including irregularities in implementing wage works. In Visakhapatnam district, 54.2 per cent of its members felt that without funds, their VSS members will lose whatsoever motivation they have now. In an OTV of this district, the percentage is as high as 66.7 per cent.

Another 33.3 per cent of the VSS members were hopeful of continuing with CFM even in the absence of external funds. Some of those respondents had made a unique arrangement to hold their member's interest in the VSS. For example, M. Kongaravaripalle (MCV, Chittoor) and Peddapalli (MCV, Visakhapatnam) have individual plots in their VSS, where they have planted cashew (the FD allowed planting of this crop in the later stage of the CFM programme; earlier, cashew was not allowed to be planted in the VSS forest). So, they have some motivation to reap definite benefits from those plots at individual level, even if the benefits from the larger portion of the VSS forest take more time to yield sustainable benefits.

Members who answered neither way were also 33.3 per cent. Actually, they mean to say that for all practical purposes, their VSS have already gone defunct. In Adilabad, 45.5 per cent of the VSS members think so. Similar are the opinions of the 60 per cent MCV members in the same district. From the district point of view, it is observed that Visakhapatnam VSS members are less hopeful, with 54.5 per cent of them feeling demotivated to continue without external funds.

By the way of conclusions on the above discussed issues, it could be surmised that the additional benefits have boosted the motivational level of an individual or a community. Irrespective of tribal and mixed-caste VSS in their respective districts in the sample study, CFM appears to have attracted the community more for its short-term and temporary benefits such as wage employment, rather than the long-term benefits occurring out of improved and regenerated forests. There are no access restrictions to any VSS member in the entire study to enter into VSS or RF to avail their domestic needs. In a couple of villages, however, final harvests are not permitted by the FD, causing much of heartburn among the members. In the guise of entry point programmes, the majority of the VSS villages in the entire sample were sanctioned funds for the construction of community halls. Instead of serving any purpose for the people, the construction of these buildings gave an opportunity to the FD officials to make money by compromising on the quality of material. Most of these buildings can now be found in a dilapidated state.

For their vested interests and by their interferences, the FD and politicians have destroyed at least a few better performing VSS at the cost of forest vegetation. Theft and grazing have come out as major conflicting causes in the study VSS in Chittoor District, followed by intra-community hostilities within their VSS. Smuggling is increasingly taking disproportional dimensions in some of the VSS in the Adilabad and Chittoor districts, due to well-organised mafias, good access to market, and also involvement of some of the FD officials. In Visakhapatnam, *podu* needs to be looked at from a new perspective to address the tribals who resort to this practice in order to beat their food insecurity in desperation. Except ITDA to some extent, coordination between VSS and other agencies were found to be minimal or of no consequence.

The three-way relationship between the NGOs, community and FD, appears to be estranged with all the parties suspecting one another. Training is important for awareness creation, but everywhere in the study, training was found to be limited to imparting basic forestry techniques and book-keeping, and to only the chairperson and vice-chairperson who seldom transfer their learning to their VSS members.

Notes

1. GO 4 (2004) introduced in addendum to GO 13 (2004), prescribes criteria for availing benefits from teak and other plantations.
2. Items like stoves, cookery utensils, plates, glasses are hired for utilisation in the public functions.
3. In an attempt to tackle this contentious issue, the government had planned a coordinated effort with the Animal Husbandry Department of the Government of Andhra Pradesh to improve the quality of livestock in forest fringe areas, rather than the number of livestock. A separate policy was also planned after deliberations with stakeholders to deal with the growing need for fodder inside and outside of the designated forests (GoAP, 2002).
4. Government has issued GO Ms. No. 78, EFS&T (For. III) Department: 17–10–2003 on the convergence of the *Velugu* project with CFM to ensure greater convergence between these two projects and the Tribal Welfare Department. Convergence with District Poverty Initiative Project (DPIP) and Andhra Pradesh Rural Poverty Reduction Programme (APRPRP) projects: these two projects, popularly called Indira Kranthi Pathakam (formerly *Velugu*) are being implemented in the state of Andhra Pradesh through financial assistance from the World Bank. Since the development objectives and majority of the target groups of these projects and the Andhra Pradesh Community Forest Management (APCFM) project overlap, a mechanism for convergence has been worked out, to ensure effective implementation strategy and to ensure non-overlap of investments, and orders in this regard have been issued in GO Ms. No. 78 EFS&T (For. III) Department: 17–10–2003.

7

Theoretical Considerations

It was two thousand years ago that a well-known Greek philosopher 'Aristotle' surmised "what is common to the greatest number has the least care bestowed upon it, everyone thinks chiefly of his own, hardly at all of the common interest" (*Politics*, Book II). But, in recent times, what made the world sit and take notice of the common pool resources was only after Hardin's groundbreaking work on 'tragedy of commons'; because if ignored consistently it presented the gravity of the situation that posed a threat to the ecosystem and biodiversity altogether. He narrated how "man is locked into a system that compels him to increase his herd without limit in a world that is limited" (Hardin, 1968: 1244). Similarly, Olson's (1965) logic of collective action also suggested that this happens because those already benefiting from incentives find themselves trapped in a rigid situation and would not forgo their individual benefits, so they find it difficult to cooperate towards collective action. As a way out, Hardin (1968) proposed two solutions to thwart the environmental problems: first, "the imposition of a government agency as regulator", and second, "the imposition of private rights". In this backdrop, APCFM in this context, boasts to have extended the 'private rights' though in some measures, to the forest dependent people, recognising them as a stakeholder 'community', and at the same time relegating FD (government agency) to a role of only a facilitator on lines of what Hardin proposed as a way out to improve the 'common pool resources'.

In the preceding chapters, the findings from the APCFM field study have already been discussed in detail. Here, in this chapter an attempt is made to theorise the findings on the democratic process prevailing in the institutions of CFM, and the levels of governance practised in it, to understand the characteristics of the 'community' that prompts them to reciprocate in their CFM institutions as found in the study. This is followed by assaying the outcome of this research on CFM in AP through the existing popular theoretical perspectives of NRM, again to understand broadly as to how the people individually and also as a community respond to the call of NRM in different context and situations.

The chapter is presented in two sections, the first is "theorising the levels of governance from the study VSS" followed by "assaying APCFM experience through theoretical perspectives of NRM" as the second. In the first, the level of governance is assessed keeping the role of community as the centre of analysis to understand the causal factors contributing to varied forms of governance in their respective VSS. The level of governance is assessed based on the broader (because people in different circumstances define governance differently in different contexts) perspective and not on the six indicators[1] advocated by World Bank which is popularly used as an indicator to assess governance level. This is followed up by listing the characteristics of the communities into 'bad' and 'good' as it implies on the overall governance of the CFM institution. The second section discusses the natural and physical; social and political; administrative and financial aspects widely, while reflecting on theoretical perspectives of NRM with that of the findings of this study in the AP context.

Theorising the Levels of Governance in the Study VSS

In the 30 VSS samples, only four (13.3%) VSS were found to be governed excellently, while another four (13.3%) VSS had good governance with a potential to turn into excellent. There were four (13.3%) VSS that were bad in terms of governance; it is

Table 7.1

Levels of Governance in the Sample VSS

Level	*Adilabad*			*Chittoor*			*Visakhapatnam*			*Overall*		
	OTV	*MCV*	***T***	*OTV*	*MCV*	***T***	*OTV*	*MCV*	***T***	*OTV*	*MCV*	***GT***
Worst	2	2	**4**	2	2	**4**	3	2	**5**	7	6	**13**
	(33.3)	(40.0)	**(36.4)**	(66.7)	(40.0)	**(50.0)**	(50.0)	(40.0)	**(45.5)**	(46.7)	(40.0)	**(43.3)**
Bad	0	0	**0**	0	2	**2**	1	1	**2**	1	3	**4**
	(0.0)	(0.0)	**(0.0)**	(0.0)	(40.0)	**(25.0)**	(16.7)	(20.0)	**(18.1)**	(6.7)	(20.0)	**(13.3)**
Good	2	1	**3**	0	0	**0**	1	0	**1**	3	1	**4**
	(33.3)	(20.0)	**(27.3)**	(0.0)	(0.0)	**(0.0)**	(16.7)	(0.0)	**(9.1)**	(20.0)	(6.7)	**(13.3)**
Excellent	0	1	**1**	1	0	**1**	0	2	**2**	1	3	**4**
	(0.0)	(20.0)	**(9.0)**	(33.3)	(0.0)	**(12.5)**	(0.0)	(40.0)	**(18.1)**	(6.7)	(20.0)	**(13.3)**
UP	2	1	**3**	0	1	**1**	1	0	**1**	3	2	**5**
	(33.3)	(20.0)	**(27.3)**	(0.0)	(20.0)	**(12.5)**	(16.7)	(0.0)	**(9.1)**	(20.0)	(13.3)	**(16.7)**

Key: OTV = Only Tribal VSS; MCV = Mixed-Caste VSS; T = Total; GT = Grand Total; UF = Unpredictable.

Source: Field Survey.

Note: Figures in parentheses are the percentages of the respective counts.

however possible to rectify their shortcomings by taking corrective measures. Whereas, a large number of 13 (43.3%) VSS are in a hopeless state of governance. While five (16.7%) VSS are also good, but the potential of the community to continue with CFM in future is suspect. This evaluation indicates that more than half of the VSS (13 + 4) are not doing well (Table 7.1) (for details on the levels of governance in each of sample VSS, see Figure A5.1 in Appendix V). If this sample is 'hypothetically' taken as an indicator for the entire state, only 1,120 VSS out of 8,412 must be doing well, in addition to another 1,120 VSS which are also close to good. This means an overwhelming 6,161 VSS are already defunct. By any standard, this is a very discouraging sign.

Worst-governed VSS

Worst-governed VSS are those, where the communities are fundamentally not serious about protecting their so-called forest. Not surprisingly, all except one of these communities were allotted VSS on the FD's initiation (for details, see constitution of VSS in Chapter 4). The 13 worst-governed VSS in the sample study are equally distributed among their respective districts and also in their social categories (7 in OTV and 6 in MCV) (Table 7.1). Most of such communities in MCV across all districts are not dependent on forest for their livelihoods, though many of their VSS members collect firewood and other items from the forest for their domestic use. Depending on availability, they also make an earning out of selling forest produce. Yet, they are not emotionally attached to their so-called forest. Other characteristics of these communities were that they are by nature very naive and weak even to 'protest' against the corrupt practices by the ground level forest staff, leave alone protecting their forest from the offenders. Not surprisingly, the majority of these communities belong to the known vulnerable groups of SC (MCV) and ST (OTV) in their respective districts. For some communities (in both OTV and MCV across all the districts), CFM is just any other poverty alleviation programme, and wage works are seen as its medium; hence, the forestry factor never came into the forefront. Another factor that delineated all these 13 VSS (especially in the OTV) communities from the CFM was FD's indulgence in extreme financial irregularities, especially in the wage works and its payment. To some extent many of the VSS members have now voluntarily withdrawn from working in any of the forest-related works. The attitude of some of the VSS members has also been a contributing factor for their worst performance. For example, members of Ratnampeta SC Colony (MCV, Visakhapatnam) refuse to work in the forest only because they feel that "such hard work is beyond their capacity and it is suitable only for the tribes"; this attitude was particularly disappointing, when 19.50 per cent of SCs are beneficiaries from the APCFM (APFD, 2005). Another example where two VSS communities whose forest was either changed to another patch (Pamulavaka, MCV, Visakhapatnam), or community was awarded a new location (Bhaktavatsala Colony, OTV, Chittoor) altogether, had a particularly demotivating effect. The allotment of VSS to communities in 'smuggling-zones' (Fakeerpet, OTV, Adilabad and Navegaon, MCV, Adilabad), was never a prudent step when the members were ill-equipped to face the danger from the organised mafias. Hence, expecting enduring motivation from them for better governance was never in the reckoning. There were other worst-governed VSS, whose members started destroying their own VSS forest (Kortheguda, OTV, Adilabad) on not receiving suitable support from the FD to combat everyday theft and smuggling from their VSS and RF. Finally, there are communities that are in no way going to leave their occupations (grazing in Veernamala Thanda, OTV, Chittoor; and *podu* in Tarlaguda, OTV, Visakhapatnam) for the sake of forest regeneration as VSS members. According to them, their traditional source of livelihood is more secure to feed them two meals a day than by the CFM.

Badly-governed VSS

Badly-governed VSS are those, where communities are either chaired by an OC member (social elite), capturing all the decision-making powers when the entire community in the VSS belonged to different social groups (for example, Galetivaripalle and Motlapalle, MCV, Chittoor), or when some communities are disillusioned with the FD over not materialising their rehabilitation promises (Gudamaliput, OTV, Visakhapatnam). Among the four VSS assessed as badly-governed, three belonged to MCV while the remaining one belonged to OTV. Of these, two VSS were from Chittoor MCV, while other two were one each from OTV and MCV of Visakhapatnam (Table 7.1). The chairperson and MC members promoting favouritism in the VSS (as in Sankaram, MCV, Visakhapatnam) also qualified in the club of badly-governed VSS. Nevertheless, these are the VSS that had shown sparks of managing their forests and still have the enthusiasm to excel if their respective grievances are addressed.

Well-governed VSS (Classified as Good Governance)

Among the four VSS (3 in OTV and 1 in MCV) qualified as well-governed (good governance), three of them were from Adilabad (2 OTV and 1 MCV) while the remaining one (OTV) belonged to Visakhapatnam (Table 7.1). None of the well-governed VSS belonged to Chittoor. The communities in this club (Bommena, OTV, Adilabad; Narayanpur Sakrinayak Thanda, OTV, Adilabad; Lalghad, MCV, Adilabad; and Borgam, OTV, Visakhapatnam) are democratic, committed and transparent in managing their VSS affairs; these characteristics are embedded in their village culture. They are pro-active in protecting their forests and also have no reservations about protecting their forests on their own in future, without external support as well. These communities profit reasonably well from sale of forest produce. Another significant characteristic of these VSS communities is that they have realised the usefulness of forests because they have seen improvement in soil moisture and water level after protecting their forests under CFM. Their forest has improved to such an extent that, now they are irked by the increase in fauna (for example in Borgam, OTV, Visakhapatnam, the members want air guns to scare the animals like foxes, pigs and bears from destroying their agriculture farms). Some sections in these VSS have small issues with the FD over funds and their rude behaviour (Bommena, OTV, Adilabad; and Narayanpur Sakrinayak Thanda, OTV, Adilabad), unfulfilled promises made while initiating the VSS (Borgam, OTV, Visakhapatnam) (The FD had promised four jobs in their department to the community members of this VSS), and indifferent attitude of the FD officials in stopping inter-state smuggling through their VSS forest route (Lalghad, MCV, Adilabad). If such minor grievances are properly addressed, these VSS can also turn into excellent ones.

Excellently-governed VSS

Four VSS, viz., Chamanpalli from MCV in Adilabad, Gopalkrishna- puram from OTV, Chittoor and Peddapalli and Pudimadaka, both from MCV in Visakhapatnam qualified for this elite group of VSS for excellently governing their VSS (Table 7.1).

The commonalities among these VSS communities are that, they are all vibrant, united and focussed to fight for their cause. They are attached to their forests, and also understand the importance of forest, not only to their lives, but to the entire biodiversity. These VSS are a strong and fearless community, courageous enough to stand against the FD's irregularities (although the FD officers have also succeeded in taking a cut from these VSS during financial transactions, the VSS members decide their share and terms). One basic characteristic most of these members possess, that stands apart from the other communities studied for this research, is that they are well aware about what is happening around them. They keep themselves informed through electronic and print media. In short, they know their rights and also how to utilise them. These VSS communities (irrespective of being OTV or MCV) maintain transparency within themselves on 'trust value'. The communities here are committed enough to invest on VSS forest plantation from their private funds when they find the monsoon coming to an end. They do not mind collecting their dues from the FD leisurely.

Unpredictable VSS

In the sample, there were five unpredictable VSS – three were from OTV and two from MCV. Adilabad has the distinction of having three VSS in this club (2 OTV and 1 MCV, whereas Chittoor and Visakhapatnam has one each from MCV and OTV (Table 7.1) These are the VSS whose members are not sure of their future commitment with CFM. Governance in these VSS is

Box 7.1

Characteristics of the Communities in the Good and Badly-Governed VSS

Bad	*Good*
• Communities whose members are socially weak by nature. • Communities allotted with VSS are reluctant to take up the challenges involved in forest management as they require physical hard work. • Absence of emotional, traditional or religious attachment with the forest among the communities. • Communities with migratory tendencies. • Communities unfamiliar with the VSS forest allotted to them. • Communities depending only on wage-labour for their livelihoods. • Communities managing VSS forest only for wage works (temporary nature) or harvesting benefits as their motivation. • Communities find 'forest work' hard or feel that it lowers their social prestige. • Majority of the community represented by numerically small social groups (especially OC) in the decision-making bodies of VSS. • Location of the VSS forest in a known smuggling zone with possible threat to the lives of their community members. • Communities persisting with their traditional occupations (podu and grazing).	• Communities that are vibrant and have a history of cohesive and participatory community culture even when the social composition is dynamic. • Communities that already have a good understanding about the importance of environment and its direct and indirect benefits. • Communities identifying themselves traditionally and emotionally with their forest. • Communities interested only in legal sanctions to their forestry rights and not in external funding. • Communities already availed with alternatives to their traditional occupations/livelihoods. • Communities necessarily depending on NTFP for their livelihoods. • Communities that have invented motivations to keep their VSS members' interest by demarcating individual plots to its members and practicing gap-plantation with their choice of species in their VSS forest. • Communities that are well informed (not necessarily with formal degrees but awareness acquired through newspapers and television).

Source: Field survey.

good because these communities are reasonably transparent in the limits of whatever the FD allows them to know about; this includes financial matters too. Barring one VSS (Patha Bellampalli, MCV, Adilabad), other community members in this category are happy with the functioning of their chair-persons. But communities here are not pro-active to continue with forest management work in future; they want to go back to their original livelihoods once the VSS funds stop, because their forest has not reached a sustainable level. Moreover, the majority of members in these VSS are motivated only by the wage works or final harvest benefits. If members of one VSS (Patha Bellampalli, MCV, Adilabad) are waiting with baited breath to cut their share of final harvest so that they can say goodbye to forestry affair forever, others (Umri Bojjuguda, OTV, Adilabad) are ready to encroach on the VSS land, since HHs in their village have increased in the last ten years and they require land for their survival.

Assaying APCFM Experience through Theoretical Perspectives of NRM

Understanding 'Community'

In the earlier section on 'Theorising the Levels of Governance in the Study VSS', it is already observed that how crucial it becomes to a concept like CFM to have a 'community' managing the NRM to posses the ingredients conducive to make success out of a programme like this. So, before going into the crux of NRM perspectives from the existing concepts, it is important to understand what 'community' in the first place means. In the dictionary of "Global Environmental Governance", 'community' is defined as "an integrated group of species inhabiting a given area" (Saunier and Meganck, 2008). Then again, defining the term 'community' is difficult, as rightly observed by Fabricius (2004: 22) "because local groupings constantly redefine and re-align themselves and reformulate their objectives". Yet, broadly, the terminology of a 'community' could be attributed to an interdependent group of people living in the same region.

The 'community' in NRM is defined by McCay (2003: 385) as: "where people who live and/or work together, share a sense of identity and belonging (therefore, some notion of boundaries and membership criteria), where they share some level of dependence on or caring for the resources in question (or streams of income coming from those resources), and where they also share many norms and goals, they are more likely to be able to develop institutions appropriate to deal with the challenges they face in using common-pool resources". For McCay (2003: 385), "community is measured by the presence, absence or strength of shared beliefs and preferences; some stability in membership; some expectation of future interaction; and direct and multiple kinds of relationships among members".

Coming to the study, all the VSS communities possessed more or less all the 'classical characteristics' especially those in OTV stratum of a 'community' defined above, but, distinguished only by the nature of its composition. If one stratum of communities constituted of only tribes or their sub-groups, the other stratum[2] comprised of a mixed caste communities. This dynamics in the sample provides for an extra understanding as to why the results in these two kind of setting are different in more than one way.

According to Agrawal and Gibson (1999) diverse groups dominate along the lines of ethnicity, gender, religion, wealth and caste. This is found to be true in MCV villages because on the strength of ethnicity and wealth, the OC communities despite being numerically fewer were found to be occupying the executive position and dominating the institution of VSS. However, the streaks of following arguments are also found in some of the MCV villages. The argument of Bardhan and Dayton-Johnson (2003) is that there is the possibility of coexistence of social or cultural heterogeneity with pronounced economic heterogeneity. To support their views, they illustrate an example of unequal agrarian societies occasionally exhibiting adherence to a hierarchal ideology. The best example that has come from the study in support of this argument is where 'caste panchayat' prevails upon all the decision in the panchayat. However, here it is more of village prestige than economic or other reasons that has worked as a binding factor in enforcing conservation ethics among its members to protect forests more aggressively.

Interestingly, in total disregard to Pimbert and Pretty (1998) and Sarin (1996) who believe that people in question present high 'social cohesion' in a condition where 'social identity or in-group feeling' among the 'community' exists because in majority of the OTV villages in the sample where all the members belong either to some group or to even a single family in their respective village are found to be squabbling over distribution of wages, sharing of benefits to an extent of registering cases on each other with the FD. This has, in fact, largely affected VSS activity in proportion to the intensity of skirmishes among its members. At the end of the day, it is to be understood that NRM institution is all about a group of people, so bonding between them is vital for the sustenance of the resources (Stern et al., 2003).

Irrespective of homogeneity or heterogeneity there tends to be always a group or class of persons enjoying superior intellectual, social or economic status, called elites. Common pool resource management has its own share of elites. Not surprisingly, in most of the studies (Reddy et al., 2004), they are found to be controlling traditional management systems, resulting in a majority of the other classes being suppressed by them (V. Das, 2003). This has come up quite evidently also in this study among the MCV villages where OC community usurps the top executive position only to have the helm of VSS affair under their control, even when they are really required to be its members from forest dependence point of view. Wade (1988b), points to the popular belief about village interests being served when it is, in reality, the personal interest of the elites. Another characteristic of elites is promotion of hierarchical relations in politics by capturing local governments through bribery and political pressures, thereby uprooting democratic participation and political accountability (Kaimowitz et al., 1998; Larson and Ribot, 2004; Pacheco, 2004; Ribot, 1999; Smoke, 2003). This is exactly what, OCs and elites from dominant BCs in the study are doing. The position of chairpersonship comes in handy to boost their status. It is being used to bargain for political favours by portraying as if entire VSS members are under their command who can vote en masse on their dictates in any form of elections. Probably this happens because "local people's ability to manage and administer revenues from natural resources is primarily weak" (Fabricius, 2004: 22). Moreover, the poor are susceptible to fall to the designs of the elites because of their poverty, over so many years. Besides, new elites that emerge out of the poor, try to squeeze out disproportionate gains through biodiversity projects (Fabricius, 2004). The reason for the poor members falling prey to such elites in the study is not any different from what has been mentioned above.

It is ironical that tribals, despite being so close to abundant forests, are subject to live in abject poverty and insecurity. Poor markets and exploitation by the local traders are the real cause that still find place in the tribal belts of the OTV villages in the study. They indulge in this activity, knowing well that their crops could be cut down by the FD, claiming it as an encroachment.

Experts are yet to reach a consensus on the reasons for continued poverty of the natural resource users. But it appears that the social systems from which they arise are structured so unequally that it justifies the Marxist view of environmental problems reflecting 'unequal distribution of resources' eluding lasting solution (Sachs, 1993). This study further strengthens the justification with an example of OTV villages.

In regard to gender and forest, women as compared to men have specific needs and interests in forests. They collect and transport the household's fuelwood used for cooking and heating; gather wild fruit, nuts, fodder, medicines and other materials; and engage in small-scale, forest-based enterprises as a source of income. As a result, forests often have special importance for women and family welfare (WCFSD, 1999: 20). Yet, women are often reported to be excluded from the CFM system (V. Das, 2003). The reason found in this research is that, many of the VSS in the sample of the study do not conduct meetings or other VSS activity as regularly as they are required to; hence, there is less scope of interaction between the members, which also means less exposure to women to test their worth. However, what comes out clearly from the study in regard to VSS is that women are consciously discriminated in wage payment so that the trend of paying less when they work elsewhere in the village is not disturbed. Instead of allowing VSS to set a precedent of paying equal wages to women, men have succeeded in setting prevailing discriminative trends into VSS also. In ultimate unfairness to women, the FD officials insist on interacting only with male members, even when women hold executive positions (chairperson or vice-chairperson) in their VSS.

Natural and Physical Aspects

Natural and physical aspects become significant in the management of resources like forest. The visibility of the common lands helps in noticing unauthorised felling if the village is situated in the uplands. Similarly, if the village is located at the bottom of the slope of forests, or inside the forests, the task of its protection becomes very easy; this cuts down on the protection costs (Saxena, 2001). As Baland and Platteau (2000) point out, achieving cooperation between the users in a location close to the resource is notably high. Also, in terms of distance, lesser the distance from the forests, better are the chances for protection. If the households live within one or two hours distance from forests, the feasibility of undertaking various activities like sapling plantation, weeding, thinning and most importantly, patrolling, becomes easier (Poteete and Ostrom, 2004). Remote villages with no easy access to roads and markets are seen to be 'retaining mutual obligation' by discouraging poaching by outsiders. In such villages, fear of reprisals from village elders also deters frequent abuse of common resources (Saxena, 2001). In unfavourable situations, where forests are situated at a distance on a 'full day's walk' from the households, not only the cost of protection increases, but also conflicts over 'the allocation of duties and benefits' erupt (Poteete and Ostrom, 2004). In the same way, a village spreading 5 to10 kms in one direction also does not help the matter, for it gives a chance for the 'free riders' to escape undetected (Saxena, 2001). In other contexts, it is found that the forests near the town are difficult to protect because of 'easy access to market' for forest timber (Tiwary, 2005).

If the preconditions described above by NRM scholars for ideal distance between the forest and the residence of the community are considered, it appears like a positive picture emerging from the study, especially in the OTV villages for being in the midst of forests, so natural protection is possible here even without any formal committees. At the same time mobilisation is also quite easy, as half of the MCV villages are at a distance of 1 to 5 kms from their forests. This implies two things – first, forests cannot be protected naturally by the VSS members; hence they have to form a specific committee to guard their forests; and second, it also indicates that primary livelihood of the VSS members is not forest; hence they are not exclusively forest-dependent communities. Moreover, most of such VSS members possess large tracts of agricultural land between the forests and their houses – a clear indication that even those who do not possess lands have an opportunity to work for others as labour. Thus, providing them with another option of livelihood away from the forests.

When it comes to size of the forest, Dolsak and Ostrom (2003) are of the opinion that the bigger areas of resources such as biodiversity, implied to common pool resources which are difficult to control and protect, while smaller ones with few access points are easy to manage, monitor and to measure the flow of resources in conformity with the usage limit.

In the same way, the size of the group protecting it, either makes or mars the outcome of the objective of collective management. A great number of researchers (Baland and Platteau, 2000; Murphree, 1998; Saxena, 2001; Agrawal, 2000) have made their views explicit in this regard. While some found that smaller groups are more productive, others contradicted them. Nonetheless, both schools of thought have their own logic in presenting their respective views.

Advocating small groups in common pool resource management, Baland and Platteau (2000) explain that when groups are small, relationships between the members are more personalised; this helps in understanding each others' 'actions and preferences' and boosts socially effective behaviour, since expected incentives are not diluted in smaller groups. Murphree (1998) further adds that 'corruption' decreases in the small institutions because collective identity makes rules' enforcement more practical, negating the evasion of responsibility. Saxena (2001: 243) also finds that "most effective local institutions develop in those small communities where people know each other". Whereas, Olson (1965) even doubted the cooperation between individuals to achieve joint benefits if the group is not small and the selective incentives are not established; Attwoood (1988) found 'collaboration' easier among small and homogeneous groups. In response to a question, "how small is small supposed to be?", Baland and Platteau (2000) recommend the ideal user community to be much smaller than the village community.

Ruling out a complete positive view on smaller groups, Poteete and Ostrom (2004: 450) point out that "smaller groups are also handicapped by limited access to the resources needed for effective collective action". On a similar line, Agrawal (2000) mentions the possible advantages of larger groups at the local level in managing resources like forests smugglers. However, he thinks 'moderate-size communities' are better equipped to follow the rules set by them for the use of the forest, while sharing monitoring duties.

In the midst of conflicting opinions over the ideal size of the group, there is always a decisive relationship between the 'group size and institutional development', and also 'between the group size and forest conditions' (Poteete and Ostrom, 2004: 450). Then again, Varughese (2000) comes up with the finding wherein population does not determine the success of the forest management institution; rather, it is found that forests studied by him were in better condition because of higher level of organisation in regard to institutional arrangements like monitoring assignments and restrictions on entry and harvesting. If the sample VSS is looked into, the average size of the forests amount to 203 hectares, and is managed by an average of 162 members. One VSS is of exceptionally big size, consisting of 12 clustered hamlets with 1,200 VSS members, where all the handicaps expressed by the scholars in such situation are found to be true. Overall, the members are happy with the size of their VSS forest and also the membership with an exception to this one village. Majority of them have been protecting their forests by forming VSS for more than a decade. However none have reached a stage of sustaining it on their own. Whatsoever be the opinion of various researchers regarding the size of the group, it can never be denied that the size of a group always remains related to its level of collective action (Marwell and Oliver, 1993).

Social and Political Aspects

Past experiences of a village in collective action is an important ingredient that presents better prospects for successful management of resources (Baland and Platteau, 2000), since the 'trust and cooperation' factor among the members is very much needed for such communities to act in complex situations. Similarly, Dolsak and Ostrom (2003) also point to the importance of trust among the users of common pool resources, while complying with agreed limits of resource use. Yet, collective action may be possible with an 'external assistance' in various forms, even when, it is not rooted in a 'long tradition of cooperation' (Baland and Platteau, 2000). However, for this new concept to flourish, autonomy has to remain with the users to build social capital, though it requires 'time' and 'resources' (Dolsak and Ostrom, 2003). AP situation in this case cannot boast of having 'formal arrangement' of protecting forests by the communities as 'institutions' like some tribal communities have in some other parts of India. However, culturally locals, especially tribals, protected their forests as a convention. Introduction of APCFM and VSS as institutions of protecting forests with the involvement of community was an experiment in its own way, which also saw enthusiasm by the people at least in the beginning of the programme. After almost a decade and a half of its practice, it is not clear yet, whether it has built a social capital as envisaged.

In the Indian setting, prejudices like caste-system, more often than 'rigid stratifications', prevent institutions from representing a 'common will' (Saxena, 2001); this ultimately results in coercion, which again is not in harmony with the principles of a sustainable collective action institution. Discounting this proposition, Bandyopadhyay et al. (1983), citing historical reality, argue that social and economic disparities were never the barrier for exploitation of community resources in India, because there were communally shared norms for the community resources, so they were used in controlled measures; and also because of the self-sufficient nature of the traditional Indian village economy. Interestingly, both the above discourses were evident in the study. MCV villages with OCs at the helm of affairs being in executive positions of VSS or dictating terms from behind the scene are found to be a distracting factor in the management of VSS. However, one VSS with heterogeneous community composition reflected the observation of Bandyopadhyay et al. (1983) because the situation in that particular village had more or less same ingredients.

An important activity of community in any NRM is participation; this is an act of sharing the activities of a group, and if a group happens to manage 'common pool resources', then participation of its members becomes utmost important, since managing 'common pool resources' is all about 'community involvement'. Empowering locals to participate and take action in their own backyards for sustainable communities is a prerequisite (Cuthill, 2002). Even while the policy trend, of late, is towards devolution of NRM to local people, yet, interpretation of their participation varies widely on ground (Fabricius, 2004). Participation in a group can be defined in at least two ways; in narrower terms, it is merely a 'nominal membership' (Chopra et al., 1990; Molinas, 1998), and in the broader sense, participation is a 'dynamic process' wherein the disadvantaged also get to voice and influence decision-making (Narayan, 1996; White, 1996). APCFM provides for this assessment with more than half of the community members belonging to this section in its entire project. Then again, there are two dimensions of participation – direct and indirect. If we take forest protection as an example, in direct participation, the stakeholders involve themselves in forest protection meetings, labour contribution and forest management through monitoring and patrolling; while in indirect participation, the individuals simply follow forest protection rules, motivate others including their own families, and see that equity, justice and transparency in forest management is ensured (Ostrom, 1990; Sarin, 1996; Silwal, 1986; Singh, Ballabh and Palakudiyil, 1996). Though cautioning about assuming mere participation by the users in NRM is an end in itself, Fabricius (2004) draws attention to the fact that the locals do not automatically become custodians of natural resources and start benefiting from them, unless the institution is endowed with suitable elements in different contexts.

The elements that influence the level of participation are well defined by Korten (1983: 181–200), according to him, "expected returns, expected cost of cooperation, attitudes, values, and skills of people, design and other characteristics of the project, and the legal, political, and institutional environment prevailing at the time" influence people's participation. Indeed, the study does vindicate to most of the issues indicated above which influence the levels of participation. When people joined the J/CFM in the beginning, they expected that the VSS forest demarcated for them would remain with them forever. They were hopeful that, the attitude of the FD would improve and become more humane towards them. They were not aware that the project is guided by mere GO and it has no constitutional status, so once they realised that this programme may not serve their livelihoods and economic security, they slowly started weaning away from active participation. As for literal patrolling of forest is concerned, very few VSS have formed such teams in the sample VSS, to keep watch on the thefts and also on animals straying into the forests. A couple of VSS employed a single person as watcher by paying about ₹ 1,200 per month. The study revealed that effective patrolling is being done in only one VSS. In most cases, the VSS members while farming in their fields near the forest keep watch and inform the other members of any unauthorised trespasses. While some VSS members cannot patrol their VSS forest because they have to go for wage-labour for their survival, others fear revenge from the offenders.

Apart from the purely economic consideration, there are other issues that are seen to be determining the participation of people in the common pool resource management. It could be anything from socio-economic, cultural, political or institutional rigidities, especially in the developing countries, that kept and continue to keep a vast number of people deficient in the basic needs of living (World Bank, 1994). To be specific, social hierarchies like religion and caste have been found to be decisive factors for the communities to participate in the participatory institutions (Shackleton et al., 2002; Deshingikar et al., 2005). In Indian context, this aspect is very much relevant. As already mentioned, the caste factor is indeed proving to be decisive in the outcome of performance in the MCV villages, as all the decisions are taken by such dominant castes despite them being numerically fewer. It is seen that they are occupying top posts in the VSS executive only to continue their control over the people, even when they have very little or no direct stakes in the forests. No matter what, token participation by merely attending meetings to indicate or to measure the level of participation is discounted by Arora (1994) and Vira, Jeffery and Sunder (1999), who believe that, in actual terms, influencing the outcome of the community decision-making is what participation is all about.

As seen above, participation in the common pool resources management institutions makes sense, only when the participants commit themselves to meaningful deliberation in expressing their opinion or judgment after due consideration in explicit and active ways; this is what politically contributes to good quality 'decision-making'. Anderson (2006) supports decision-making by local resource users, because he believes improvements materialise only in such conducive atmosphere. In the instances of governments not devolving the right to decision-making to its local people in the management of natural resources, they have to contend with unimproved 'custodianship' and unchanged attitude from the communities (Fabricius, 2004). In the same way, several other researchers like Singleton (1998), Blair (2000) and Larson (2002) agree that in the absence of 'popular decision-making', no positive outcome in the decentralised environmental governance is possible.

In AP, need for effective decision-making is felt right from the initiation of CFM in the villages where at least 50 per cent of the HHs have to give their consent to form VSS in their villages. However, in reality, majority of the VSS in both OTV and MCV villages are simply announced as formed and the signatures of the two (male and female each) HH members were taken later to complete the procedural formality. But, this act of overlooking the democratic voice is seen to be having a bearing on the final outcome of the overall programme where committees are formed without proper consent, because the VSS formed without popular consent are the ones found to be failing in achieving the objectives of this concept. Absence of popular decision-making can be gauged by taking into account as to how the executive heads are elected barring a couple of VSS in each stratum of OTV and MCV villages. These positions were either hijacked authoritatively by the OC dominant elites in their respective villages or they have been handpicked by the FD and installed to work as their stooges. Perhaps, because of such possibilities there is no guarantee that everyone affected would participate 'automatically' in the decision-making process even when power is devolved or decentralised (Engel, 2004) on paper.

The 'cost of participation' for the 'poor' section of participants in the affairs of 'common pooled resource management', is a decisive factor, because they cannot afford to lose their usual labour that fetches them a wage to sustain a day's living (Lupanga, 1988; Behera and Engel, 2004). Exactly for this reason, majority of the members in MCV villages preferred going to alternate livelihood works because the forest activities undertaken under CFM to create wage works to its members to sustain their interest until their forest reaches a sustainable level, was not fetching them the minimum wages. Besides, the wages paid in the forest activity under CFM was much less than what is paid by others in the village or from nearby for similar work. This demotivated many of its members from participating in VSS work or activities there. The reason for such low wages was monetary malpractices by the local FD. Regarding the all-important document 'micro-plan' – which also required popular participation by the VSS members – was found to be prepared by the NGOs or FD officials on their own. With such precedents already set-in, expecting regular participation by all the members in the meetings only amounted to a fraud. In the end, all talk about effective decision-making in the decentralised environmental governance proves to be meaningful only when downward accountability to resource users is guaranteed (Crook and Manor, 1998; Agrawal and Ribot, 1999; de Oliveira, 2002; Ribot, 2002). The applicability of "resource users get a voice to hold officials responsible for their actions" (Anderson, 2006), appears to be totally missing in the study villages.

Although common resource management is a group-oriented entity, leadership is an important ingredient that influences the outcome of such institutions in a positive way, provided the leader of the group in question is 'effective' and 'charismatic' (Baland and Platteau, 2000: 337). In the same way, results can be reversed in case of ineffective leadership. Nevertheless, it is the necessity or the occasion that makes the 'leaders'. In simple words, a leader is someone holding a sway over others, resulting in mutual rise in motivation and morality (Burns, 1979). This extraordinary feature of leadership plays a vital role in ensuring that 'the game is played sequentially', paving the way for cooperation in game-theoretical terms (Baland and Platteau, 2000: 338).

According to Parnell (1995), a good leader preferably drawn from cardinal stakeholders provides vision and inspiration to both the members and management to cooperate with their honesty, skill and benevolent nature to fulfil cooperative purpose. In the study chairpersons are the leaders who are looked up to accomplish these needs by their members. Baland and Platteau (2000) reason that those leaders from the Third World, who are exposed to the outside world in one or the other way and have developed a non-parochial outlook and who have also acquired knowledge of present-day challenges to nature are the ones who become good leaders to represent 'collective action'. Indeed this trait was noticed in a couple of VSS in each of the stratums in the study. And in fact, these VSS leaders were aptly found to be taking along their MC and GB members while taking all decisions. Leaders of OTV villages, who make a case of representing cardinal stakeholders, but, because of their very poor awareness level of CFM and its working, and also for their timid nature, they have been dominated in every aspect of deliverance in the VSS by the local FD.

Sometimes, good leaders are not necessarily efficient ones. Wade (1988a) feels that, to be an efficient leader one must have two qualities – competency with an understanding of main stakes, and intentions that can be trusted as good by the followers. The leader's actions should not be seen as self-centred; instead, power wielding should be identified with the welfare of the larger whole. The irony of heads in APCFM VSS was that despite the leaders (chairpersons) possessing these qualities, in more than half of the sample they were helpless because they have been completely dominated by the FD when it comes to taking decisions that made any difference. However, when it comes to charismatic leadership, there is no dearth of scholars endorsing a view of such leaders playing a very important role successfully in mobilising people over a common goal or issue, in the co-operatives (Baviskar, 1980; Singh and Kelley, 1981; Baviskar and Attwood, 1991; Shah, 1995). In the sample of 30 VSS, only one charismatic leader was functioning with gutso. That too, in an odd situation, as far as his village is concerned, because non-VSS members in this village belong to non-tribals including dominant and powerful OC. But, the key to his success happens to be because of complete backing of the FD, indicating clearly how important is the role of FD, in making this programme into a success.

Interestingly, there is also a school of thought that believes only good leadership is not enough for successful collective action, because to achieve high levels of institutional performance, one need not depend entirely on leadership traits (Israel, 1987). Nevertheless, it always remains an enigma to understand, why people always behave as they do – differently under a leader of different kind or without one altogether.

Administrative Aspects

For administration of any organisation or an institution, rules and regulations are central to it. In general, 'rules', as understood from the lexicons, is a kind of dominance or power through legal authority. It could even be defined as a generalisation of something accepted as true to be used as a basis for reasoning or conduct. In other words, rules prescribe actions of permissions, omissions and sanctions in specific contexts (Crawford and Ostrom, 1995). For the institutions of common pool resources, rules imply to its members on their membership, participation, rights and duties. Hence, rules could be seen as important tools that facilitate institutions to function in an order and also under certain norms. Rules are important to institutions because of various reasons, the foremost being defining the limits of the institution and its entity. This is followed by the determination of entry and exit considerations (Gupta, 1990), access to use and excluding others from common property rights (Libecap, 1989; Ascher, 1995). According to Ostrom (1990), Tucker (1999) and Bardhan (1999), rules enhance performance of the institution because they are framed and managed by users; this makes enforcement and monitoring easy. At the same time, the staff involved is accountable to the users. With respect to forestry, rules are enforcement of boundaries, deciding yield levels for harvesting forest produce and distributing resource costs and benefits (Rietbergen, 2001). In regard to APCFM, all the above-mentioned rules appear more or less to be in place, as far as its statutory order is concerned, and the by-laws exercised at the start of the programme by the respective VSS members.

Strange it may appear to mention that, with an exception of a few VSS in the sample, most of the forest, including RF is open for all, and obviously, the members are found to be enjoying all the benefits that are available in their forest and RF without any access restrictions. So, no headaches on aspects of rule-making or violating; however, it is important to mention that conflicts occur among the community members when somebody violates the rules but in the sample villages, conflicts of different nature have beleaguered almost every village; thefts, smuggling or grazing menace are some of the examples that cause conflicts with other villages. Some VSS also face trouble from within their own community or from the non-VSS households in the village. Serious conflicts resulting in physical injuries are also reported from some VSS while defending their forest from the offenders.

Similarly, encroachments on forest land are observed in all the sample VSS villages, be it in the scheduled areas or in the plains. While in some VSS villages the issue was closed after the court's judgment (hence not reported in the research), in others there are new encroachments. However, the nature of encroachments in the plains and tribal areas is very different. If it was purely a fallout of populist adventurism by the political establishments in the latter, food insecurity in the former keeps the issue alive.

Corruption in general terms denotes dishonesty or lack of integrity. And when applied to someone in authority, it is an inducement, or more seriously, an offence or violation of one's duty at the cost of one's integrity and honesty. In the arena of NRM, corruption is widespread due to many reasons, the major one being forest officials who are ill-equipped to deal with people-centred programmes like NRM; this is born out of the officials' indifferent attitude towards the new bottom-up approach that is fast making inroads into the management of natural resources, especially forests (Fabricius and de Wet, 2002). The indifferent attitude of the FD was evident in majority of the sample VSS – fiercer were they in the OTV villages. The senior officers are still not able to come to terms with the concept of letting their power to the community. However, the younger officials are found to be more compassionate towards the communities as such.

Corruption also includes the ill-treatment of poor people, while extending respect to the private landowners (ibid.). This insensitivity breeds out of ethical failure with respect to prevalent illegal practices at all levels of forest-related decision-making. The height of this sort of treatment was observed in the OTV villages where the elected executive members (chairperson or vice-chairperson) are literally taken captives by the forest officials before withdrawing money from their VSS accounts, and also after the withdrawal to snatch a share out of it. Sometimes, the FD officers threaten the VSS members of holding back wage works to their VSS, if they refuse to pay the officials their share. While dealing with adamant VSS members, the forest officials threaten to file a false case against them on charges of being sympathisers of Naxalites. Interestingly, some of the FD officials have also reported reverse threats from aggressive VSS members. Such members threaten the FD officials of framing them in 'atrocity cases'. In a couple of instances, they actually booked a few officers under the atrocity act.

Not surprisingly, large scale misuse of public resources for private gain by top-level political elites damages forest resources more than the indulgence of petty bribery by the low-ranking officials (WCFSD, 1999). It could be because of such apathetic characteristics of the state officials, Winston Churchill described "bureaucracy as a riddle wrapped in a mystery inside an enigma" (cited in Bandyopadhyay, 1996: 3110). The commonest of corrupt practices forest officials indulge in, range from "secretly selling harvesting permits to illegally under-pricing wood by a company (a practice called 'transfer pricing'), negotiating illegal timber agreements, false certification of species or volumes cut in public forests, illegal logging, and trafficking sensitive government information related to forests" (WCFSD, 1999: 48). Most of these characteristics of corruption was reported from the MCV villages in Adilabad and Chittoor where the timber of high price is found. This naturally results in an unprecedented amount of revenue loss to the governments. Such unethical activities go unabated because the offenders are very well aware of the inefficiencies of government mechanism compounded by non-existent or lenient supervision on part of the authorities as observed by WCFSD (1999).

All the VSS in the sample have availed entry point benefits, mostly in the form of buildings, viz., community halls, bus shelters, bridges or temples. In some instances, the community was provided with income generating sources like honey boxes, incense stick-making machines and tent houses. Nevertheless, the funds released for building purposes have proved to be a mechanism worked out by the FD officials of FSO, FBO or guard to siphon off a large portion of the money by compromising on the quality of the construction material.

The major players contributing to such corrupt practices could be anyone from corrupt political leaders to incoming foreign industrialists, big local companies, the powerful and the elite, including the public officials already mentioned (WCFSD, 1999). This kind of nexus was exposed when the respondents explained how the local FD officials collude with construction mafias based in cities, to smuggle out teak and make huge money by using a local community as foot soldiers for paltry sum. It is not that all these corrupt practices are hidden from the common public, particularly in those areas where this kind of activity occurs; rather, the story is universal. In consequence to these developments, the Food and Agriculture Organisation (FAO), the World Bank and other concerned bodies have been recommending reforms through their reports in the last two decades. Unfortunately, their efforts are being thwarted at every step by industrialists and politicians with vested interests (ibid.).

Despite the serious charges, the role of the FD and FSO in particular to the success of APCFM programme is central, because he is the one officer who being a signatory to transfer funds into the VSS account, has every opportunity to manipulate financial dealings. Besides, he is the main link between community and FD and interacts most with the VSS members, only second to the FBO or guard. Being an officer, he has more authority at his disposal. His role becomes decisive among the poor and illiterate communities. In spite of their issues with the FD, the majority of the VSS members do not support the view of dissolving the FD completely, because they believe that without some kind of authority, the forest will soon disappear. Defending themselves, the forest officials blame the casual approach of the communities towards CFM and also for the difficult conditions they work in.

Presence of NGOs was much needed in creating awareness among the poor, illiterate tribes. In the sample VSS, this was missing in all OTV because these tribes reside in very remote hamlets devoid of even basic necessities, and the NGO's ground staff did not want to go there. Even in the MCV, except for one VSS, their presence was as good as non-existent. In regard to other departments, working in the same jurisdiction as that of VSS, only ITDA in OTV villages is found to have established some amount of confidence among the tribals to work with, as they are more sensitive to tribal's concerns and livelihoods.

Financial Aspects

For institutions managing natural resources through community-based approach, expected benefits in the form of labour wages or individual share in the 'commons' always top their motivation, and rightly so, because it is they who strive hard to protect the commons and to bring it to a fruitful stage. Hence, Upadhyay (2003) recommends realistic hope for significant benefits to the managers of commons; to instil confidence in them, and for that to come through, the community and authority should be clear about their stands on the gains, and the consequences of failing to live up to the agreement by both parties. As emphasised by Rangachari and Mukherji (2000), better protection possibilities are always preceded by secure tenure and assured access to the resources, benefits and more voice in regard to resources. Gupta (1990) also asks for clear 'resource allocation mechanism' that describes as to who and what, when and where gets their share of benefits. The power of benefits could be gauged with an example of Maharashtra Sugar Cooperation, which shows successful cooperation even among different classes when their respective economic interests are served to satisfaction (Attwood, 1988). When it comes to the APCFM experience, the only complaint the VSS members have as far as benefits are concerned is about FD's denial to allow the members to harvest the timber that has come of age.

Funds are imperative to the success of any activity, and a development project like 'common pool resources management' is no different. It is agreed by many scholars like Fiszbein (1997), Kaimowitz et al. (1998) and de Mello (2000) that natural resource governance at local levels cannot do much without a secure source of funding. The importance of external aid is highlighted by Baland and Platteau (2000) as well. The story in the developing countries in regard to financial resources is acute. Yet, the behaviour of external funders is one of impatience; they find it difficult even to wait for the institutions to develop into successful ones, due to their shorter time-frame objective (Morrow and Watts Hull, 1996); for instance, environment conservation schemes take decades rather than years to accomplish their objectives (Fabricius, 2004).

With increasing reports of wage works emerging as the backbone to sustain the CFM programme (Reddy et al., 2004), the members in the sample VSS were of the view that they agreed with such a notion wherein the CFM lasts as long as it provides wage works and not after it; one-third of the total respondents were sure that VSS will lose its meaning in the absence of monetary motivation. Some VSS have already weaned away from CFM because in such VSS, forest has not reached any sustainable level, and they do not see it reaching any beneficial stage because of poor management by the FD and the chairperson, due to rampant corruption on all matters including irregularities in implementing wage works. In one district, majority of its members felt that, without funds, their

VSS members will lose whatsoever motivation they have now. In an OTV of this district, such voice was heard overwhelmingly. Wage work has outscored all other factors of motivation to form VSS in the sample. The majority of the VSS members appeared content with narrower and temporary benefits rather than the long-term benefits they could reap by protecting forests to a sustainable level.

Only a couple of VSS were hopeful of continuing with CFM in the absence of external funds. They have made a unique arrangement to hold their member's interest in the VSS by allocating individual plots in their VSS to its members, where they have planted cashew (the FD allowed to plant this crop in the later stage of the CFM programme; earlier, cashew was not allowed to be planted in the VSS forest). So they have some motivation to reap definite benefits from those plots at individual level, even if the benefits from the larger portion of the VSS forest take more time to yield sustainable benefits. All the VSS members in the study expressed insufficiency of funds; most of the VSS members are under the impression that CFM (irrespective of sponsors) has a small budget, not knowing the actual fund sanctioned to their VSS, thanks not only to the FD's irregularities in the financial matters, but also to the members' overall ignorance level. In case no VSS forest reaches any meaningful sustainability in terms of forest produce, then without external funding, the future sustainability of the institution appears bleak.

Notes

1. World Bank supported indicators for the 212 countries as perceived by Kaufmann et al. (2008) are presence of: (1) voice and accountability; (2) political stability and absence of violence; (3) government effectiveness; (4) regulatory quality; (5) rule of law; and (6) control of corruption.
2. This stratum had a couple of villages where the entire VSS had either only SCs or fisherfolk as its members.

8

Conclusions: Challenges of CFM

Neumann and Hirsch (2000) find no community more vulnerable than the forest-dependent communities, which are the poorest and the weakest. According to Angelsen and Wunder (2003), NTFP collectors are the poorest of all, because they take to it as a last resort of employment. Their position becomes more volatile due to the compulsions of dispersing naturally reproduced products with seasonal and annual fluctuations in quantity and quality of production, further complicated by the small markets for such products. According to statistics, about 275 million (27.5 crore) landless people and small farmers in India are estimated to gather resources from their adjacent forests (WCFSD, 1999). Equally poor are those practicing shifting cultivation; in fact, they are much more deprived, both in economic and political terms among the other forest resource competitors.

Against such a backdrop, PFM was initiated in the early 1990s in AP. It was natural for forest-dependent communities to enliven their hopes of better future through this government-initiated programme. Such expectations were obvious because they were to be the major beneficiaries. As claimed by the state's FD, many GOs on J/CFM were introduced for enhancing the cause of the 'forest-dependent communities'. However, different reviews coming from the field on different subjects of the CFM were less of sporadic successes and more of failures. Hence, this research was intended to study the causes for such outcomes by choosing to assess the basic aspect of the programme, i.e., the 'democratic process' and 'governance' in the institutions of CFM and its bearing on the forest-dependent people particularly tribals. Governance, because in the Indian context, it means "evolution of effective policies through participation and their implementation for the general welfare of the people, especially the poorest and the weakest" (Pinto, 2001: 233).

The most significant concept in the APCFM is that, it is aimed at upgrading the initiatives taken under JFM. While JFM was more of a partnership between the forest-dependent communities and the Government of AP, CFM was expected to be more of a democratic process through delegation of the decision-making process by decentralising the entire process of planning and implementation with APFD and Government of AP. The role of FD was envisaged as facilitators and providers of technical and infrastructural support. CFM is an approach for forest development through a democratised participatory approach, which empowers the forest-dependent local communities. It is aimed to balance the local needs with external and environmental needs through increased productivity of the forest resources, reduced dependence on forests through substitution of demand and alternate livelihood opportunities, upgradation of living standards and inculcating a sense of ownership and pride among the forest-dependent communities. Despite the fact that CFM is claimed to be more democratic than JFM, the structure of the hierarchy above VSS gives the impression of a top-down exercise of authority and power, still resting with the FD.

Suggestions Specific to APCFM

Based on the findings from the field on the governance and democratic process, and assessing the challenges this decentralised forest management institution is facing at the bottom level of the VSS, the following key recommendations are made in order to strengthen the CFM with corrective measures for 'better forest' and 'better institutional conditions' for the communities to come out with their full potential and accomplish the APCFM vision in right perspective. Power, to begin with needs to be vested with right and deserving people so that all important positions of VSS chairpersonship and vice-chairpersonship should necessarily go to the caste/class of the numerically major community in those VSS composed of multi-community members, so that they can identify themselves with the power centre. The 15–member MC should be amended such that it represents proportional strength of each caste in the VSS. In GO 13 (2002), proportional representation is provided only for SC and ST members. Further, the existing set-up of a 'cabinet system' of executive with 15 members of the MC electing two heads to executive positions was expected to be democratic in functioning; however, it is increasingly found to be turning into a 'solitary executive' for all practical purposes, as the chairperson and vice-chairperson are seen to manipulate all VSS decisions (most of the time in collusion with FD), especially finances. Hence, it is suggested that the system should be changed into a 'plural form of executive' by empowering all the 15 MC members to equal power authority. This not only will bring down corruption within the community, but also leaves lesser scope for the FD to manipulate, as they do at present by overpowering the two elected executive heads, especially of the VSS in agency areas.

Transparency in the affairs of running VSS is equally vital, especially in those issues related to funds. Hence, the already existing norm (which is understood as optional by the community) that of displaying of the balance-sheet of all financial transactions by painting on a board or on the wall in a prominent place in the village should now be made compulsory for every VSS by linking this activity with the release of future funds.

Turning to the main issue of protecting the forest, allowing individual plots (for planting species of VSS member's choice to enhance their income subject to FD conditions) around the outward stretch of VSS boundary would help in safeguarding the forest because VSS members, while working on their individual plots can keep watch both on intruders and cattle alike, by sealing the fringe forests, because their plots cut off the entrance route into the forests. Similarly, to prevent people from practising *podu*, the government can do well by providing all the food essentials to the tribals through a PDS with special privileges, viz., providing free ration (this will not be a burden on the government treasury; besides it can be viewed as a barter for improving forest condition, rather than treating it as a populist measure) to eliminate food insecurity permanently. Food insecurity has been found to be the main reason for the poor tribals to practice the risky and unpredictable option of podu. The PDS staff should also be made accountable in order to contain their oppressive behaviour with the poor tribes.

Likewise, wage works, which has become a main motivation for poor members to join this programme needs a relook and complete control with regard to the payment procedures. Preparation of estimates and joint account system have proved to be ineffective and more dangerous because records now show only the chairperson and vice-chairperson to be responsible for the withdrawal of money, when in actuality the story is different in many places. The payment mode can be adopted from the Mahatma Gandhi National Rural Employment Guarantee Scheme (MGNREGS), wherein, the money is directly deposited into the accounts of individual members.

As an individual security measure and to further motivate the people towards forest protection activities, and also to take it as an occupation for those who are not traditionally forest-dependent communities, the VSS members should be covered by insurance against animal attacks, snake bites, attacks from offenders, allergies, injuries during tree-felling and also from lightning while working in the forest. This act will build confidence among the people to involve themselves freely with more assurance.

Finally, to overcome the absolute high-handedness of the FD in the agency areas, the TWD[1] can be delegated with the facilitator's role at VSS level in the tribal regions to build confidence among the tribals. This policy can be explored even while the FD oversees the CFM activities at the apex level to determine broader policies. This step will also help in removing the policing-image to people-oriented programme like CFM while ensuring an end to a long-standing strife between the FD and the tribals. This can be achieved by bringing change in the attitude of the FD officials to being more compassionate towards the forest-dependent people in order to deal with the challenges of the changing times of institutional governance; this will be possible by training the young staff at the primary level of their recruitment to be sensitive to the feelings of the 'communities', and also make them see the point in accepting the importance of 'genuine' forest-dependent communities in the protection of the forests.

Looking Ahead

In the broader sense, good governance is determined by factors like technical and managerial competence in public administration, accountability of public officials for their actions, predictability, the rule of law and an adequate and accessible information system.

The governance of 'CBNRM institutions' is not any less challenging. The J/CFM has been functional in AP for more than a decade. The APFD has been governing it through the local institutions (VSS) managed by 'local communities'. Yet, APCFM with the enormous number of VSS in it could not soar to the height of envisaged success in terms of enhanced forests (VSS and RF) and sustainable livelihoods for the 'communities' managing them. The conclusion from the research, points to APFD's 'poor technical and managerial competence' or 'poor policy' for indiscriminately scaling up the number of VSS by thrusting them upon many unwilling communities. More than half of the VSS members would have dissuaded themselves from constituting this institution, if opinions were elicited from them in reality according to GO 13 (2002). The casualty of this policy was the piling up of 'communities' with 'no motivation' which yield no positive output. Another reason for CFM not performing up to the mark was the FD's folly in not identifying the right 'community' or the 'composition of the community' to manage the VSS forests; a good number of non-performing or non-forest-dependent people grabbed the membership for their vested interests. The presence of such members also gave an impression of 'communities' per se not responding positively to the CFM altogether.

The canons of CFM got further diluted when a good number of VSS 'communities' were kept away even from testing their 'transparency and accountability level' in the institutional affairs by the ground level staff of the FD by manipulating all aspects of the democratic process to their own advantage. This is the story in the majority of the VSS in tribal areas ever since the inception of J/CFM. In some VSS, the respective chairperson and vice-chairperson were found to be conveniently joining hands with the FD only to keep the entire VSS community away from practising the affairs democratically. This happened most often when there was no match between the elected executive heads, especially the chairperson, and the rest of the VSS community in terms of 'caste' and 'class'.

However, communities of successful VSS had characteristics of 'will' and 'foresight'. When a community considered this programme honestly with a long-term vision and worked towards regenerating forest instead of eyeing short-term benefits like wage-employment, they have been triumphant. Besides, communities possessing in-built attributes of participatory decision-making, transparent and accountable values found themselves placed in a better position to face the challenges of managing this programme. Then again, the FD's hostile role and the community's performance were directly proportional to the later's 'resilience' level and their 'vulnerability' to cope with everyday institutional challenges. This again was determined by certain 'pre-conditions' of the respective communities.

On the whole, the APCFM urgently needs to 'prune' the number of VSS to only the performing communities by 'redefining the word 'community' to represent real 'forest-dependent' ones. For permanent financial assistance, CFM can also be merged with the MGNREGS.

Note

1. Tribal Welfare Department (TWD) was a contender with the FD for the implementation of the JFM when the 'participatory' concept was under consideration (Rangachari and Mukherji, 2000).

Appendices

Appendix I
Forest Vegetation in India and Andhra Pradesh

India is distributed into four regions, viz., the Himalayan range, the alluvial northern plains, the mid-western desert and the peninsula plateau. It has diverse vegetation in 'tropical wet evergreen forest to dry alpine scrub' (FAOUN, 1999). The recorded forest area of India is 76.52 million (7.65 crore) hectares that is 23.28 per cent of its total geographic area. The forest area is classified into three categories, namely, Reserved Forests (RF) (54.44%), Protected Forests (29.18%), and Unclassified Forests (16.38%) (GoI, 2003). The state Forest Departments (FDs) are controlled by the Ministry of Environment and Forests (MoEF) with the help of inputs received from the Ministry of Rural Development, Ministry of Finance and Ministry of Commerce.

As per APFD (2004) the forest cover in the state is 23.20 per cent of its total geographic area spreading into 63,814 sq. kms. As far as the legal status of Andhra Pradesh's (AP's) forest is concerned, 79.10 per cent is reserved, 19.38 is protected and remaining 1.52 is unclassified. The state's forest could be classified into five different types. They are southern tropical (25.25%); southern tropical moist deciduous (25.22%), southern tropical dry deciduous (44.55%); literal forests (4.48%); and tidal swamp mangroves forests (0.50%). About 54 per cent of the total forest in the state is situated in hilly areas (one-fifth of which is very hilly), and the remaining 44 per cent on the plains where the topography varies from flat to gently rolling. Teak is the major timber, estimated at 25.7 (2.57 crore) million cubic metres, or nearly 13 per cent of the total stock. Red Sanders is stated to be only 0.12 million (1.2 lakh) cubic metres forming less than 0.1 per cent of the total stock of wood, most of which is found in the Nallamali region. Bamboo is abundant in the catchments covering an area of about 10,000 sq. kms in the East Godavari and Adilabad districts.

Figure A1.1

Map of Andhra Pradesh showing its Forest Cover

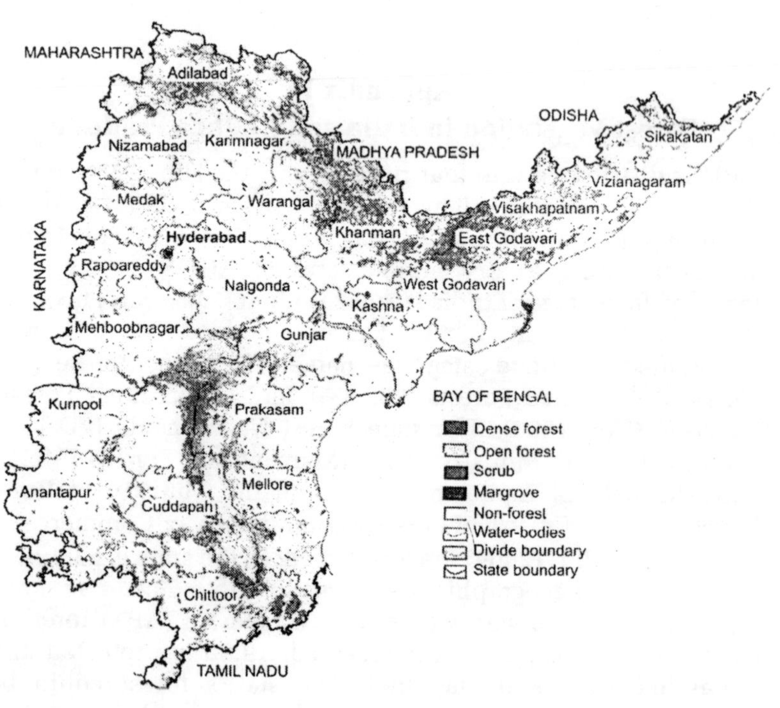

Source: Forest Survey of India (1999).

Table A1.1

Details of the Forest Area in the Study Districts

Forest Details	*Adilabad*	*Chittoor*	*Visakhapatnam*
Geographic area (in sq. kms)	16,128	15,152	10,807
Forest area	7,231	4,520	4,411
Forest area to the total geographic area of the district (in per cent)	44.8	29.9	39.3
District-wise forest area to total AP forest (in per cent)	11.32	7.09	6.92

Source: Forest Survey of India (2006).

Appendix II
VSS Secondary Data

Table A2.1

The number of VSS in each of the Districts in AP under different Projects

R	SL	Districts	N	Divisions	RN	SN	BT	FDA VSS	RIDF VSS	CFM VSS	Forest Area$^{\theta}$
Telangana	1	Adilabad	1.	Adilabad	5	24	58	60	31	325	1830.35
			2.	Bellampally	4	21	56	30	—	190	1540.56
			3.	Kagaznagar	4	14	39	30	—	89	858.81
			4.	Mancherial	4	24	50	—	—	113	1205.83
			5.	Jannaram	4	14	34	—	—	74	607.95
			6.	Nirmal	5	19	59	—	—	201	1021.24
	2	Nizamabad	1.	Nizamabad	3	14	52	25	82	119	750.31
			2.	Kama Reddy	4	18	60			83	939.58
	3	Medak	1.	Medak	6	20	95	43	139	202	953.91
	4	Hyderabad	1.	Hyderabad	—	—	—	—	—	—	—
	5	Rangareddy	1.	Hyderabad Total	—	—	—	57	106	—	
	6	Karimnagar	1.	Karimnagar (E)	4	18	53	—	68	135	1298.81
			2.	Karimnagar (W)	5	26	116	—		234	1251.13

Cont'd…

...*Cont'd*

	7	Warangal	1.	Warangal (N)	6	33	99	55	95	92	2393.70
			2.	Warangal (S)	4	21	60	34		113	1319.43
	8	Khammam	1.	Khammam	4	18	82	—	—	110	1246.19
			2.	Bhadrachalam (N)	4	16	52	28	—	26	1863.82
			3.	Bhadrachalam (S)	4	25	78		—	31	1632.27
			4.	Paloncha	6	25	78	50	—	86	2843.64
			5.	Kottagudem	6	19	85	—	—	101	1538.04
	9	Mahabubnagar	1.	Mahabubnagar	4	11	54	—	41	200	573.18
			2.	Achampet	5	18	94	44	—	33	2454.35
	10	Nalgonda	1.	Nalgonda	3	11	46	60	47	—	838.30
Costal Andhra	11	Srikakulam	1.	Srikakulam	5	22	43	41	95	241	686.41
	12	Vizianagaram	1.	Vizianagaram	4	15	50	67	62	190	1192.04
	13	Visakhapatnam	1.	Visakhapatnam	4	14	39	—	414	286	1201.94
			2.	Narsipatnam	8	21	55	—		286	2304.20
			3.	Paderu	3	8	20	—		304	1160.13
	14	East Godavari	1.	Kakinada	6	18	83	—	97	466	3242.44
	15	West Godavari	1.	Eluru	4	12	40	60	97	—	811.86
	16	Nellore	1.	Nellore	6	29	46	—	52	148	2519.37
	17	Krishna	1.	Krishna Total	2	9	29	36	19	—	663.21
	18	Guntur	1.	Guntur Total	4	15	60	60	67	—	1619.41
	19	Prakasham	1.	Giddalur	4	17	52	49	39	—	1948.60
			2.	Markapur	4	13	48	28		—	2476.39

Cont'd...

...Cont'd

Rayalaseema	20	Kadapa	1.	Proddatur	5	8	45	27	—	88	1563.55
			2.	Kadapa	5	13	45	24	40	95	1955.69
			3.	Rajampet	5	10	45	69	—	54	1498.09
	21	Chittoor	1.	Chittoor (E)	7	27	111	96	183	127	2452.00
			2.	Chittoor (W)	5	22	95	85		119	2061.94
	22	Kurnool	1.	Atmakur	4	14	26	25	—	—	1288.81
			2.	Kurnool	3	10	40	60	87	—	1192.10
			3.	Nandyal	4	9	20	—	—	—	1054.44
	23	Anantapur	1.	Anantapur Total	5	15	70	60	183	—	1969.78
	—	Wild Life Circle	1.	Tirupati (WL)	—	—	—	28	—	—	—
	—	—	1.	N Sagar	—	—	—	26	—	—	—

Key: R =Region, N =Serial Number, RN=Range, SN=Section, BT=Beat, WL=Wild Life; FDA = Forest Development Agency; RIDF = Rural Infrastructure Development; CFM = Community Forest Management; θ = Forest Area in sq. kms.

Source: APFD (2006).

Appendix III
Summary of J/CFM Government Orders

Table A3.1

Highlights of the GOs that Evolved J/CFM Programme in AP

Year	*GO*	*Highlights of the GO*
1992	MS No.218, 28.08.1992	'Social Forestry' experience established the fact that neither regeneration nor prevention of the degradation of forests could be achieved without participatory involvement of the local people who depend on the forests for usufruct and cattle grazing. This development culminated into issuance of this GO, under the guiding principles of 1988 National Forest Policy.
1993	MS No.181, 24.08.1993	This order was issued for constituting 'AP state level committee' to coordinate JFM.
1993	MS No.182, 24.08.1993	This order was issued to constitute 'District Forestry Committee' to implement JFM at the district level.
1993	MS No.183, 24.08.1993	This order was issued to facilitate the implementation of the concept of JFM in a smooth way in the tribal areas, with the Project officer of the ITDA as its Chairman.
1993	MS No.224, 11.11.1993	This order was issued, approving the revised Annexure I and II of GO 218. The order defined the constitution of VSS, constitution of MC, functions and responsibilities of the FD, usufruct sharing rights and a format of MoU that is signed between the various parties involved in this activity.
1996	MS No.10, 31.10.1996	This GO was issued to define sharing of compounding fees to the tune of 25 per cent (agreed during the second state level committee meeting held on 26.8.1995) with the VSS members for better forest protection and prevention of smuggling of forest produce. The order also contained directions to constitute a 'three-member committee' to scrutinise the cases apprehended by the members of VSS and recommend the award to be given to such VSS.

Cont'd...

...Cont'd

1996	MS No.173, 07.12.1996	This order makes reference to incorporate changes to the earlier orders to give more incentives to the members of the VSS with respect to sharing of benefits from the reserved items like 'beedi leaves'. The order also mentions the prohibition of 'horticulture' in the name of JFM, maintenance of bio-diversity, assurance to ensure people's interests before joining JFM. It lays emphasis on places where good leadership is available or NGOs are active enough to provide interface between the government and the people. It also mentions to associate an officer of not less than the rank of FRO with the JFM. The order also finds mention for the constitution of VSS of the local village communities and a direction for the already existing VSS to carry out the forest programme jointly with the FD as per the rules annexed to this order and guidelines issued thereon by the Government of India.
1997	MS No.115, 25.09.1997	This order modified the GO 173, pertaining to usufruct rights, whereupon the VSS were entitled to 50 per cent of the net income from '*beedi* leaves' after deducting harvesting and transporting cost and in case the required amount is more than 50 per cent of the income, the proposal was made to be approved by the GB of VSS.
1997	MS No.167, 15.12.1997	This GO was regarding the constitution of the EDCs to improve the state's biodiversity. The proposal was envisaged for about 200 villages living in and around the vicinity of the forests.
1998	MS No.21, 05.03.1998	This order was specific to the issue of sharing compounding fees with the VSS for better forest management and prevention of smuggling of forest produce. The order clearly mentions that whenever the VSS members apprehend smugglers transporting forest produce illegally, the VSS concerned will be sanctioned an incentive amount subject to the defined conditions.

Cont'd...

...Cont'd

1998	MS No.112, 22.09.2000	This was a controversial GO that tried to let industries like Indian Tobacco Company (ITC) Bhadrachalam, Reliance Industries and Murugappa Industries into the scheme of Forest Management to support the VSS in regenerating the degraded forests, with an assurance of not disturbing the 'Basic Structure' of VSS as defined in the GO 173.
1999	MS No.66, 04.05.1999	This order considered changing the system of sale of '*beedi* (Abnus) leaves' from weight basis to standard bag basis, after reviewing the earlier GO 173. It also contained references to other related issues such as collection and accounting.
2000	MS No.43, 07.04.2000	This order had clauses added to the earlier GO 21, pertaining to the incentives provided for the VSS members over a seizure of forest produce.
2002	MS No.13, 12.02.2002	This GO rechristianed 'JFM' into 'CFM'. The government, after careful consideration, decided to modify all the earlier orders issued on the 'JFM' to pave the way for the implementation of the 'CFM' in the state, with immediate effect. It also contained a 'faint' proposal to provide legal status to CFM.
2004	MS No.4, 12.01.2004	This was an Addendum to GO 13, 2002. It was also an effort to issue simple statements in clear and unambiguous words to interpret incremental volumes as share of VSS. It contained VSS entitlement to all NTFPs and all intermediate yields.

Key: ITDA = Integrated Tribal Development Authority; MoU = Memorandum of Understanding; FD = Forest Department; NGO = Non-Government Organisation; FRO = Forest Range Officer

Source: APFD.

Appendix IV
Officially Recognised Scheduled Tribe Groups in Andhra Pradesh

Table A4.1
Scheduled Tribes of AP

S.No.	*Tribes*
1.	Andh, Sadhu Andh (Agency Areas of Adilabad District)
2.	Bagata (Agency Areas of Visakhapatnam District)
3.	Bhil (Agency Areas of Srikakulam and Vizianagaram Districts – North Coastal Area)
4.	Chenchu (Agency Areas of Mahbubnagar, Nalgonda, Kurnool, Prakasam and Guntur districts – Nallamala Forests)
5.	Gadabas, Bodo Gadaba, Gutob Gadaba, Kallayi Gadaba, Parangi Gadaba, Kathera Gadaba, Kapu Gadab (Agency Areas of Visakhapatnam District – North Coastal Area)
6.	Gond, Naikpod, Rajgond, Koitur (Agency Areas of Adilabad District)
7.	Goudu (Khammam, East and West Godavari Districts)
8.	Hill Reddys (Khammam, East and West Godavari Districts)
9.	Jatapus (Agency Areas of Srikakulam and Vizianagaram Districts – North Coastal Area)
10.	Kammara (Khammam, East and West Godavari Districts)
11.	Kattunayakan (Warangal, Khammam)
12.	Kolam, Kolawar (Agency Areas of Adilabad)
13.	Konda Doras, Kubi (Khammam, East and West Godavari Districts)
14.	Konda Kapus (Khammam, East and West Godavari Districts)
15.	Kondareddis (Khammam, East and West Godavari Districts)
16.	Kondhs, Kodi, Kodhu, Desaya Kondhs, Dongria Kondhs, Kuttiya Kondhs, Tikiria Kondhs, Yenity Kondhs, Kuvinga (Agency tracts of North Coastal Area)
17.	Kotia, Bentho Oriya, Bartika, Dulia, Holva, Sanrona, Sidhopaiko (Agency tracts of North Coastal area)
18.	Koya, Doli Koya, Gutta Koya, Kammara Koya, Musara Koya, Oddi Koya, Pattidi Koya, Rajah, Rasha Koya, Lingadhari Koya (ordinary), Kottu Koya, Bhine Koya, Rajkoya (Khammam, East and West Godavari District)

Cont'd...

...Cont'd

19.	Kulia (Agency Areas of North Coastal Area)
20.	Malis (excluding Adilabad, Hyderabad, Karimnagar, Khammam, Mahbubnagar, Medak, Nalgonda, Nizamabad and Warangal Districts)
21.	Manna Dora (Khammam)
22.	Mukha Dora, Nooka Dora (Khammam, East and West Godavari Districts)
23.	Nayaks (in the Agency tracts North Coastal Area)
24.	Pardhan (Adilabad)
25.	Porja, Parangiperja (Agency Areas of Visakhapatnam District and North Coastal Area)
26.	Reddy Doras (Khammam East and West Godavari Districts)
27.	Rona, Rena (Agency Areas of North Coastal Area)
28.	Savaras, Kapu Savaras, Maliya Savaras, Khutto Savaras (Agency Areas of Srikakulam and Vizianagaram Districts – North Coastal Area)
29.	Sugalis, Lambadas, Banjara (Adilabad, Warangal, Nizamabad, Khammam)
30.	Thoti (Adilabad, Hyderabad, Karimnagar, Khammam, Mahbubnagar, Medak, Nalgonda, Nizamabad and Warangal Districts)
31.	Valmiki (in the Scheduled Areas of Vishakhapatnam, Srikakulam, Vizianagram, East Godavari and West Godavari Districts)
32.	Yenadis, Chella Yenadi, Kappala Yenadi, Manchi Yenadi, Reddi Yenadi
33.	Yerukulas, Koracha, Dabba Yerukula, Kunchapuri Yerukula, Uppu Yerukula (Mahaboobnagar, Warangal, and West Godavari)
34.	Nakkala, Kurvikaran (Agency Areas of Srikakulam and Vizianagaram Districts – North Coastal Area)
35.	Dhulia, Paiko, Putiya (in the districts of Vishakhapatnam and Vizianagaram)

Source: Census of India (2001).

Appendix V
Levels of Governance

Figure A5.1

Levels of Governance in each of the Sample VSS

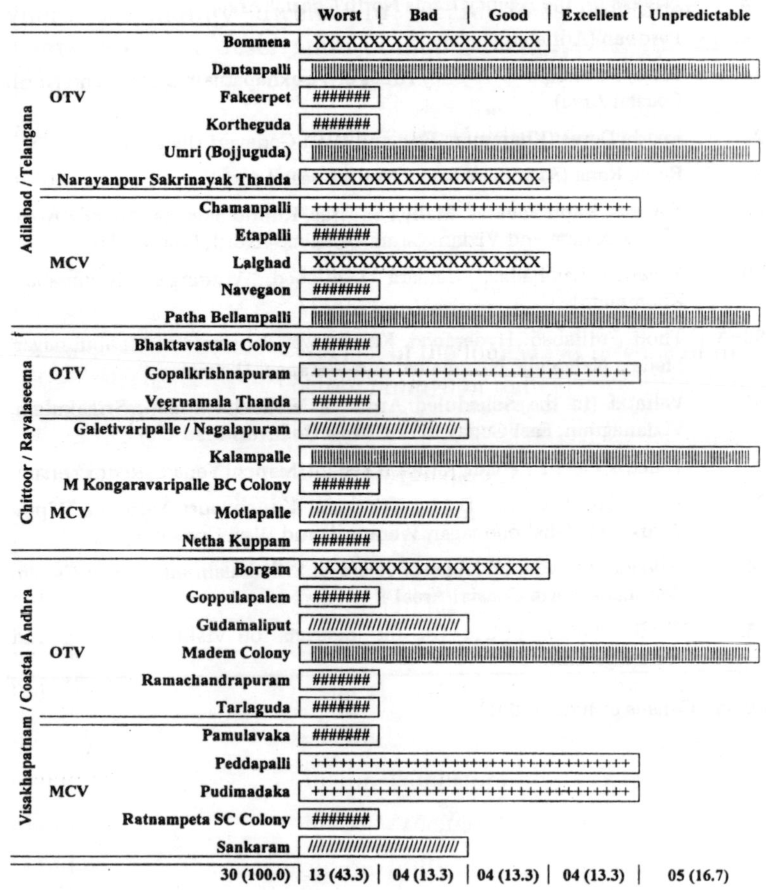

Key: OTV = Only Tribal VSS; MCV = Mixed-Caste VSS; T = Total; GT = Grand Total.

Source: Field survey.

References

Acheson, James (1989): 'Where Have All the Exploitings Gone? Co-Management of the Marine Lobster Industry', in Fikret Berkes (ed.), *Common Property Resources*, Belhaven, London, pp. 199–217.

Agrawal, Arun (2000): 'Small is Beautiful, but is Larger Better? Forest Management Institutions in the Kumaon Himalaya, India', in Clark C. Gibson, Margaret McKean and Elinor Ostrom (eds), *People and Forest: Communities, Institutions, and Governance*, The MIT Press, Cambridge, Massachusetts, London, England.

Agrawal, Arun and Clark C. Gibson (1999): 'Community and Conservation: Beyond Enchantment and Disenchantment', *World Development*, Vol. 27, No. 4, pp. 629–49.

Agrawal, Arun and J. Ribot (1999): 'Accountability in Decentralization: A Framework with South Asian and African Cases', *Journal of Developing Areas*, Vol. 33, No. 4, pp. 473–502.

Alam, M. (1991): 'Eastern India in the Early Eighteenth Century "Crisis": Some Evidence from Bihar', *Indian Economic and Social History Review*, Vol. 28, No. 1.

Anderson, Krister (2006): 'Understanding Decentralised Forest Governance: An Application of the Institutional Analysis and Development Framework', *Science, Practice and Policy*, Vol. 2, No. 1, pp. 25–35 (http://ejournal.nbil.org).

Andhra Pradesh Forest Department (APFD) (1999): 'Facts and Figures', Hyderabad, Forest Department, Andhra Pradesh.

—— (2003): 'Forest at a Glance', Hyderabad, Forest Department, Andhra Pradesh.

—— (2004): 'Facts and Figures', Hyderabad, Forest Department, Andhra Pradesh.

—— (2005): 'Current Status of Implementation of JFM in Andhra Pradesh', Hyderabad, November 22 (http://forest.ap.nic.in).

—— (2006): 'Activities of Forest Department for the Meeting of AP Legislative Committee on Forests, Wildlife and Environment Protection', Hyderabad, January.

Angelsen, A. and S. Wunder (2003): 'Exploring the Forest-Poverty Link: Key Concepts, Issues and Research Implications', CIFOR Occasional Paper No. 40, Centre for International Forestry Research, Bognor, Indonesia.

Arnold, David (1982): 'Rebellious Hillmen: The Gudem-Rampa Risings 1839– 1924', in Ranajit Guha (ed.), *Subaltern Studies I: Writings on South Asian History and Society*, Oxford University Press, Delhi, pp. 88–142.

Arnold, J.E.M. (1992): *Community Forestry: Ten Years in Review*, FAO, Rome.

Arora, D. (1994): 'From State Regulation to People's Participation: Case of Forest Protection Committees in India', *World Development*, Vol. 30, No. 12, pp. 2153–67.

Article 51A (G) (1990): 'Constitution of India', in S.C. Kashyap (ed.), *National Policy Studies*, published for Lok Sabha Secretariat by Tata McGraw-Hill Publishing Company Limited, New Delhi.

Ascher, William (1995): *Communities and Sustainable Forestry in Developing Countries*, ICS Press, San Francisco.

Attwood, D.W. (1988): 'Social and Political Preconditions for Successful Cooperatives: The Cooperative Sugar Factories of Western India', in D.W. Attwood and B.S. Baviskar (eds), *Who Shares? Cooperatives and Rural Development*, Oxford University Press, New Delhi, pp. 69–90.

Badgaiyan, S.D. (1990): 'The Political Economy of Tribal Development', in A. Bose, U.P. Sinha and R.P. Tyagi (eds), *Demography of Tribal Development*, Indian Association for the Study of Population (IASP), B.R. Publishing Corporation, Delhi.

Bahuguna, V.K., K. Mitra, C. Capistrano and S. Saigal (eds) (2004): *Root to Canopy: Regenerating Forests through Community-State Partnerships*, Commonwealth Forestry Association, India Chapter and Winrock International India.

Baland, Jean-Marie and Jean-Philippe Platteau (2000): *Halting Degradation of Natural Resources: Is There a Role for Rural Communities?*, Oxford University Press, Oxford.

Bandyopadhyay, D. (1996): 'Administration, Decentralisation and Good Governance', *Economic and Political Weekly*, Vol. 31, No. 48, November 30, pp. 3109–14.

Bandyopadhyay, J., Vandana Shiva and H.C. Sharatchandra (1983): 'The Challenge of Social Forestry', in F. Walter and K. Sharad (eds), *Towards a New Policy*, Indian Social Institute, New Delhi, pp. 49–72.

Bardhan, Pranab (1999): 'Water Community: An Empirical Analysis of Cooperation on Irrigation in South India', Working Paper, Department of Economics, University of California, Berkeley.

Bardhan, Pranab and Jeff Dayton-Johnson (2003): 'Unequal Irrigators: Heterogeneity and Commons Management in Large-Scale Multivariate Research', in Elinor Ostrom, Thomas Dietz, Nives Dolsak, Paul C. Stern, Susan Stonich and Elke U. Weber (eds), *The Drama of the Commons*, National Academy Press, Washington, DC.

Bartlett, A.G. and Y.B. Malla (1992): 'Local Forest Management and Forest Policy in Nepal', *Journal of World Forest Resource Management*, Vol. 6, pp. 99–116.

Baviskar, B.S. and D.W. Attwood (1991): 'Fertile Grounds: Why do Co-operatives Flourish in Western India?', *IASSI Quarterly*, Vol. 9, No. 4, pp. 82–99.

Baviskar, B.S. (1980): *The Politics of Development: Sugar Co-operatives in Rural Maharashtra*, Oxford University Press, Delhi.

Becker, C. Dustin, Abwoli Y. Banana and William Gombya-Ssembajjwe (1995): 'Early Detection of Tropical Forest Degradation: An IFRI Pilot Study in Uganda', *Environmental Conservation*, Vol. 22, No. 1 (Spring), pp. 31–38.

Behera, Bhagirath and S. Engel (2004): 'The Four Levels of Institutional Analysis of Evolution of Joint Forest Management (JFM) in India: A New Institutional Economics (NIE) Approach', paper presented at the Annual Meetings of the International

Association for the Study of Common Property (IASCP), Oxaca, Mexico, October 9–13.

Berkes, Fikret (1996): 'Social Systems, Ecological Systems, and Property Rights', in Susan Hanna, Carl Folke and Karl-Goran Maler (eds), *Rights to Nature: Ecological, Economic, Cultural, and Political Principles of Institutions for the Environment*, Island Press, Washington, DC, Covelo and California.

Beteille, Andre (1965): 'Caste, Class and Power: Changing Patterns of Stratification in a Tanjore Village', *Studies Review*, Vol. 27, No. 2, pp. 59–112.

Bhatt, C.P. (1990): 'The Chipko Andolan: Forest Conservation based on People's Power', *Environment and Urbanisation*, Vol. 2, Nos 17–18, pp. 7–18.

Biswas, Kallol, Dharudu Murali, Reddappa Reddy and K. Govindappa (1997): 'People and Forest; Mutual Survival: A Case Study on the VSS/FPC of Nainayana Cheruvu, Anantapur District', for the Department of Social Work, April, Sri Krishna Devaraya University, Anantapur, Andhra Pradesh.

Blair, Harry (1996): 'Democracy, Equity and Common Property Resource Management in the Indian Subcontinent', *Development and Change*, Vol. 27, No. 3, pp. 475–99.

— (2000): 'Participation and Accountability at the Periphery: Democratic Local Governance in Six Countries', *World Development*, Vol. 28, No. 1, pp. 21–39.

Blockhus, Jill M., Mark Dillenback, Jeffrey A. Sayer and Per Wegee (1992): *Conserving Biological Diversity in Managed Tropical Forests*, International Union for the Conservation of Nature, Gland, Switzerland.

Bromley, Daniel, David Feeny, Margaret McKean, Pauline Peters, Jere Gilles, Ronald Oakerson, C. Ford Runge and James Thomson (eds) (1992): *Making the Commons Work: Theory, Practice, and Policy*, ICS Press, San Francisco.

Burns, James McGregor (1979): *Leadership*, Harper and Row Publishers, New York.

Census of India (2001): *Provisional Population Total: Andhra Pradesh*, Office of the Registrar General of India, New Delhi.

Centre for World Solidarity (CWS) (2003): *A Study on VSS/FPC Sustainability and the Role of GCC in Connection with Programme in Andhra Pradesh*, Draft Report, Secunderabad, Andhra Pradesh.

Chandhoke, Neera (2003): 'Governance and the Pluralisation of the State: Implications for Democratic Citizenship', *Economic and Political Weekly*, Vol. 38, No. 28, pp. 2957–68.

Chaudhry, Kamala (1984): 'Managing Forests for Development', *Financial Express*, New Delhi, February 5.

Chopra, K., G.K. Kadekodi and M.N. Murthy (1990): *Participatory Development: People and Common Property Resource*, Sage Publications, New Delhi.

Cleghorn, H. (1964): *Forests and Gardens of South India*, W.H. Allen, London.

Crawford, S. and E. Ostrom (1995): 'A Grammar of Institutions', *American Political Science Review*, Vol. 89, No. 3, pp. 582–600.

Crook, R. and J. Manor (1998): *Democracy and Decentralisation in South Asia and West Africa*, Cambridge University Press, New York.

Cuthill, M. (2002): 'Exploratory Research: Citizen Participation, Local Government and Sustainable Development in Australia', *Sustainable Development*, Vol. 10, No. 2, pp. 79–89.

D'Silva, Emmanuel and B. Nagnath (2002): 'Behroonguda: A Rare Success Story in Joint Forest Management', *Economic and Political Weekly*, Vol. 37, No. 6, pp. 551–57.

Das, P.K. (2003): 'Growth Models and India's Policies', *Indian Journal of Public Administration*, Vol. XLIX, No. 2, April–June, pp. 157–64.

Das, Vidhya (2003): 'Democratic Governance in Tribal Regions: A Distant Dream', *Economic and Political Weekly*, Vol. 38, No. 42, pp. 4429–32.

de Mello, L. (2000): 'Fiscal Decentralization and Intergovernmental Fiscal Relations: A Cross-Country Analysis', *World Development*, Vol. 28, No. 2, pp. 365–80.

de Oliveira, J. (2002): 'Implementing Environmental Policies in Developing Countries through Decentralization: The Case of Protected Areas in Bahia, Brazil', *World Development*, Vol. 30, No. 10, pp. 1713–36.

Deshingikar, P., C. Johnson and J. Farrington (2005): 'State Transfers to the Poor and Back: The Case of the Food-for-Work Programme in India', *World Development*, Vol. 33, No. 4, pp. 575–91.

Dewees, P.A. and N.C. Saxena (1997): 'Tree Planting and Household Land and Labour Allocation: Case Studies from Kenya and India', in J.E.M. Arnold and P.A. Dewees (eds), *Farms, Trees and Farmers: Responses to Agricultural Intensification*, Earthscan, London, pp. 242–67.

Directorate of Census Operations (1997): *Census of India 1991: Andhra Pradesh – District Census Handbook Adilabad*, Series 2, Government of India.

—- (1998): *Census of India 1991: Andhra Pradesh – District Census Handbook Visakhapatnam*, Series 2, Government of India.

Disaster Management Department (2008): 'Seasonal Condition', Government of Andhra Pradesh, Hyderabad.

Dolsak, Nives and Elinor Ostrom (2003): 'The Challenges of the Commons', in Dolsak and Ostrom (eds), *The Commons in the New Millennium: Challenges and Adaptations*, The MIT Press, Cambridge, Massachusetts and London.

Engel, S. (2004): 'Designing Institutions for Sustainable Resource Management and Environmental Protection', Habilitation Thesis, Faculty of Agriculture, University of Bonn, Germany.

Fabricius, C. and C. de Wet (2002): 'The Influence of Forced Removals and Land Restitution on Conservation in South Africa', in D. Chatty and M. Colchester (eds), *Conservation and Mobile Indigenous People: Displacement, Forced Resettlement and Conservation*, Berghahn Books, Oxford, pp. 142–57.

Fabricius, Christo (2004): 'The Fundamentals of Community-based Natural Resource Management', in Christo Fabricius, Eddie Koch, Stephen Turner and Hector Magome (eds), *Rights, Resources and Rural Development: Community-based Natural Resource Management in South Africa*, Earthscan, London and Sterling, VA.

Farrington, John and Pari Bauman (2002): 'Panchayat Raj and Natural Resources Management: How to Decentralise Management over Natural Resources', *Situation Analysis and Literature Review*, Andhra Pradesh, October.

Feeny, David, Fikret Berkes, Bonnie J. McCay and James M. Acheson (1990): 'The Tragedy of the Commons: Twenty-two Years Later', *Human Ecology*, Vol. 18, No. 1, pp. 1–19.

Fisher, R.J. (1991): 'Studying Indigenous Systems of Common Property Forest Management in Nepal: Towards a More Systematic Approach', Working Paper No. 30, East-West Centre, Honolulu, Hawaii.

Fiszbein, A. (1997): 'The Emergence of Local Capacity: Lessons from Colombia', *World Development*, Vol. 25, No. 7, pp. 1029–43.

Food and Agricultural Organisation of the United Nations (FAOUN) (1999): 'Forestry Profile: India' (http://www.faao.org/infosylva/vr/is_country).

Forest Peoples Programme (FPP) and Samata (2005): 'Andhra Pradesh Community Forest Management Project: A Preliminary Independent Evaluation of a World Bank Forestry Project', May (www.forestpeoples.org).

Forest Survey of India (1999 and 2006): *Forest Atlas of India*, Ministry of Environment and Forests (MoEF), Dehradun.

Gadgil, M. and R. Guha (1992): *This Fissured Land: An Ecological History of India*, Oxford University Press, Delhi.

Ghai, D. (1992): 'Conservation, Livelihood and Democracy: Social Dynamics of Environmental Changes in Africa', Discussion Paper No. 33, United Nations Research Institute for Social Development, Paris.

Gibson, C. (2001): 'Forest Resources: Institutions for Local Governance in the Americas', in J. Burger, E. Ostrom, R.B. Norgaard, D. Policansky and B.D. Goldstein (eds), *Protecting the Commons: A Framework for Resource Management*, Island Press, Washington, DC, pp. 71–89.

Gogia, S.P. (2002): *Andhra Pradesh Forest Laws*, Asia Law House, Hyderabad.

Government of India (GoI) (1980): 'Report of the Committee for Recommending Legislative Measures and Administrative Machinery for Ensuring Environmental Protection', New Delhi.

— (1990): 'Involving of Village Communities and Voluntary Agencies for Regeneration of Degraded Forest Lands' (Letter No. 6–21/89–PP dated June 1), Ministry of Environment and Forests (MoEF), New Delhi.

— (2000): 'Guidelines for Strengthening JFM', Ministry of Environment and Forests (MoEF), Forest Protection Division, New Delhi.

— (2003): 'Forest Resources in India: An Overview' (http://envfor.nic.in/fsi/sfr99/chp2/t21b.html).

Gopal, K.S. and Sanjay Upadhyay (2001): 'A Report on Livelihoods and Forest Management in Andhra Pradesh', prepared for the Natural Resources Management Programme, Andhra Pradesh, September.

Government of Andhra Pradesh (GoAP) (2002): 'Andhra Pradesh State Forest Policy – 2002', Environment Forest Science and Technology (EFS&T) (For. III) Department, Government of Andhra Pradesh, Hyderabad.

Government Order (GO) 13 (2002): Ms. No. 13, Environment Forest Science and Technology (EFS&T) (For. III) Department, Government of Andhra Pradesh, February 12.

—- 237 (1993): Ms. No. 237, Environment Forest Science and Technology (EFS&T) (For. II) Department, Government of Andhra Pradesh, November 26.

Government Order (GO) (1986): Ms. No. 445, Forests Animal Husbandry and Fisheries (For. VI) Department, December 21.

Gupta, H.S. (1997): 'Legal Provisions for Joint Forest Management', *The Indian Forester*, Vol. 123, No. 6, June.

Gupta, Anil K. (1985): 'Sociology of Stress: Why do Common Property Resource Management Projects Fail?', proceedings of the Conference on Common Property Resource Management, April, BOSTID and National Council, Washington, DC, pp. 305–22.

—- (1990): 'Eco-sociology of Household Risk Adjustment and Commons: Performance in an Uncertain World', presented at the International Conference on Designing Sustainability on the Commons, International Associations for the Study of the Common Property, Duke University, USA, September, p. 24.

Hague, Frederic (1985): 'World Commission on Environment and Development (WCED) Public Hearing', Oslo, October 28–29, quoted in WCED, *Our Common Future*, Oxford University Press, Delhi, p. 164.

Hajer, Maarteen (1995): *The Politics of Environmental Discourses: Ecological Modernisation and the Policy Process*, Oxford University Press, Oxford.

Hardin, G. (1968): 'The Tragedy of the Commons', *Science*, Vol. 162, pp. 1243–48.

Harrison, S.R. and A. Ghose (2000): 'Small-Scale Forestry Systems in India', in S.R. Harrison, J.L. Herbohn and K.F. Herbohn (eds), *Sustainable Small-Scale Forestry*, Edward Elgar Publishing Ltd., Cheltenham, Glos.

Harrison, S.R., J.L. Herbohn and K.F. Herbohn (eds) (2000): *Sustainable Small-Scale Forestry*, Edward Elgar Publishing Ltd., Cheltenham, Glos.

Rangachari, C.S. and S.D. Mukherji (2000): *Old Roots, New Shoots: A Study of Joint Forest Management in Andhra Pradesh*, Winrock International/The Ford Foundation, Mehta Press, Delhi.

Rao, K. Mohan (1990): *The Kolams: A Primitive Tribe in Transition*, Book Links Corporation, Hyderabad, p. 223.

Rao, Kameshwar K., P.V. Prasad Rao, M.D. Iqbal, K.V. Padmavati Devi, T.S. Ramakrishana and P. Ramesh (2000): 'Community Forest Management and Joint Forest Management in the Eastern Ghats, Andhra Pradesh', in N.H. Ravindranath, K.S. Murali and K.C. Malhotra (eds), *Joint Forest Management and Community Forestry in India: An Ecological and Institutional Assessment*, Oxford and IBH Publishing Co. Pvt. Ltd., New Delhi.

Rao, P., Kamala Manohar and D.L. Prasad Rao (1982): 'Tribal Movements in Andhra Pradesh', in K.S. Singh (ed.), *Tribal Movements in India*, Manohar, New Delhi.

Rao, Raman A.V. (1958): *Economic Development of Andhra Pradesh: 1766–1957*, Popular Prakashan, Bombay (Mumbai).

Rao, Sitaram (1979): *Introduction to Social Forestry*, Oxford and IBH Publishing Co., New Delhi.

Ravinder, D. (2003): 'Forest and Grazing Policies in Andhra Pradesh: Contestations from Civil Society', Unpublished Seminar Paper, CESS, Hyderabad.

Reddy, M. Gopinath and K. Anil Kumar (2010): 'Political Economy of Tribal Development: A Case Study of Andhra Pradesh', Working Paper No. 85, Centre for Economic and Social Studies, Hyderabad, February.

Reddy, Redappa, V.G. Sreedhar, K. Bhaskar, C. Sudhakar, K. Govindappa and M. Muninarayanappa (2000): *Impact Assessment Study of Joint Forest Management in Anantapur District*, Department of Rural Development and Social Work, Sri Krishnadevaraya University, Anantapur, March.

Reddy, V. Ratna, Bhagirath Behera and D. Mohan Rao (2001): 'Forest Degradation in India: Extent and Determinants', *Indian Journal of Agricultural Economics*, Vol. 56, No. 4, October– December, pp. 631–47.

Reddy, V. Ratna, M. Gopinath Reddy, Madhusudan Bandi, V.M. Ravi Kumar, M. Srinivasa Reddy and Oliver Springate-Baginski (2007): 'Participatory Forest Management in Andhra Pradesh: Implementation, Outcomes and Livelihood Impacts', in Oliver

Springate-Baginski and Piers Blaikie (eds), *Forests, People and Power: The Political Ecology of Reform in South Asia*, Earthscan, London, pp. 302–34.

Reddy, V. Ratna, M. Gopinath Reddy, Velayutham Saravanan, Madhusudan Bandi and Oliver Springate-Baginski (2004): 'Participatory Forest Management in Andhra Pradesh: A Review', Working Paper No. 62, Centre for Economic and Social Studies, Hyderabad, October.

Ribot, J.C. (1999): 'Decentralisation, Participation and Accountability in Sahelian Forestry: Legal Instruments of Political-Administrative Control', *Africa*, Vol. 69, No. 1, pp. 23–65.

— (2002): *Democratic Decentralisation of Natural Resources: Institutionalising Popular Participation*, World Resources Institute, Washington, DC.

Rich, R., M. Edelstein, W. Hallman and A. Wandersman (1995): 'Citizen Participation and Empowerment: The Case of Local Environmental Hazards', *American Journal of Community Psychology*, Vol. 23, No. 5, pp. 657–76.

Rietbergen, Simon (2001): 'The History and Impact of Forest Management', in Julian Evans (ed.), *The Forests Handbook – Volume 2: Applying Forest Science for Sustainable Management*, Blackwell Science, London.

Robbins, P. (1998): 'Authority and Environment: Institutional Landscapes in Rajasthan, India', *Annals of the Association of American Geographers*, Vol. 88, No. 3, pp. 410–35.

Roy, S.B. (1997): 'Social Indicators towards Institutionalisation of Development Programme: A Case Study from Joint Forest Management', *The Indian Forester*, Vol. 123, No. 6, June.

Sachs, W. (ed.) (1993): *Global Ecology*, Zed Books, London.

Samata and Coastal Rural Youth Network (CRY-Net) (2001): 'Joint Forest Management in Andhra Pradesh: A People's Perspectives', Hyderabad.

Sarin, M. (1996): 'From Conflict to Collaboration: Institutional Issues in Community Management', in M. Poffenberger and B. McGean (eds), *Village Voices, Forest Choices: Joint Forest Management in India*, Oxford University Press, Delhi, pp. 165–209.

Sarin, M., L. Ray, M.S. Raju, M. Chatterjee, N. Banerjee and S. Hiremath (1998): *Who Gains? And Who Loses? Gender and Equity Concerns in Joint Forest Management*, Society for the Promotion of Wasteland Development, New Delhi.

Sarin, Madhu (2003): 'Real Forests versus Forests on Paper? Challenges Facing Forest Conservation', *The Hindu: Survey of India's Environment*, February.

Saunier, Richard E. and Richard A. Meganck (2008): *Dictionary and Introduction to Global Environmental Governance*, Earthscan, London and Sterling, VA.

Saxena, K.B. (2005): 'Disempowering Masses: Development as Destitution', Alternative Economic Survey 2005–06 (www.daanishbooks.com/).

Saxena, Naresh C. (1999): Forest Policy in India, Policy and Joint Forest Management, Series 1, World Wide Fund for Nature, India.

— (2001): 'The New Forest Policy and Joint Forest Management in India', in Julian Evans (ed.), *The Forests Handbook: Volume 2: Applying Forest Science for Sustainable Management*, Blackwell Science, London.

Schimmel, Annemarie, Corinne Attwood and Burzine K. Waghmar (2004): *The Empire of the Great Mughals: History, Art and Culture*, Reaktion Books, University of Chicago, Chicago.

Scott, James C. (1998): *Seeing Like a State: How Certain Schemes to Improve the Human Condition Have Failed*, Yale University Press, New Haven and London.

Shackleton, S., B. Campbell, E. Wollenberg and D. Edmunds (2002): 'Devolution and Community-based Natural Resource Management: Creating Space for Local People to Participate and Benefit', Natural Resource Perspectives No. 76, Overseas Development Institute, London.

Shah, S.A. (1997): 'Reinventing Tropical Forest Management in India', *The Indian Forester*, Vol. 120, No. 6, June.

Shah, Tushaar (1995): *Making Farmers Co-operative Work: Design, Governance and Management*, Sage Publications, New Delhi.

Sharma, Jitendra (1997): 'Joint Forest Management: Some Fundamentals Reviewed', *The Indian Forester*, Vol. 123, No. 6, June.

Shen, S. and A. Contreras-Hermosilla (eds) (1995): 'Environmental and Economic Issues in Forestry', World Bank Technical Paper No. 281, The World Bank, Washington, DC.

Sills, David L. (1972): *International Encyclopedia of Social Science*, Macmillan, New York, Reprinted edition.

Silva, Eduardo (1994): 'Thinking Politically about Sustainable Development in the Tropical Forests of Latin America', *Development and Change*, Vol. 25, No. 4, pp. 697–721.

Silwal, U.K. (1986): 'Attitude, Awareness, and Level of People's Participation in Community Forestry Development Programme', Nepal Forestry Research Paper Series No. 3.

Singh, S.P. and Paul Kelley (1981): *Amul: An Experiment in Rural Economic Development*, Macmillan India Ltd., Delhi.

Singh, K., V. Ballabh and T. Palakudiyil (eds) (1996): *Cooperative Management of Natural Resources*, Sage Publications, New Delhi.

Singh, K.S. (2003): *People of India: Andhra Pradesh*, Anthropological Survey of India, Affiliated East-West Press Pvt. Ltd., New Delhi.

Singleton, S. (1998): *Constructing Cooperation: The Evolution of Institutions of Co-Management*, University of Michigan Press, Ann Arbor, MI.

Sivaramakrishnan, K. (1999): *Modern Forests: Statemaking and Environmental Change in Colonial Eastern India*, Stanford University Press, Stanford, California.

Smoke, P. (2003): 'Decentralisation in Africa: Goals, Dimensions, Myths and Challenges', *Public Administration and Development*, Vol. 23, No. 1, pp. 7–16.

Springate-Baginski, Oliver and Piers Blaikie (eds) (2007): *Forests, People and Power: The Political Ecology of Reform in South Asia*, Earthscan, London, pp. 302–34.

State Forest Departments (2006): 'Measuring Milestones', proceedings of the National Workshop on Joint Forest Management (JFM), workshop organised by Ministry of Environment and Forests (MoEF), Government of India (GoI) and Winrock International, New Delhi, India, October 17.

Stern, Paul C., Thomas Dietz, Nives Dolsak, Elinor Ostrom and Susan Stonich (2003): 'Knowledge and Questions After 15 Years of Research', in Stern, Dietz, Dolsak, Ostrom and E.U. Weber (eds), *The Drama of the Commons*, National Academy Press, Washington, DC.

Sunder, N., Roger Jeffery and Neil Thin (2001): *Branching Out: Joint Forest Management*, Oxford University Press, New Delhi.

Sunder, Nandini (2000): 'Unpacking the "Joint" in Joint Forest Management', *Development and Change*, Vol. 31, No. 2, pp. 255–79.

Suryakumari, D. (2001a): 'A Light Shade of Green: Forests and Their People', *Humanscape*, Vol. VIII, Issue XI, December (www.humanscapeindia.net).

—— (2001b): 'Involvement of Women in Joint Forest Management (JFM) in Andhra Pradesh State: Grass Roots Concerns', *Energia News*, Vol. 4, Issue 2, July, pp. 13–14.

Thakur, Prabhir (1984): 'Forestry in India: Its Conservation and Planning', *Indian and Foreign Review*, Vol. 21, No. 19, July 31.

Tiwary, Manish (2005): 'Panchayats versus Forest Protection Committees: Equity and Institutional Compliance in Rural Development Forestry', *Economic and Political Weekly*, Vol. 40, No. 19, pp. 1999–2005.

Thompson, J.T., and K. Schoonmaker Freudenberger (1997): Crayting institutional arrangements from community forestry. Community Forestry Field Manual, Rome. Food and Agriculture Organisation of the United Nations, pp. 154.

Trautmann, T.R. (1982): 'Elephants and the Mauryas', in S.N. Mukherjee (ed.), *India, History and Thought: Essays in Honour of A.L. Basham*, Subarnarekha, Calcutta (Kolkata), pp. 254–73.

Tucker, Catherine M. (1999): 'Common Property Design Principles and Development in a Honduran Community', *Praxis: The Fletcher Journal of Development Studies*, Vol. 15, pp. 47–76.

United Nations Food and Agriculture Organisation (UNFAO) (1990): 'Interim Report on the Forest Resources Assessment 1990 Project', Item 7 of the Provisional Agenda, Committee on Forestry, Tenth Session, September 24–28, FAO, Rome.

Upadhyay, J.K. (1997): 'Village Resource Development Programme of Village Forest Committees in Bilaspur Forest Circle, Madhya Pradesh: A Case Study', *The Indian Forester*, Vol. 123, No. 6, June.

Upadhyay, Sanjay (2003): 'JFM in India: Some Legal Concerns', *Economic and Political Weekly*, Vol. 30, No. 35, pp. 3629–31.

Varughese, George (2000): 'Population and Forest Dynamics in the Hills of Nepal: Institutional Remedies by Rural Communities', in Clark C. Gibson, Margaret A. Mckean and Elinor Ostrom (eds), *People and Forests: Communities, Institutions, and Governance*, The MIT Press, Cambridge, Massachusetts, London.

Venkatraman, A. and J. Falconer (1998): 'Rejuvenating India's Decimated Forests through Joint Actions: Lessons from Andhra Pradesh', Joint Forest Management Andhra Pradesh (http://www.jfmindia.org).

Vira, Bhaskar, Roger Jeffery and Nandini Sunder (eds) (1999): *A New Moral Economy for India's Forests: Discourses of Community and Participation*, Sage Publications, New Delhi.

Wade, R. (1988a): *Village Republics: Economic Conditions for Collective Action in South India*, Cambridge University Press, Cambridge.

— (1988b): 'Why Some Indian Villages Cooperate', *Economic and Political Weekly*, Vol. 23, No. 16, April 16, pp. 773–76.

White, S. (1996): 'Depoliticizing Development: The Uses and Abuses of Participation', *Development in Practice*, Vol. 6, No. 1, pp. 6–15.

Wiersum, K.F. (1986): *Social Forestry and Agro-forestry in India*, Report No. 456, Department of Forest Management, Wageningen Agricultural University, The Netherlands.

World Bank (1994): 'The World Bank and Participation', Operations Policy Development, Washington, DC.

World Commission on Forests and Sustainable Development (WCFSD) (1999): *Our Forests, Our Future*, Report of the World Commission on Forests and Sustainable Development, Cambridge University Press, Cambridge.

Yumnum, A.S. (1996): 'Property Rights, the Hills and the Tragedy of the Commons of Manipur', in R.K. Sen and K.C. Roy (eds), *Sustainable Economics Development and Environment: India and Other Low Income Economies (LIEs)*, Atlantic Publishers and Distributors, New Delhi, pp. 99–105.

Index